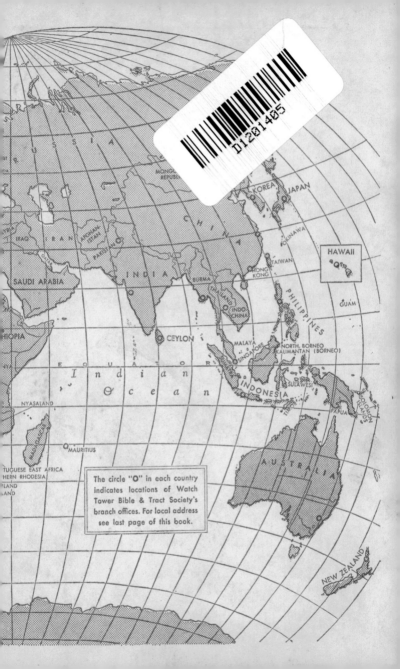

The circle "O" in each country indicates locations of Watch Tower Bible & Tract Society's branch offices. For local address see last page of this book.

"YOUR WILL
Be Done On Earth"

"Our Father in heaven, your name be revered!
Your kingdom come!
Your will be done on earth as well as in heaven!"

—Matthew 6:9, 10, An American Translation.

First Edition
ONE MILLION COPIES

PUBLISHERS

WATCHTOWER BIBLE AND TRACT SOCIETY
OF NEW YORK, INC.
INTERNATIONAL BIBLE STUDENTS ASSOCIATION
Brooklyn, New York, U.S.A.

Made in the United States of America

DEDICATED

to Man's Loving Creator,
who has willed
a perfect government of
righteousness over
the earth.

Abbreviations of Bible versions quoted or cited in this book

AS – American Standard Version, by the American Committee of Revision

AT – An American Translation, by J. M. P. Smith and E. J. Goodspeed

AV – Authorized or King James Version of 1611

JPS – The Holy Scriptures according to the Masoretic Text, A New Translation, by The Jewish Publication Society of America

Le – The Twenty-four Books of the Holy Scriptures, by Isaac Leeser

LXX – Greek Septuagint Version of the Hebrew Scriptures, in an English translation

Mo – A New Translation of The Bible, by James Moffatt

Ro – The Emphasised Bible, a New Translation, by J. B. Rotherham

RS – Revised Standard Version, by the Division of Christian Education of the National Council of the Churches of Christ in the United States of America

Ibidem, Latin, meaning "In the same place."

Any quotation not followed by any specific abbreviation is from the New World Translation of the Holy Scriptures. (*NW*) Other versions of the Bible are quoted or cited, but not with the name of the translations abbreviated.

CONTENTS

CHAPTER 1

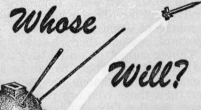

Whose Will?

UMANKIND is swiftly moving toward a new world. Soon the great troubles that have disturbed this world since the year 1914 will reach their

Armageddon* climax. This old world will not be able to endure that overwhelming trouble, the like of which man has never before gone through since the beginning of human existence. The worst ever, yet it will be the last world trouble, and the thankful survivors of it will enter into a new world that gives promise of wonderful things.

² For important reasons there has to come a new world. Things cannot go on as they are and on the same foundations. There has to be an all-embracing change. This change has to come by powers other than those who are responsible for mankind's woes for these thousands of years. That change will make all things new. The world, the whole system of things, will be healthily new. As we think about this desirable new world, some vital questions arise. Will that new world be fashioned and built by human scientists of today or of the future? During that world, which will always stay new, whose will is it that must be done and will be done on earth? Is it to be the will of some imperfect, selfish, dying human creature? Or is it to be the will of someone unselfish, perfect, undying, someone higher and more powerful than the most outstanding human creature? Is it to be the will of someone on earth or of someone in outer space or of someone beyond outer space?

³ Particularly since October of 1957 all informed men and women have interested themselves in outer space. They have been expressing themselves from a new viewpoint, that of cosmic space. They say we have entered into the nuclear space age. They say we must conquer outer space with the use of nuclear energy, the mighty energy

---

* See The Holy Bible, at Revelation (Apocalypse) 16:16.

---

1. Why is humankind rapidly moved toward a new world?
2. Why must a new world come, and what questions arise about it?
3. Since 1957, why have informed persons interested themselves in outer space?

bound up in the nucleus of the atoms of which all matter is made up, the terrific energy that has been made known to us by the explosion of fiendish bombs of scientific invention. But why conquer outer space? That the conquerors may gain control of man's everlasting home, this planet earth. They say that the point of control is somewhere out there in outer space. For them, the so-called ultimate weapon of war is not enough; the "ultimate position" is supremely necessary. To the shock of many, one noted lawmaker said:

[4] "There is something more important than any ultimate weapon. That is the ultimate position— the position of total control over earth lies somewhere out in space. This is the future, the distant future, though not so distant as we may have thought. Whoever gains that ultimate position gains control, total control, over the earth, for purposes of tyranny or for the service of freedom."*

[5] That ringing statement, spoken to wake up the threatened people to the "peril of the hour," expressed the fear of a one-sided "spatial imperialism" by some political, military world power. The will of the world power that gained the "ultimate position" along with the "ultimate weapon" would then be the controlling will of the earth. So comes the question, Who should control outer space? Believing that now the "sky is the limit" for men, worldly-wise men suggested that the members of that international organization, the United Nations, should all rule out an "ultimate position"

* Statement by American Senator Lyndon B. Johnson, the Senate majority leader and chairman of the Preparedness subcommittee to a meeting of Democratic Senators on January 7, 1958, as quoted by the New York *Times* of January 8, 1958.

4. What did one noted lawmaker say regarding outer space?
5. What fear did that statement express, and hence what answer is given to the question as to who should control outer space?

for any nation and that all member nations should unite in a drive to conquer space for the purposes of world peace. Said one editorial writer: "Control of outer space may well be the key to the future; and for the sake of world peace, even human survival, this must be a matter not of national prestige but of collective security."* International control was seen as the only practical answer to all the questions that man's invasion of outer space with rockets and man-made moons had raised. International law, a "law of the world," was seen to be needed for keeping man's conquest of space from being misused by any nation or group of nations.

⁶ Religion has stepped into the discussion of the opportunities and dangers of man's space age. One week after the Soviet Union launched its first satellite, Sputnik No. 1, to orbit around our globe, the Vatican newspaper "The Roman Observer"† encouraged exploration into outer space. Under date of October 11, 1957, it said: "God has no intention of setting a limit to the efforts of man to conquer space." It said that the Roman Catholic Church's viewpoint on outer space had not changed since its Pope Pius XII addressed an astronautical congress in Rome, Italy, in 1956. "On that occasion," said the Vatican newspaper, "Pope Pius XII told 400 delegates from twenty-two nations that 'the more we explore into outer space, the nearer we become to the great idea of one family under the Mother-Father God.' "‡ Yet facts to date reveal that the exploration of outer space in man's

---

* The New York *Times* as of January 16, 1958, editorial page.

† In Italian *L'Osservatore Romano*.

‡ According to an Associated Press dispatch from Rome, dated October 11, 1957, and published in the American press.

---

6. (a) What did one religious newspaper say on the conquering and exploring of outer space? (b) But whom has such exploration put foremost?

way brings the physical scientists foremost to view. A paid newspaper article entitled "Will We Do the Job in Science?" paid a compliment to the Russian scientists and then spoke of our being on "the threshold of a space age in which the side that is strongest in science will inherit the earth— or what's left of it."*

[7] Those words cast a doubt on the third beatitude of Jesus Christ's famous Sermon on the Mount: "Blessed are the meek: for they shall inherit the earth."† Yet, can it possibly be that someday soon the meek or mild-tempered ones will actually inherit this earth under oppression of no kind? For an answer that question, like other vital ones, depends upon whose will is to be done on earth in the oncoming new world.

[8] Amid their fears, anxieties and ambitions the nations of this world are forgetting something. What? There is a power that already has the "ultimate position," not the ultimate position toward merely this tiny earth but that toward all the planets, moons and suns of the immeasurable universe that telescopes can bring to our view. It is the intelligent, divine Power that created the earth and man and beast and bird upon it, yes, that created all the stars, the sun and the moon that shine down upon us here at the earth. Self-centered, self-reliant man does not want to think of this intelligent, divine Power or of any responsibility that man owes to this almighty Power as his Creator. Man tries to laugh off the existence of such an intelligent creative power, because man's tiny, short-lived satellites or sputniks have

---

* Quoted from page 38 of the New York *Times* as of March 26, 1958.

† Quoted from The Holy Bible, Matthew 5:5, Authorized Version of 1611. See *AV* on page 3.

---

7. On what beatitude did those words cast a doubt, and upon what does fulfillment of that beatitude depend?
8. As regards the "ultimate position," what are the nations forgetting?

not run into him while orbiting about us in outer space. How foolish! For His ultimate position is not somewhere out in distant space as far as human scientists could shoot their farthest satellite or sputnik.

⁹ Let unreasoning man know that the all-scientific, almighty Creator's ultimate position is in the invisible realm, into which man with all his science cannot rocket himself. Necessarily the Creator holds the "ultimate position" because he is the Most High, the Supreme One over all the universe. He is the living, creative Center around which all creation revolves. He rightfully holds the spatial imperialism everywhere, for he is Sovereign over all heaven and earth and over all the space between them. With no nation or group of nations will he divide and share his spatial imperialism. Against him no disdainful earthly nations can win. He is God!

A SYMBOLIC VISION OF HIM

¹⁰ Although we cannot see him, yet we dare not ignore the Most High, the almighty Sovereign God. We cannot escape his laws in any part of the boundless universe, including the law that no man of dust can see him and keep on living. God could not break this law even to favor his prophet Moses, through whom he gave the matchless Ten Commandments. When Moses asked God to cause him, a mere man, to see the divine glory, God told Moses: "You are not able to see my face, because no man may see me and yet live."* That rule has held true regardless of how scientists have tried to discover the secret of life. God is not created matter, as man is. He is spirit, impossible for

---

* Quoted from the sacred Bible, Exodus 33:20.

---

9. Where does the Creator hold the ultimate position, and why does he hold the spatial imperialism everywhere?
10. Why may we not dare to ignore God, and why can we not see him?

earthly eyes to see, even aided by the most far-seeing telescope or the most powerful electronic microscope.

[11] Centuries ago Jesus Christ explained it to a Samaritan woman, saying: "God is a Spirit, and those worshiping him must worship with spirit and truth."* Despite his invisibility in the spirit realm, human creatures can intelligently worship him with truth and get the unspeakable blessing out of it. One man who worshiped this great unseen One as divine Ruler immortal exclaimed: "Now to the King of eternity, incorruptible, invisible, the only God, be honor and glory for ever and ever."† Taking this prayerful exclamation seriously, how can we dare to leave God out of mind?

[12] "No man has seen God at any time," wrote a follower of Jesus Christ nineteen centuries ago.‡ He was a personal friend of Jesus and leaned on his bosom; yet he had not seen God. Since no man, not even John the son of Zebedee who thus wrote, has seen God, we have no description of what he is like. We cannot imagine what he is like. For us to paint a picture or to sculpture an image to stand for him would mean to fool ourselves and to belittle him and to insult him. It would pull him down in our esteem rather than lift us up in a pretense at worshiping him. It would not be worshiping him with spirit, which is not materialistic like an image; nor worshiping him with truth, which is not imaginary. But this all-glorious, unseeable God helps us to understand and appreciate things about himself by likening them to things that we see and know well. He even speaks about

---

* See The Holy Bible, John 4:24.
† *Ibidem*, 1 Timothy 1:17.
‡ *Ibidem*, John 1:18.

11. How must we and can we worship him?
12. Since we have no description of God, how does he help us to understand and appreciate things about himself?

himself as if he had a nose, eyes, a mouth, ears, hands and feet, and a pulsating heart. Thus he may give a vision of himself by the use of symbols. He gave John the son of Zebedee an awe-inspiring vision of himself, that John might describe the vision to us and let us, as it were, into the very presence of God in his "ultimate position" in heaven.

[13] John saw more and learned more than all the modern-day scientists have learned or could learn by all the satellites or sputniks that they rocket up into outer space, equipped with scientific measuring instruments, radiocasting apparatus and televising sets. John saw farther than into outer space with its visible suns and planets, galaxies and meteors and comets, and its cosmic rays. John was then the last living of the twelve apostles of Jesus Christ. What he saw was a revelation, made possible not by modern-day scientific instruments but only by the operation of God's invisible active force or spirit. The book in which John describes this miraculous vision is called The Revelation to John. It is put last in the books of the Holy Scriptures, The Holy Bible. John was then suffering for being a Christian, "for speaking about God and bearing witness to Jesus," John says. He was being kept as a prisoner on the penal island of Patmos, not far from the coast of Asia Minor, now Asiatic Turkey. (Revelation 1:9) What did John see that is of value and importance to us in this nuclear space age?

[14] From the glorified Jesus Christ in heaven John had just received seven messages for seven Christian congregations in Asia Minor. "After these things I saw, and, look! an opened door in heaven, and the first voice that I heard was as of

---

13. How did John see and learn more than all modern-day scientists?
14. Into what was John invited, and by following him where do we get and what may we see?

a trumpet, speaking with me, saying: 'Come on up here, and I shall show you the things which must take place.' " (Revelation 4:1) By following John through this opened door that led beyond outer space, where man-made moons orbit around the earth, we enter as if into the presence of the supreme, almighty Sovereign God. Knowing that no man can see God's face and keep living, we do not expect to see his shape or any of his features. We could not endure the actual sight of him any more than we could endure a hydrogen bomb explosion close up. What we do see through John's vision is glorious, brilliant, dazzling. We are also shown things that must take place in universal history.

[15] As soon as John answered the invitation to come up through the opened door in heaven he came under the operation of God's active force or spirit, to see what we humans cannot normally see. "And, look! a throne was in its position in heaven, and there is one seated upon the throne." The position of this throne is the ultimate for superiority. It is the throne of the Most High, who dominates all creation seen and unseen, upon whom all creation depends for existence and for universal orderliness. It is the throne of the King of eternity, a perpetual King higher than all emperors, kings, dictators and rulers of the earth, who perish.

[16] What is he like? Like a man in figure, in shape? No! "And the one seated is, in appearance, like a jasper stone and a precious red-colored stone, and round about the throne there is a rainbow like an emerald in appearance." He is like highly polished gems, precious, glowing, beautiful, that attract the eye and win delighted admiration.

---

15. Under what force did John come, and whose throne did he see?
16. What was the enthroned One like in appearance, and what do these things call to our attention?

There is nothing horrifying about him, nothing
fiendish that would even suggest that he would
torture his earthly creatures, human souls, forever and ever in conscious torment in a fiery hell.
He is lovely in appearance and pleasant to look at,
causing one to lose oneself in wonderment. About
his throne there is further glory, the appearance
of calmness, serenity. The appearance of a perfect
rainbow of emerald indicates that, reminding one
of the enjoyable, quieting calm that follows a
storm. It reminds one of the first rainbow that
God put into the sky after the global flood to serve
as a heavenly sign to Noah and to all of us his
descendants, to signify that never again would
there be a global deluge. That was when God said:
"No more will the waters become a deluge to bring
all flesh to ruin. And the rainbow must occur in
the cloud and I shall certainly see it to remember
the covenant of eternity between God and every
living soul among all flesh that is upon the earth."
(Genesis 9:12-16) Human scientists who want to
control the weather on earth from an "ultimate
position" in outer space will never be able to destroy God's covenant symbolized by the rainbow.

[17] Before God began creating he was all alone
in space, from time without beginning. But whom
of his creatures did God choose to call into his
presence? With whom does he surround himself?
In the close-up vision John tells us: "And round
about the throne were four and twenty thrones:
and upon the thrones I saw four and twenty elders
sitting, arrayed in white garments; and on their
heads crowns of gold." (Revelation 4:4, *AS*) Who
are these "elders," these twenty-four persons of advanced age, enthroned around God's own throne?
John knew of "elders" in the Jewish community,
in the congregation of ancient Israel. Fifteen centuries before John, when the prophet Moses re-

17. With whom was God seen to surround himself, and why did
these not picture the "apostles of the Lamb"?

ceived the Ten Commandments from God, Moses had associated with him seventy of the older men or "elders" of the nation of Israel. (Exodus 24: 1, 9, AS) John, however, was an "elder" or older man of the Christian congregation. He was a special "elder," because he was one of the "twelve apostles of the Lamb [Jesus Christ]," who served as twelve foundations for the Christian congregation, like twelve foundation stones of the walls of the new Holy City. (Revelation 21:14) But those crowned and enthroned "elders" whom John saw sitting around God's throne could not picture the twelve apostles of Jesus Christ, for they were twenty-four in number, or twice the number of the twelve apostles.

[18] In the congregation of ancient Israel "elders" were representatives of the entire congregation of Israelites. Likewise since John's day the Christian "elders" have stood for the entire congregation of Christians or spiritual Israelites. According to this rule, the twenty-four "elders" seated on thrones about God picture the entire congregation of Christians who prove faithful till death and who are rewarded with a resurrection out of death to life in heaven and to a throne in the heavenly kingdom of God.*

[19] This congregation of faithful Christians who win the heavenly reward finally becomes 144,000 in number, or six thousand times twenty-four. John himself is used to give us this final number of them, in Revelation 7:1-8; 14:1-5. John was

---

* Twenty-four was the number of the divisions into which King David divided the priests of the nation of Israel to serve at Jerusalem's temple. The Christian congregation will be a "royal priesthood."—1 Chronicles 24:1-19; Luke 1:5-24, 57-67; 1 Peter 2:9; Revelation 20:6. See *The Watchtower* in its issue of April 15, 1956, pages 253-256.

---

18. Whom do the twenty-four "elders" represent?
19. How great in number does this congregation finally become, and what promises has Jesus Christ given them?

used to pass on to them these messages from the
glorified Jesus Christ in heaven: "Prove yourself
faithful even with the danger of death [or, faithful till death], and I will give you the crown of
life." "He that conquers will thus be arrayed in
white outer garments, and I will by no means blot
out his name from the book of life, but I will make
acknowledgment of his name before my Father
and before his angels." "To the one that conquers
I will grant to sit down with me in my throne,
even as I conquered and sat down with my Father
in his throne." (Revelation 2:10; 3:5, 21) What
these twenty-four "elders" say and do in this
vision to John further proves that they symbolize
the 144,000 who make up the final congregation.

[20] It was only nineteen hundred years ago that
the Christian congregation was begun, on earth.
As regards the presence of any members of it in
heaven, their presence in heaven could date only
from after the setting up of God's kingdom, for
which faithful Christians have prayed during all
these centuries. Despite these facts, God views the
members of the congregation as "elders" or persons of advanced age in comparison with all others
of his intelligent creation in heaven and on earth.
It is clear, therefore, that it is not the years of
actual life of the members of the congregation
but their advancement in knowledge, in official
training and in loyal godly devotion that has paved
the way to their being clothed in white, crowned
and enthroned as "elders" around God's throne.

[21] How have they been chosen to be "elders"
in God's own presence? Certainly this has been by
no democratic election carried on by any nation
or people on earth, in the east or in the west. It
has been by God himself, for God does not see the

20. Are they "elders" in years toward all creation, and what has
paved the way to their being enthroned as persons of advanced
age?
21. How have they been chosen to be "elders" in God's presence?

way any man or nation sees, but by his own standards God chooses who is to be given a seat within his immediate circle. So these symbolic "elders" are chosen theocratically, from the supreme place of authority above, and not from the people below on earth.

²² Since God surrounds himself with a circle of twenty-four symbolic elders, does this mean he has what might be called a Senate, an intimate Council of heavenly officers with whom he goes into consultation and takes counsel, asking their advice and acting according to the majority opinion or vote? No; for he is all-wise. He needs no counsel from any of his creatures. The prophet Isaiah rightly asked concerning this great Creator: "Who has taken the proportions of the spirit of Jehovah, and who as his man of counsel can make him know anything? With whom did he consult together that one might make him understand, or who teaches him in the path of justice, or teaches him knowledge, or makes him know the very way of real understanding? Look! The nations are as a drop from a bucket; and as the film of dust on the scales they have been accounted." (Isaiah 40:13-15) The Christian congregation represented by the twenty-four "elders" have therefore only the honor of serving as foremost heavenly officials of the Ancient of Days, the Creator.

²³ In the vision to John, God and his twenty-four "elders" sat enthroned in a setting like the interior of the temple of worship in the ancient city of Jerusalem. From the description that is written down in the Bible, John knew that there were ten golden lampstands in the holy chamber of the temple that King Solomon had built a thousand

---

22. Does God therefore have a Senate, and as what do the twenty-four "elders" have the honor of serving?
23. According to the things before God and the "elders," what kind of interior was suggested to John?

years before. Five lampstands were to the right and five to the left before the innermost room or Most Holy. In the courtyard of the temple there was also a great copper basin of water, so large that it was called a sea. (1 Kings 7:23-26, 44, 49) With water from it the priests washed their hands or the sacrifices.

[24] Relative to God's throne John says: "And out of the throne there are lightnings and voices and thunders proceeding; and there are seven lamps of fire burning before the throne, and these mean the seven spirits of God. And before the throne there is, as it were, a glassy sea like crystal." In King Solomon's temple of long ago God did not sit enthroned in its Most Holy, but there was a miraculous light that hovered above the sacred golden chest or ark that contained the two stone tablets upon which the finger of God had written the Ten Commandments. However, in the vision to John, God is seen as if seated enthroned in his heavenly temple.

[25] The flashes of lightning from his throne aptly reminded John that "God is light." At earth's creation He was the One that said: "Let light come to be." (1 John 1:5; Genesis 1:3) From his power go forth not only the actual lightnings but also all the flashes of enlightenment, of knowledge, of understanding and of wisdom to his creatures in heaven and on earth. From the One sitting upon the divine throne the power of voice comes, also the sound waves produced by the organs of speech, and especially divine messages that are carried by the voice. Sometimes the divine messages thunder in their impressiveness and in pronouncing judgment upon his enemies. "The glorious God himself has thundered." (Psalm 29:3)

---

24. How did God's sitting enthroned here differ from what was true of King Solomon's temple of long ago?
25. As pictured by what John saw and heard, what things go forth from God's throne?

His prophecies of things to come have foretold of his coming to his great spiritual temple for the purpose of judging men.—Malachi 3:1.

[26] God's spirit or active force is invisible to human eyes, but it can cause creations to move and to work. It can produce results that our feeble eyes can see and that our other senses can perceive. By his spirit or active force God can cause enlightenment, revealing things that no ordinary human mind could think up or understand, through light shed on long-hidden sacred secrets. His spirit is like "seven lamps of fire" burning before God in his heavenly temple, not to give him light but to make things light for those who come into his presence. Those seven lamps of fire, John says, "mean the seven spirits of God." Not that seven spirit persons are meant by these seven spirits, but that the spirit or active force of God is to be looked upon in a sevenfold way. Seven being the Bible number that stands for spiritual completeness or perfection, the seven spirits denote the complete fullness of God's spirit. The fully needed amount of his spirit or active force he uses for enlightening those who serve him in his spiritual temple. In their turn, these enlightened ones reflect the spiritual light to other creatures to bring them a knowledge of God's truth.

[27] Those seven symbolic lamps of fire must have shed their light upon the "glassy sea like crystal," at which priests could wash. So, too, the sevenfold spirit of God works only through an organization or group of creatures that is clean in his eyes. His spirit operates through a cleansed organization and helps the members to keep the organization and its offerings to God clean. Remember that the great "sea" of King Solomon's temple

---

26. What is meant by the "seven lamps of fire," and why should lighted lamps be before him?
27. Upon what did those seven lamps shine, and what did this fact picture?

could hold about 19,600 gallons of water and was "for the priests to wash in it." (2 Chronicles 4: 2-6) Like clean water, God's truth is cleansing and purifying in its power. Those who are admitted into God's presence, like the twenty-four elders, need such water of truth, in order to carry out their priestly duties acceptably to God and for the good of all men of good will. True to this picture, the congregation of 144,000 faithful followers of Jesus Christ are spoken of as receiving from him a cleansing "with the bath of water by means of the word, that he might present the congregation to himself in its splendor, not having a spot or a wrinkle or any of such things, but that it should be holy and without blemish." (Ephesians 5:25-27) God believes in religious cleanness. He has near him what is clean.

JUSTICE, POWER, LOVE AND WISDOM IN HIS CREATURES

[28] Let us not be surprised at what we see further in the vision to John. Let us not think that in heaven there are animals that are found on earth. The dog Laika that lived for a few days imprisoned in the Russian Sputnik No. 2, rocketed into outer space on November 3, 1957, got no higher than the orbit in which this man-made satellite zoomed around the earth till it fell to destruction on April 14, 1958. But in God's holy presence there are creatures that have qualities pictured by certain animals here on earth. We see these as John tells us more details of his marvelous vision. "And in the midst of the throne and around the throne there are four living creatures that are full of eyes in front and behind. And the first living creature is like a lion, and the second living creature is like a young bull, and the third living creature has a face like a man's, and the

---

28. What four living creatures were seen at God's throne?

fourth living creature is like a flying eagle."—Revelation 4:6, 7.

[29] Being in the midst of God's throne and around his throne, these four living creatures symbolize an organization of God's creatures having the four prominent qualities or attributes that were found first in the Creator himself and that he put in creatures whom he made in his image and likeness. The Holy Bible tells specially of God's four principal qualities or attributes, which are justice, power, love and wisdom, in perfect balance and harmony. These are live or living qualities, not existing separate or detached, but embodied in God himself and also in all his godlike creatures. Since the living creatures full of eyes before and behind are four in number, they together would picture God's organization of godlike creatures in the perfectness of a square, with its four sides equal and in perfect balance, right-angled.

[30] All these creatures are marked by a combination of the four outstanding godlike qualities. These set them apart from mere brute beasts of the earth. The fact that the first living creature is like a lion pictures that God's properly balanced organization has courageous justice. Jesus Christ, God's first creation, is spoken of as God's righteous or just one, and he is called "the Lion that is of the tribe of Judah." (John 5:30; Acts 3:14; 7:52; 22:14; Revelation 5:5) The fact that the second living creature was like a young bull points to the power or strength with which God has filled the organization of his godlike creatures. In keeping with this fact the apostle Paul said: "For all things I have the strength by virtue of him who imparts power to me." And to Christians he wrote: "Finally, go on acquiring power in the Lord and

---

29. What do these living creatures symbolize, and to what does their number four point?
30. What does the first creature's likeness to a lion picture, and the second creature's likeness to a young bull?

in the mightiness of his strength."—Philippians
4:13; Ephesians 6:10.

³¹ As regards the third living creature, it had
a "face like a man's." Now it is said of man's
Maker: "God is love." (1 John 4:16) Man, who
is made in God's image and likeness, should cor-
respondingly be love, expressing love above all
other things of which he is capable. So the man's
face on the third living creature symbolizes that
God's organization of faithful sons has love and
hence works no evil to fellow creatures. "He that
does not love has not come to know God, because
God is love." (1 John 4:8) Combined with this
love and with justice and power is wisdom, heavenly wisdom; and this is pictured by the flying
eagle that the fourth living creature resembles.
The eagle flies high in the heavens and is far-
sighted. "An eagle flies upward" and "builds its
nest high up, . . . far into the distance its eyes
keep looking." (Job 39:27-29) "For a foolish one
true wisdom is too high," but not for the far-
sighted, high-aiming ones of God's faithful organization. They are swift like the eagle in acting
according to God's wisdom.—Proverbs 24:7.

³² The symbolic four living creatures were full
of eyes in front and behind. In like manner those
who are members of God's just, powerful, loving
and wise organization are awake, alert, on the
watch. They especially take note of God in all
things and observe all his indications of what he
wants them to do. This remarkable feature about
them is made noticeable in the further description
of them: "And as for these four living creatures,
each one of them respectively has six wings; round
about and underneath they are full of eyes. And
they have no rest day and night as they say:

31. What did the third creature's having a face like a man's picture, and the fourth creature's being like a flying eagle?
32. What is pictured in that the four living creatures have many
eyes in front and behind and declare Jehovah's holiness day and
night?

'Holy, holy, holy is Jehovah* God, the Almighty, who was and who is and who is coming.' " (Revelation 4:8) From this it is plain that these four many-eyed living creatures picture those who can talk and who recognize God and appreciate his holiness, his almightiness and his purposefulness, and who, besides, know his name.

33 Long before John, the prophet Isaiah also had a vision of God at his temple. At that time Isaiah saw heavenly creatures called seraphs standing above God's throne. Like the four living creatures, these also had three pairs of wings. How did they use these wings? "With two he kept his face covered, and with two he kept his feet covered, and with two he would fly about. And this one called to that one and said: 'Holy, holy, holy is Jehovah of armies. The fullness of all the earth is his glory.' "—Isaiah 6:1-3.

34 Manifestly, with three pairs of wings, the four living creatures whom John saw could either fly or speed up their movement forward; they could either cover parts of themselves or cover other creatures protectively; and they would have plenty of vision to know how to use those wings that were full of eyes round about and underneath. Such peculiarities speak of similar powers of swift movement, protectiveness and awakeness, awareness, on the part of God's faithful servants pictured by the four living creatures. For example, we are told by Psalm 34:7: "The angel of Jeho-

---

* Nine Hebrew translations of the book of Revelation have the name "Jehovah" or "Yahweh" here, instead of the title "the Lord." These Hebrew translations, listed as J[7, 8, 11-14, 16-18], are identified for us on pages 31, 32 of the *New World Translation of the Christian Greek Scriptures*. See therein the footnote a on Revelation 4:8.

---

33. What equality in wings did the prophet Isaiah see in his vision of Jehovah in his temple?
34. What did the four creatures' having each three pairs of wings make possible, also the wings' being full of eyes?

vah is camping all around those fearing him and
he rescues them." Day and night God's just,
powerful, loving and wise organization can render
any needed service. Why? Because they "have
no rest day and night" as they tell continually,
with a threefold emphasis, how holy Jehovah God
the Almighty is. So we should appreciate God's
universal organization.

³⁵ The true Christian congregation is in full harmony with what the symbolic four living creatures
do and say. John shows that when telling us more
of what he saw in vision. He says: "And whenever the living creatures offer glory and honor
and thanksgiving to the one seated upon the
throne, the one that lives for ever and ever, the
twenty-four persons of advanced age fall down before the one seated upon the throne and worship
the one that lives for ever and ever, and they cast
their crowns before the throne, saying: 'You are
worthy, Jehovah,* even our God, to receive the
glory and the honor and the power, because you
created all things, and because of your will they
existed and were created.' "—Revelation 4:9-11.

³⁶ Do the political rulers of today, or do even
the religious rulers of today, inside and outside
Christendom, fulfill that symbolic vision? Do
they take off their crowns, their diadems, their
miters, their official turbans or headdress and cast
them before the One sitting in the "ultimate position" on the supreme throne of the universe, the

---

* Six Hebrew translations of the book of Revelation
have the name "Jehovah" or "Yahweh" here, instead
of the title "the Lord." In the *New World Translation
of the Christian Greek Scriptures* these are listed as
J⁷, ⁸, ¹³, ¹⁴, ¹⁶, ¹⁸. See therein the footnote b on Revelation
4:11, and pages 31, 32.

35. How did the twenty-four elders show that the Christian congregation is in agreement with what the living creatures do and
say?
36. Having in mind those twenty-four elders, what questions do
we ask concerning political or even religious rulers on earth today?

immortal One, who lives and reigns forever and ever? Do they get down off their thrones or official seats and fall down before this God and Creator and surrender to him their governing power and authority, confessing that He is the one worthy to receive the glory, the honor and the power, because he is the Creator of all things? Do they thus copy the twenty-four "elders"? Or do they try to make heroes and gods out of themselves for people to idolize and worship, requiring them to 'give to Caesar what belongs to God'? Do they seek to gain the "ultimate position" in outer space and to seize world domination and to enforce their will on the peoples of the earth? Or do they show willingness to hand over national or tribal sovereignty to the supreme, everlasting kingdom of God? The worldly events of our day give the unprejudiced, unmistakable answers to these pointed questions.

[37] Those who are really symbolized by the twenty-four "elders" honestly declare that all power comes from God the Creator and that they deserve no glory or honor. God the Creator they acknowledge as worthy of receiving glory, honor and power and therefore worthy of receiving worship, submission and obedience. Since he is Creator of all things, he is also our Creator. In no other way did we come into existence. We did not will ourselves into existence on this earth. No; but as the twenty-four "elders" said to God on his throne: "Because of your will they existed and were created." Since it is because of God's will that we were created and have existence today, then we were created for God's will. We exist only for his will, all of us. Quite properly we should desire and try to learn what his will is and then do it. Otherwise we shall disastrously miss the purpose of our creation and existence.

---

37. To whom do those pictured by the "elders" give the glory, and why should we try to learn what his will is and to do it?

[38] The greatest man ever on earth appreciated that very fact. He was a man of prayer to God. His name was Jesus. His father was not a Hebrew, an Israelite or a Jew, but was God himself, as the facts to be discussed herein will show. For that reason he called no man his father but spoke of God as his heavenly Father. Because Jesus, when thirty years old, was anointed and received the spirit of God he was called Jesus Christ. In The Holy Bible we find written the "book of the history of Jesus Christ," "the good news about Jesus Christ." (Matthew 1:1; Mark 1:1) He was the greatest teacher ever on earth. He had learners or disciples, and he sent out special disciples to preach. These he called apostles, or sent-forth ones.—Mark 3:7, 9, 13, 14.

[39] Jesus taught his disciples to pray to God in an acceptable way. The simplest, yet greatest pattern of prayer that he taught them is given in his well-known Sermon on the Mount. He told them not to pray hypocritically or according to mere form: "But when praying, do not say the same things over and over again, just as the people of the nations do, for they imagine they will get a hearing for their use of many words. So, do not make yourselves like them, for God your Father knows what things you are needing before ever you ask him." (Matthew 6:5-8) In this way he taught them to recognize God as their Creator and Life-giver, hence as their Father, the Provider of what things they are needing. Then he added:

THE MODEL PRAYER

[40] "This, therefore, is the way you are to pray: 'Our Father in heaven, your name be revered!

---

38. Who as the greatest man ever on earth appreciated that fact, and whom did he send out to preach?
39. In what way did he tell them that they should pray, and to whom?
40. What was the model prayer that he taught them?

Your kingdom come! Your will be done on earth as well as in heaven! Give us today bread for the day, and forgive us our debts, as we have forgiven our debtors. And do not subject us to temptation, but save us from the evil one.' "—Matthew 6:9-13, *An American Translation.*

[41] In Jesus' day on earth the Caesar of the Roman Empire ruled a large part of the inhabited earth, including the Middle East, where Jesus lived. Jesus did not teach his learners, his disciples, to pray to a nameless divine Person, an unnamable God, a God who as soon as his title "God" is mentioned is recognized in the same way by everybody, regardless of which one of the millions of so-called gods that a person may be worshiping. Jesus Christ many times spoke of the personal name of God his Father. Before he began to preach in a meeting place in his home town of Nazareth he took the book of Isaiah and read to his listeners chapter 61, verses 1 and 2, which say: "The Spirit of the Lord Jehovah is upon me; because Jehovah hath anointed me to preach good tidings." (*AS;* Luke 4:16-21) From this it is seen that God has a personal name.

[42] God has a name that sets him apart from every other person or thing that is called by the title "god." He honors and respects his own name and will allow nobody to live forever that speaks wrongly of his name or that shames his name. He puts his own name behind the promises, the prophecies, the statements of purpose that he makes, so that he may not be mistaken for anyone else whom men worship as a god. In regard to his

41. Was it to a nameless God that he taught them to pray, and how did he personally show the answer to this question?

42, 43. How does God set himself apart from every other one that is called "god," and with what Hindu statement does his Word disagree in this matter?

name his written Word, the Bible, disagrees with
the following recent statement:*

[43] "Names of gods do not make religion any
more than the names of men and women make
up their personality. Names are originally given
and used without any idea of comparison or contrast with other names. . . . Whether it be God,
Jehovah, Bhagwan, Ishwar, Allah, Hari, Siva or
Rama, it is the same Being that in vague manner
is recalled by every devotee when he utters the
name which he has been brought up to associate
with the mystery of the universe and the idea of
worship."

[44] To the contrary, Jesus taught his disciples to
pray, not to a so-called Mother-Father God,† or
to a nameless God, but to a God whose name Jesus
himself knew and the Israelite high priests knew.
If God's personal name, which is Jehovah, did not
count, why did Jesus open the model prayer,
teaching: "Our Father in heaven, your name be
revered [or, be sanctified, NW]"? Those listening
to Jesus' Sermon on the Mount were believers,
not in the gods of India or other lands like it, but
in the God whom Jesus himself worshiped. Christ's
own name honors the name of this God and heavenly Father, for the name Jesus means "Jehovah
is Salvation."—Matthew 1:21.

[45] This Jehovah was the One to whom Jesus'
disciples were to pray as "Our Father in heaven."
God gave himself this name before ever there was
an Abraham, an Israelite, a Jew or a Christian;
and God has stuck to that name ever since. The

---

* Quoted from the book *Hinduism—Doctrine and
Way of Life*, by C. Rajagopalachari (1956), printed at
the Hindustan Times Press, New Delhi, page 3, paragraph 1.

† See page 8, paragraph 6.

44. What was known about the God to whom Jesus was teaching
his disciples to pray?
45. (a) Who gave God that name, and how long have men known
and used it? (b) When will it be revered and sanctified, and why?

first man and woman on earth knew and mentioned his name. (Genesis 4:1) More than five hundred years before the flood of Noah's day men in general were using God's exclusive name. Yes, for during the days of the first man's grandson they were doing so: "Then began men to call upon the name of Jehovah." (Genesis 4:26, *AS*) In the new world toward which humankind is rapidly moving, the name of Jehovah will be revered, hallowed, sanctified or held sacred by all human creatures that survive into that coming world. Jesus Christ taught his disciples to pray that it might be so. For nineteen centuries since then his faithful, obedient disciples have prayed that it might be so. It will be so, because the heavenly Father who respects his own name will answer the prayer that his beloved Son and the disciples of his Son have prayed continually in faith.

⁴⁶ But one important question before leaving this prayer. It is this: Who will rule the planet earth and decide what the people on earth must do? The answer to that question will determine whose will is to be done on earth. There is an answer to the question, and it will be given by an able government. Whose government? God's own government. Addressing the model prayer to his own Father and the Father of his disciples, Jesus prayed: "Your kingdom come! Your will be done on earth as well as in heaven!"

⁴⁷ During the coming new world this earth will not be governed by some government from this earth, from men. It will not be governed by some government of great wealth, power and scientific achievements that gets control of man's "ultimate position" in outer space, and that with this advantage forces the peoples of earth to do its will

46. According to Jesus' model prayer, what will make certain whose will is to be done on earth?
47. Why will the government of the new world not be one from outer space?

or else take the consequences from outer space.
Earth will be governed by a government higher
than man's "ultimate position" in outer space.
It will be governed by a truly heavenly government, by God's kingdom, in answer to the prayer
of all lovers of a righteous, perfect, sinless government, a theocratic government.

48 Since there are so many who are called gods
today, how could we know whose government God's
kingdom really was unless we knew the name of
this God, this Father in heaven to whom Jesus
addressed the model prayer? But no uncertainty
exists as to whose kingdom is prayed for. It is the
kingdom of the great Life-giver in heaven, whose
name is to be revered and hallowed. That heavenly
King is Jehovah God the Almighty, whom the
twenty-four symbolic "elders" called worthy to
receive the glory, honor and power. The earth and
man upon it were created because of Jehovah's
will. It is right and inescapable that his will should
be done on earth. His will is being done up in
heaven, where he reigns as Sovereign of the universe. On earth his will is not being done by men
whom the Creator has permitted to live. His will
is done up in heaven, which is so immeasurably
bigger than our small earth. During the new world
his will is certain to be done on earth just as it is
done on a vaster scale in heaven.

49 When the will of that One is done on earth
whom John saw in his inspired vision, the One
who is so radiantly beautiful in himself and who
surrounds himself with an organization of creatures acting with justice, power, love and wisdom,
how grand it will be on earth in the new world!
For thousands of years the changeless, irresistible
purpose of Jehovah God has been working to that

48. Because of the many so-called gods, how is it known whose
government personally the Kingdom is, and why is it inescapable
that his will should be done on earth?
49. To what grand end respecting the earth has God been working, and what will its realization mean for the earth?

grand end. Regardless of what has been the turn
of events on earth, he in his all-might has always
been in command of the situation. He has always
been ahead of man and devil. He has permitted
nothing to interfere with the perfect outworking
of his purpose, his will.

[50] Knowing the end of his works from the beginning of them, he has seen thousands of years
ahead of his creatures. (Isaiah 46:10) From the
beginning he has worked steadily, unswervingly
toward his goal. The end is now plainly in sight.
By making a swiftly moving survey of the known
events of human history over thousands of years
in the light of prophecies given over God's own
name, we shall appreciate more his faithfulness
to his promise and prophecy, and his perfect foresight and ability to carry out his righteous purpose. As never before we shall understand the
meaning of what is now occurring on earth.
Through this we shall receive still greater assurance that the will of Jehovah God will be done on
earth as well as in heaven.

---

50. Why has God seen thousands of years ahead of humans, and
how shall we receive greater assurance that his will is going to
be done here?

CHAPTER 2

Why It Must Be Done On Earth

LIVING on this earth is becoming more and more dangerous for mankind, not only physically but also morally and spiritually. This ought not to be so. But it is so. Yet there is no other place for mankind to move to. Mankind cannot move away from the trouble to the much smaller moon or to the other planets such as men have named Venus, Mercury and Mars. The earth's moon and the planets of our solar system were not prepared for man to live there in comfort, happiness and eternity. Boast as men may of shooting a rocket to or around the moon, or of sending a manned, atom-powered spaceship there and beyond, no nation is prepared to evacuate its people from this earth to the moon or any other planet of our solar system. Besides, what sane man wants to live there or could live there? Man is bound to this planet. He will have to stay here when the danger reaches its highest pitch. He will find himself trapped in a destructive trouble that is largely of his own making.

[2] Because of the advances of worldly science the nuclear space age suddenly broke in upon mankind. Because it was practically forced upon us by ambition, rivalry and fears of a grasping, greedy enemy, not by love, it has not proved to be such a wonderful time to live in for people of this world. Any spreading of modern conveniences, any lifting of the people's standard of living, any increases in the number of scientists, any enlargement of man's understanding of the secrets of outer space and of the structure of our earth, all this has left the more important situation still unchanged. It is still a split-up world. More than just a chasm divides East and West. In numberless ways the people are divided as to whose political, social and religious will they want to rule them. Dictatorial powers or systems of rule take control of the people in large areas; even popular

1. Why is there no other place for man to move to, and how will he find himself trapped in destructive trouble?
2. Why is this nuclear space age not such a wonderful time in which to live, and what has scientific advance left unchanged?

governments find it necessary to take over more power in order to keep operating or to protect themselves. So the people find themselves forced to bow down to the will of distracted, powerfully armed and heavily financed rulers.

[3] Despite protests, the test explosion of atomic and nuclear weapons of war continued, polluting the air and the sea, even the rainfall and the snow. Nations are willing to call a halt to the production and testing of further weapons of holocaustic destruction of human lives only because they feel overstocked with them, or feel they have reached the ultimate weapon and no further testing is needed. Fear of radioactive fallout from nuclear explosions spreads around the globe and stirs unrest among the helpless, who feel victimized. For the sake of security and to get surprises ready for the suspected enemy, the invention and making of more hideous weapons of destruction continues. With the ICBM (intercontinental ballistic missile) or with the atomic or modernized submarine equipped to hurl IRBM's (intermediate-range ballistic missiles) from underneath the water and able to conceal itself under the polar icecap, the "splendid isolation" of any continent is a thing of the past. All continents are within range of war missiles, all civilian populations also. Strategic bombing of population or industrial centers is just as vital to winning a hot war as tactical bombing of people in the war camp or on the firing lines. In the unavoidable total warfare and regimentation of the citizenry all the people supporting and supplying the men in uniform must suffer equally with those firing the scientific weapons of war.

[4] To add to the scare, the control of the weather

3. Why is the isolation of any continent now a thing of the past, and why in further total warfare must all the people as well as the firers of weapons suffer?
4. What possibility does control of the weather take on as compared with nuclear weapons?

takes on the possibility of being more deadly than nuclear warfare. The chairman of the American Advisory Committee on Weather Control warned that control of the weather by the enemy could work more disastrous results to the United States of America than atomic discoveries. About the same time the director of the Laboratory of Earth Sciences at the Massachusetts Institute of Technology backed that warning up, saying: "International control of weather modification will be as essential to the safety of the world as control of nuclear energy is now." And he urged America to keep ahead or abreast of Soviet Russia.*

[5] A peaceful coexistence has been recommended for nations that follow radically different political ideas and systems. Coexistence does not mean brotherly love between nations. It means a risky putting up with each other while the rivalry and race for worldly advantages and domination goes on in ways less noisy than launching deadly missiles armed with atomic and nuclear warheads. Merely the temperature of the war is different— cold. At the World Conference of Religions in New Delhi, India, during November of 1957, Jawaharlal Nehru as India's Prime Minister mentioned to the delegates that the world had taken a "mighty turn" toward the adventure of interplanetary travel. He said no one was sure how the new forces would at last be put to use. One thing had become clear to him, though, and that was that if the "cold war" kept on it would be a hard thing for this world to survive.† Other voices besides his have been raised in warning.

---

* Howard T. Orville and Dr. Henry G. Houghton, respectively, as reported in the New York *Times* under date of January 28, 1958.

† The New York *Times* as of November 18, 1957, page 3.

---

5. What does coexistence of opposed nations really mean, and how hard would "cold war" at last make it for this world?

⁶ If mankind and animalkind are yet to be preserved on an earth fit to live in, a will higher than that of the selfishly divided, suspicious nations needs to be carried out on earth. It must be the will of more than just anyone in the spirit realm who is higher and more powerful than earthly nations. Why so? Because the Holy Bible warns us that the nations are in the grip of the worst enemy of man and of man's Creator, namely, Satan the Devil. He is, in fact, the invisible "ruler of this world," "the god of this system of things." (John 12:31; 14:30; 2 Corinthians 4:4) What, then? For the survival of man and animal on earth as an everlasting home the supranational will that has to be done on earth is that of God the Creator, who says: "I am Jehovah. That is my name; and to anyone else I shall not give my own glory, neither my praise to graven images." (Isaiah 42:8) His will must be done on earth if man and beast are to enjoy life on earth forever. In this way his purpose in creating man and animals on earth will have to be proved just, righteous, good and loving. His purpose will thus have to be vindicated, justified, to his immortal glory. Those praying the model prayer that Jesus taught pray for God's purpose to be vindicated by his will being done on earth as well as in heaven.

THE EARTH EVERLASTING

⁷ How, though, can we make sure that it is the Creator's will for the earth to stay in existence to eternity and for it to remain an inhabited planet always? We cannot make sure of this by going to the contradictory religions of Christendom. We can positively make sure of it by going to the Creator's own written Word, the Holy Bible. By

---

6. For man's preservation on earth, whose supranational will must be done here, and how will that affect the purpose in man's creation?

7. How can we make sure that it is the Creator's will for the earth to exist forever?

his spirit or active force he is the Creator of the Bible, even though he did use faithful men of God in the producing of it. "For you know this first, that no prophecy of Scripture springs from any private release. For prophecy was at no time brought by man's will, but men spoke from God as they were borne along by holy spirit." (2 Peter 1:20, 21) Religious priests keep the Bible from the people and interpret or misinterpret it according to their creeds or man-made statements of belief. However, God produced the Bible for all the people to read or to have read to them, to know for themselves what God himself says in his Book.

[8] Jesus Christ had the thirty-nine books of the Hebrew Scriptures, from the book of Genesis to the book of Malachi, which had been written under inspiration of God's spirit before Jesus lived on earth. From those books Jesus knew what God's will for this earth was and what his purpose was in creating it and putting man on it. In harmony with this knowledge from those Hebrew Scriptures Jesus composed the model prayer for his followers. He told them to pray to the Father in heaven: "Your kingdom come! Your will be done on earth as well as in heaven!" Let us ask ourselves, then: Is Jesus here teaching men to pray for the earth to be destroyed by fire or any other means and to be emptied of human and animal creatures? Since the heavenly Father's kingdom is to come to this earth in answer to Jesus' own prayer, why should this earth be destroyed at that time or at any time afterward? God's kingdom comes to stay here for all future time. He does not need to destroy the earth on account of the people on it. No, not when God's will is then being

8. (a) In harmony with what writings did Jesus compose his model prayer? (b) When God's kingdom comes, why should the earth not be destroyed?

done by people on earth under God's kingdom the same as it is being done up in heaven. Why destroy the earth any more than destroy the heavens, where holy spirit creatures are doing God's will the same as human creatures will be doing it here under his kingdom?

[9] Manifestly, God's kingdom comes to earth and his will is then done on earth because it is his purpose for the earth to remain forever as part of the universal realm over which he is the King of eternity, the Most High Sovereign. God's will being done here under his kingdom will make a delightful change on this earth. Why then destroy this territory of his kingdom? Why remove the people doing God's will on earth from this territory of his kingdom? That is not what God will do, for he inspired wise King Solomon of old to write this proverb: "In the multitude of people there is an adornment of a king, but in the lack of population is the ruin of a high official." (Proverbs 14:28) It was because the first man did not keep on doing the will of his Creator that God sentenced him to die and return to the dust of the earth. (Genesis 3:17-19) When God's will is done by the people on earth under God's kingdom, he will give them the right to eternal life on this territory of his kingdom realm. For the sake of this he will preserve this earth to his everlasting glory as its Creator.

[10] Christendom, however, will argue through its priests and clergymen that the coming of Christianity changed matters for the earth. But how could that be so? Jehovah God used Jesus Christ as the very Leader in Christianity, and it was this Leader of Christianity himself that gave us the

---

9. God's kingdom will come and his will will be done because of what divine purpose concerning the earth?
10. How does the model prayer prove that the coming of Christianity did not change matters for the earth?

prayer for God's kingdom to come and for God's will to be done on earth as well as in heaven!

[11] The Leader of Christianity could not be wrong in what he taught about the earth. He was not wrong. Holy men of God, who were borne along by God's spirit in order to speak and write prophecy before Christ's day, had no hope or desire to go to heaven's unknown realm. In fact, they had no invitation from God to go to heaven, nor was the way then open for men to go to heaven. They did not expect, when they died, to go to heaven. They did not look forward to the total destruction of this earth and its moon in a universal conflagration. True, they expected a future life, but not a future life in heaven. Their hope was to return from the dead to a renewed life on this earth, but then when God rules over the Middle East and over all the rest of the earth.

[12] The coming of Jesus Christ to earth did not prove that their hope was a mistaken one. His coming did not change the future for them and open the way to heaven for them. Long after Abraham, Isaac, Jacob (Israel), Moses, King David, the prophet Isaiah and even the prophet Malachi died, Jesus Christ the Son of God came down from heaven to earth in a miraculous way. He did not say that those holy men of old were up in heaven when he left. Jesus, as the Son of man on earth, said to a Jewish ruler: "No man has ascended into heaven but he that descended from heaven, the Son of man." (John 3:13) When the Baptizer, John the son of Zechariah, was in prison and soon to have his head chopped off, Jesus said: "Among those born of women there has not been raised up a greater than John the Baptist; but a person that is a lesser one in the

---

11. What was the hope and desire of ancient holy men of God respecting their future?
12, 13. (a) Why did Jesus' coming to earth not prove that their hope was a mistaken one? (b) In this regard, what did Peter say, to confirm what Jesus himself had said?

kingdom of the heavens is greater than he is."
(Matthew 11:11) After Jesus himself was put to
death on a torture stake but was resurrected from
the dead on the third day and later went back to
heaven to his Father, the apostle Peter preached
to over three thousand Jews and said that the
resurrected Jesus was in heaven but King David
was not up there.

¹³ Said Peter: "It is allowable to speak with
freeness of speech to you concerning the family
head David, that he both deceased and was buried
and his tomb is among us to this day. Actually
David did not ascend to the heavens, but he himself says, 'Jehovah said to my Lord [that is, to
Jesus Christ], "Sit at my right hand, until I make
your enemies a stool for your feet."'" (Acts 2:
29, 34) Those dead men like David still wait for
God's kingdom to come.

¹⁴ Jesus spoke of himself as going to heaven
because he had come down from there only for
thirty-three years and a half. He spoke of his
congregation of faithful followers, those pictured
by the twenty-four "elders" in the Revelation to
John, as invited to go to heaven to be with him.
To these he gave instructions to prepare them
to go to heaven. But this did not mean that Jesus
Christ had changed God's original purpose concerning humankind as a whole.

¹⁵ Jesus did not open the way for all the God-
fearing ones of mankind to go to heaven. For the
sake of humankind in general, he prayed for God's
kingdom to come to the earth where dead humankind lies buried and for the heavenly Life-giver's
will to be done on earth as well as in heaven. Will
King David and John the Baptist want to do God's
will on earth under His kingdom? Certainly. Hence

14. Why did Jesus speak of himself as going to heaven, and what
effect did the invitation to his followers to go to heaven have on
God's purpose toward mankind?
15. For whose benefit in general did Jesus pray for God's kingdom to come, and what do confused men need to re-examine?

confused men need to re-examine the Bible to learn what the Creator's will was for man at the beginning. Then they will see that God's will and purpose have been made more sure because Christ came.

GOD'S PURPOSE FOR THE EARTH

[16] Earth's Creator is pointed out to us by name. In the prophecy of Jeremiah we read the difference between him and all the false gods: "But Jehovah is in truth God. He is the living God and the King to time indefinite. Because of his indignation the earth will rock, and no nations will hold up under his denunciation. This is what you men will say to them: 'The gods that did not make the very heavens and the earth are the ones who will perish from the earth and from under these heavens.' He is the Maker of the earth by his power, the One firmly establishing the productive land by his wisdom, and the One who by his understanding stretched out the heavens. At his voice there is a giving of a turmoil of waters in the heavens by him, and he causes vapors to ascend from the extremity of the earth. He has made even sluices for the rain, and he brings forth the wind from his storehouses." (Jeremiah 10:10-13) Jehovah is therefore the God who is meant when the Holy Bible opens with the words: "In the beginning God created the heavens and the earth."—Genesis 1:1.*

[17] No proof of creature life on the other planets of our solar system has been established by astronomers and scientists, but the Creator's direct pur-

---

* For a Scriptural discussion of the earth and its living creatures see the book *"New Heavens and a New Earth"*, chapters 3 and 4.

---

16. By what identification does Jeremiah 10:10-13 point out the earth's creator, and who therefore is meant in Genesis 1:1?
17. How did this planet earth start off, and how does God, according to his own statement, not want it to end?

pose for our earth was different. In its case he did not desire it to be an empty, lifeless planet at its start; he does not desire it ever to end up in that condition. Let us ask him about this. "This is what Jehovah has said, the Holy One of Israel and the Former of him: 'Ask me even about the things that are coming concerning my sons; and concerning the activity of my hands you people should command me. I myself have made the earth and have created even man upon it. I—my own hands have stretched out the heavens, and all the army of them I have commanded.' For this is what Jehovah has said, the Creator of the heavens, He The true God, the Former of the earth and the Maker of it, He the One who firmly established it, who did not create it simply for nothing, who formed it even to be inhabited: 'I am Jehovah, and there is no one else. In a place of conceal-ment I spoke not.' " (Isaiah 45:11, 12, 18, 19) He formed this earth to be inhabited for all time.

[18] Those inspired words through the prophet Isaiah are in full agreement with the written rec-ord about the preparation of this earth for the realizing of God's purpose. When he had made this earth a most interesting place by putting fish and sea monsters in its waters and birds in its trees and skies and animals and insects of all kinds on its land, he revealed for whom he had really made this earth to be an everlasting home. "And God went on to say: 'Let us make man [a·dam'] in our image, according to our likeness, and let them [man multiplied] have in subjection the fish of the sea and the flying creatures of the heavens and the domestic animals and all the earth and every creeping animal that is creeping upon the earth.' And God proceeded to create the man [a·dam'] in his image, in God's image he created

18. After creating the living creatures lower than human, what further did God say regarding the earth and its then living crea-tures?

him; male and female he created them." (Genesis 1:26, 27) It was not said of the other creatures, all those lower than man, that God had created them in his image and according to his likeness. Only man was thus created.

[19] While this fact raised man far higher than all the fish, birds and brute beasts, it also argued that man was created perfect, that he was a perfect creature to begin with, fully able to display on earth some image, some likeness, of his perfect Creator. Of course, all the other creatures were also made perfect, each one in its own family kind. The perfection of the inanimate material universe, which is now billions of years old, came from this same Creator. Why should there be less than perfection in the creating of living and intelligent creatures? "For I shall declare the name of Jehovah. Do you attribute greatness to our God! The Rock, perfect is his activity." (Deuteronomy 32: 3, 4) So God gave mankind a perfect start. In that way he knew that his will could be done on earth perfectly by human creatures in his image and likeness.

[20] The Creator did not keep his will concerning mankind to himself, to be guessed at by us. Because man was created in God's image and likeness he could tell man and woman what his purpose and will regarding them was. He could give them commands that they could understand and fulfill in perfection. "Further, God blessed them and God said to them: 'Be fruitful and become many and fill the earth and subdue it, and have in subjection the fish of the sea and the flying creatures of the heavens and every living creature that is creeping upon the earth.' "—Genesis 1:28.

19. What argues for the perfection of God's creation of man, and so what did God know could then be done on earth?
20. What did God tell man and woman his purpose in creating them was, and why?

[21] God blessed them; he spoke for their good, not for their injury as if they were cursed. On the preceding day or time-period of creation God had blessed the fish and the winged flying creatures that he had made. That blessing meant for them to multiply in their natural habitat, for "God blessed them, saying: 'Be fruitful and become many and fill the waters in the sea basins and let the flying creatures become many in the earth.'" (Genesis 1:22, 23) So God's blessing upon man and woman meant for them to multiply their kind and fill this earth, not fill heaven or provide a population for heaven; no more than God's blessing upon the fish and flying creatures meant for them to provide fish and winged, flying creatures for angels in heaven. Two human creatures were not enough for this earth of 196,940,000 square miles (510,071,000 square kilometers) of surface. Hence perfect man and woman were to fill earth with their perfect kind to the measure of fullness that fish and birds fill their part of this earth and surroundings with their kinds.

[22] Since man and woman were created perfect and were put under a blessing and not under a curse or a condemnation to death, the time would come when they would fill the earth to the right, needed, comfortable fullness, with nobody dying but every born child growing up to full growth. Then the need to multiply would pass, and the birth of further children would stop. There was no command to produce further children in order to transplant the surplus human population to the moon or to other planets in our solar system. "Fill the earth and subdue it," was God's command to the first human male and female. "Subdue it," that is, the earth, not the moon, not so-called

21. What did God's blessing upon them mean, and why?
22. When would the need to multiply humankind cease, and what was man to subdue?

Venus or Mercury or Mars. But how subdue the
earth?

[23] God created perfect man in a part of the earth
near the Middle East of today, for the Bible account
associates the rivers Euphrates and Tigris (Hiddekel) with their original home. It was a pleasant
location in which to create man, and it was well
called Eden, which means "Pleasure." But more
than that. "Jehovah God planted a garden in Eden,
toward the east, and there he put the man whom
he had formed. . . . Now there was a river issuing
out of Eden to water the garden, and from there
it began to be parted and it became, as it were,
four heads. . . . And the name of the third river
is Hiddekel [Tigris]; it is the one going to the
east of Assyria. And the fourth river is the
Euphrates. And Jehovah God proceeded to take
the man and settle him in the garden of Eden to
cultivate it and to take care of it." (Genesis 2:
8-15) Then, in the interest of increasing the human race, God gave this first man Adam a perfect
wife. God had built her up from a rib taken from
Adam's body to be his helper, a complement of
him.

[24] To this perfect human pair their Creator gave
the command to use their reproductive organs
and to produce children and fill the earth with
them. But along with this filling of the earth with
the human kind they must "subdue it." All these
perfect children were meant to live in an Edenic
garden or Paradise. The original one in which
Adam and Eve were settled would become too
small after a great increase in their family, with
children, grandchildren, great-grandchildren, and
so on, with no one dying because of paying the
penalty for sin. So it would become necessary for

23. In what general location did God situate man's Edenic home,
and for increasing the human race what did he give man?
24. What were the man and woman commanded to do, and what
effect would this have upon their Paradise home and the doing of
God's will?

them all to subdue the earth outside the initial garden or Paradise of Eden by spreading out the garden's boundaries, gradually cultivating the as yet uninhabited parts until the Paradise garden embraced the whole earth, from east to west and from the North Pole regions to the South Pole. This earth-girdling Paradise would require the constant attention and care of them all. Together with this garden care they were to have in subjection all the living creatures moving through earth's waters and over its land or through its skies. Thus God's will, which began to be done in the original Paradise of Eden, would finally be done everywhere on earth.

²⁵ This was the glorious, God-honoring climax that Jehovah God envisioned for all the earth. When that grand, loving purpose was fully realized, why would God want to destroy the Paradise earth? Or why would he want to depopulate Paradise by taking those doing his will in it somewhere else, leaving Paradise untended and no longer a place where the divine will was done just as it is done up in heaven? It is not Scriptural for us to think of God's doing that, for it would bring to nothing his grand purpose.

²⁶ Today, after almost six thousand years of human history, men in general are ruining the surface of the earth by their wars and commercial exploitation of the land. They are making a sewer of its atmosphere and are polluting and radioactivating its waters. They are filling the earth with imperfect children, illegitimate and legitimate, who are no more doing the will of God than their parents are doing. God's will has never yet been done over all the earth by all humankind as God indicated to man in Eden was the divine pur-

25. When that glorious climax was reached, what would it be unscriptural for us to think that God would want to do?
26. What, however, has man been doing to earth, water and air, and what divine purpose must be realized to justify man's creation?

pose. That divine purpose must yet be realized in order to justify God's creation of the first man. God must yet be vindicated in the matter of having his will done on earth as well as in heaven. Jesus prayed that God should be vindicated in that way.

[27] God has not changed his purpose in this regard, not even since his Son Jesus Christ came to earth. Regarding his stated purposes he says: "I, Jehovah, change not; therefore ye, O sons of Jacob, are not consumed." (Malachi 3:6, *AS*) He will not be obliged to consume all humankind off the face of the earth or to destroy the earth. He will not quit with his purpose unrealized in a confession of defeat. He will not let his purpose be blocked by an opposer, a Satan, or by a liar and slanderer, a Devil. For deliverance from that wicked one Jesus taught us to pray. He ended his model prayer for us, saying: "And do not bring us into temptation, but deliver us from the wicked one." (Matthew 6:13) Almighty God will answer that part of his Son's prayer too; and this means that the wicked "ruler of this world," "the god of this system of things," will have to go. The presence of the "wicked one," Satan the Devil, and God's will being done on earth as well as in heaven do not harmonize. So Satan the Devil and his invisible demons and his visible human agents will have to go. An everlasting earthly Paradise filled with perfect doers of his will is a future certainty. The kingdom of the heavenly Father, for the coming of which Jesus taught his disciples to pray, will see to that.—Revelation 20:1-3.

[28] This was why, when the sympathetic evildoer was dying on a stake alongside Jesus and said to him: "Remember me, my Lord, when you come

---

27. By whom will God not let his purpose be blocked, and for what deliverance did Jesus teach us to pray, and by what means? 28, 29. For that reason, what did Jesus on the stake say to the sympathetic evildoer, and what vision did he later give to John on Patmos to show God's purpose unchanged?

in your kingdom," Jesus said to him: "Truly I say to you today, You will be with me in Paradise."* On the third day after this Jesus was resurrected from the dead, but not the sympathetic evildoer. Forty days later, as his faithful apostles looked on, Jesus Christ ascended from the Mount of Olives east of Jerusalem and disappeared into the heavens, to return to his Father above, the King of eternity. That was in the spring of 33 (A.D.). Years later, about A.D. 96, Jesus from heaven made known to the apostle John on the island of Patmos that the heavenly Father's purpose concerning the earthly Paradise under the kingdom of God was still unchanged. Jesus gave John a prophetic vision of the coming of God's kingdom to earth in a glorious way. Then John said:

²⁹ "With that I heard a loud voice from the throne say: 'Look! the tent of God is with humankind, and he will reside with them, and they will be his peoples. And God himself will be with them. And he will wipe out every tear from their eyes, and death will be no more, neither will mourning nor outcry nor pain be any more. The former things have passed away.' And the one seated on the throne said: 'Look! I am making all things new.' Also he says: 'Write, because these words are trustworthy and true.' "—Revelation 21:3-5.

³⁰ In harmony with this vision of things that "must shortly take place" the tent of God will be

---

* Luke 23:42, 43, Lamsa's *The Gospels from Aramaic* (1933) and *The Modern New Testament* (1940) and the marginal reading of *The Holy Bible from Ancient Eastern Manuscripts* (1957) and *Gospel Light* (1939), pages 303, 304. Also Rotherham's *The Emphasised Bible;* and the *New World Translation*.

30. How will it not be a strange thing then that God should dwell with men, and so how will that evildoer come to be with Jesus in Paradise?

with men. In a representative way God will dwell with men on earth, and not men with God up in heaven. This is not strange. Thousands of years ago Jehovah God dwelt representatively with the ancient Israelites by the sacred tent of worship

that the prophet Moses constructed when they were encamped on the Sinai Peninsula on their way from Egypt to the land of Palestine. (2 Samuel 7:5-7) Because this symbolic "tent of God" comes down to be with men during the new world, Jesus Christ as God's High Priest will be representatively at the earth. Our earth is then to be made a Paradise of pleasure, without tears, death, mourning, outcry or pain, with all former things of sin and death having passed away, and with God on his throne making all things new for humankind on earth. So it will come true that,

when the sympathetic evildoer is resurrected from
his centuries-long sleep of death to life on earth,
he will be with Jesus in Paradise.

[31] This hope of an earthly Paradise restored and
made earth-wide is not a materialistic hope, to
turn men away from the joys of heaven, which
many religious leaders of Christendom say is the
destiny of members of their religious systems.
This hope is no more materialistic than Adam's
obeying God for a time in Eden in order to remain
alive in the first paradise was selfishly materialistic in its aim. " 'The first man Adam became a
living soul.' The first man is out of the earth and
made of dust." (1 Corinthians 15:45, 47) Adam's
God-given hope could be no more than an earthly
hope, the same hope that all the holy men of God
entertained, from the first martyr Abel down to
John the Baptist, yes, and down to that sympathetic evildoer dying alongside Jesus.—Hebrews
11:3-40.

[32] This does not conflict with the heavenly hope
that God puts in the hearts of the followers of
Jesus Christ. These God makes his spiritual children by the use of his holy spirit or active force,
to start them in a new way of life, a heavenly life.
These comparatively few Christians, pictured by
the twenty-four "elders" in the vision to John,
are said to be begotten or engendered by God
through the means of his life-giving spirit. So
they set their affections and keep their minds
fixed on the things above. In the resurrection from
the dead they expect to be born like Jesus Christ
into the fullness of spirit life in heaven, changed,
transformed indeed.—1 Corinthians 15:42-54.

[33] The heavenly hope of these 144,000 faithful
ones of the true Christian congregation does not

31. Why is this hope of an earthly Paradise not a materialistic
one, and what was the God-given hope of men from Abel to the
dying evildoer on the stake?
32, 33. Why does this not conflict with the heavenly hope that
God puts into the hearts of followers of Jesus Christ?

leave the rest of mankind with nothing to hope for. That gleaming hope of an earthly Paradise, where God's will is to be done on earth as well as in heaven, is the blessed hope reserved for them according to God's unchanged loving purpose. The realizing of the heavenly hope by the faithful, world-conquering congregation of Christ takes place before the realizing of the earthly hope by faithful men of pre-Christian times and by faithful men of good will toward Jehovah God today. The realizing of the heavenly hope by the Christian congregation also works for the realizing of the earthly hope by believers of mankind.

[34] All the above is why God's fatherly will needs to be done on earth as well as in heaven. This will mean more than an unending happiness for the righteous ones of mankind in their earthly Paradise home. It will also show forth God's holiness, his respect for his name, his changelessness in his perfect will, his faithfulness to his word, and his invincible power and ability expressed in his kingdom, his heavenly government through his Son Jesus Christ. The saving and preserving of the human race on earth under God's kingdom is therefore made sure and certain. Let men rejoice! God's all-powerful kingdom will take complete control over the earthly home of man regardless of the long-permitted interference and opposition of all man's enemies under Satan the Devil. The events of our day are being controlled in that direction in fulfillment of God's prophecy. This we shall see as we read on.

---

34. Why will God's will in being done on earth mean more than endless happiness for righteous mankind, and why should men now rejoice?

The Need Of A Sanctuary

DOWN through thousands of years of time men have felt the need of sanctuaries, sacred places or holy buildings at which to worship the gods of their religions. But any holiness claimed for such things has not

saved them from desecration, robbery or destruction. Invading conquerors have plundered them
for their treasures; worshipers of rival gods have
polluted them in disgust; wars have brought on
their destruction by fire and bombs; earthquakes
have shaken them to their foundations and sent
their walls and pillars crashing to the ground. At
Baalbek in the valley between the Lebanon and
the Anti-Lebanon Mountains stand today the gi-
gantic ruins of the greatest temple to Jupiter in
all antiquity, the havoc upon it being climaxed by
an earthquake of twenty-seven days in 1759. The
magnificent temples to Jehovah that once crowned
Mount Moriah in Jerusalem are no more. They
suffered destruction by Gentile hands, and for
years pious Jews were accustomed to use what is
said to be the outside western wall of the ancient
temple area as a wailing wall. Nothing has seemed
to have a permanent holiness or sanctity. Why
has this been so? Is there no real sanctuary?

² In the days of the prophet Jeremiah the temple
at Jerusalem was being profaned by the very ones
that carried on religious services in it. Jeremiah
tells of God's indignation in these words to the
hypocritical worshipers: " 'Has this house upon
which my name has been called become a mere
cave of robbers in your eyes? Here I myself also
have seen it,' is the utterance of Jehovah." (Jeremiah 7:11) For the purpose of correcting wrong
ideas about his sanctuary, God inspired his prophet Isaiah to say: "This is what Jehovah has said:
'The heavens are my throne, and the earth is my
footstool. Where, then, is the house that you
people can build for me, and where, then, is the
place as a resting place for me?' " (Isaiah 66:1;

1. How have buildings regarded by men as sanctuaries not been
saved from desecration, robbery or destruction, and what questions does this fact raise?
2. By whom did Jeremiah show that Jehovah's temple was being
profaned, and when will God's great footstool be treated as holy?

Acts 7:48-50) Compared with the heavens where Jehovah sits enthroned as universal King of eternity, the earth is his footstool. This place of his feet should be holy. It will be treated as such when his will is fully done on earth as well as in heaven.

³ At the beginning of man's existence this earthly footstool of Jehovah God was not defiled by sinful creatures. The garden or Paradise that the Creator planted in Eden was part of his footstool. It especially was a holy place, because there Jehovah God conversed with man and, as it were, went "walking in the garden about the breezy part of the day." (Genesis 2:15-17; 3:8) Having been planted by him and being surpassingly beautiful, it was "the garden of Jehovah." (Genesis 13:10) It was "Eden, the garden of God." (Ezekiel 28: 13, *AS*) This made it in fact a sanctuary, a sacred, holy place, where what is sinful must not enter, where what is sinful could not dwell. In its holiness it was a place of happy, joyous living for the first human pair, Adam and Eve. They had pleasure in living in holiness, in obedience to the will of their God and heavenly Father. This is taken as an example of the happiness of Jehovah's spiritual children when he transforms their earthly condition to one of overwhelming spiritual prosperity. Speaking of this transformation for his spiritual organization, he prophetically said: "He will for certain comfort all her devastated places, and he will make her wilderness like Eden and her desert plain like the garden of Jehovah. Exultation and rejoicing themselves will be found in her, thanksgiving and the voice of melody."—Isaiah 51:3.

⁴ However, it was not long before sin did try to establish itself and take up its dwelling in that

---

3. Why was the garden of Eden, in fact, a sanctuary, and of what is the happiness of living in holiness in it used as a picture?
4. What other sons of God were there then besides the perfect Adam, and so by whom did sin try to establish itself in the sanctuary in Eden?

Edenic sanctuary. How did such a thing ever start
in God's holy universe? By the fall of a son of
God to selfish desire that this unfaithful son permitted to enter his heart and that he cultivated.
True, the human family of today traces its line
of descent back through Noah to the "son of Enos,
the son of Seth, the son of Adam, the son of God."
(Luke 3:38) Adam was an earthly son of God,
because God was his Creator and Life-giver. But
there were then other sons of God in existence,
not on earth in the flesh, but in heaven; and these
had watched the creating of our earth and of the
first man. Jehovah God himself said so, when he
asked the man Job: "Where did you happen to be
when I founded the earth? Tell me, if you do know
understanding. Into what have its socket pedestals
been sunk down, or who laid its cornerstone, when
the morning stars joyfully cried out together, and
all the sons of God began shouting in applause?"
(Job 38:1, 4, 6, 7) It was a self-enticed spirit son
of God that became leader in sin in God's holy
universe and that speedily introduced it into the
earth at God's sanctuary in Eden.

⁵ Long afterward in human history a Middle
Eastern king, the monarch of the Mediterranean
seaport of Tyre, took a line of action similar to
that of the unfaithful spirit son of God. So God
likened the king to the original sinner and inspired
his prophet Ezekiel to say to the symbolic king
of Tyre: "You were the signet of perfection, full
of wisdom and perfect in beauty. You were in
Eden, the garden of God; . . . You were blameless
in your ways from the day you were created, till
iniquity was found in you. In the abundance of
your trade you were filled with violence, and you
sinned; so I cast you as a profane thing from the
mountain of God, . . . Your heart was proud because of your beauty; you corrupted your wisdom

5. What monarch did Ezekiel liken to that original sinner, and
how did this sinner draw himself into sin?

for the sake of your splendor. . . . By the multitude of your iniquities, in the unrighteousness of your trade you profaned your sanctuaries." (Ezekiel 28:12-18, *RS*) The spirit son had had an interest in the real Eden, man's first Paradise home. He had the gift of freedom of will, but he willed in a selfish way as he began to see selfish opportunities there in Eden. His studying these selfish possibilities caused him to be tested. God was not to blame for this: "When under trial, let no one say: 'I am being tried by God.' No; for with evil things God cannot be tried nor does he himself try anyone. But each one is tried by being drawn out and enticed by his own desire. Then the desire, when it has become fertile, gives birth to sin; in turn, sin, when it has been accomplished, brings forth death."—James 1:13-15.

⁶ By deciding to do wrong to God and thus to sin and then by taking the steps to satisfy the selfish desire by which he was enticed, this spirit son of God changed himself from a son of God into a disowner of God his Father, from a coworker with God into an opposer of God, from a truth-telling praiser of God into a lying slanderer of God. He turned himself into Satan the Devil, whom God could not own as his son. He did this by trying to convert Adam and Eve from perfect, righteous, sinless children of God into bad persons such as he could now originate, sinners against their Creator. That is why John writes: "He who practices sin originates with the Devil, because the Devil has been sinning from when he began. For this purpose the Son of God was made manifest, namely, to break up the works of the Devil. . . . The children of God and the children of the Devil are evident by this fact: Everyone who does not practice righteousness does not originate with God, neither does he who does not love his brother.

6. From what into what did he change himself, and how did he desecrate God's Eden sanctuary?

. . . we should have love for one another; not like [Adam's son] Cain, who originated with the wicked one and slaughtered his brother [Abel]. And for the sake of what did he slaughter him? Because his own works were wicked, but those of his brother were righteous." (1 John 3:8-12) Through introducing sin, Satan desecrated God's Eden sanctuary.

[7] By keeping the Paradise of Eden a holy place or sanctuary it would be possible for Adam and Eve to live in it with their children forever. In this garden spot God had planted a special tree, which he called the "tree of the knowledge of good and bad." As long as God did not want man to eat of it, man's eating of it would be wrong, disobedient to his heavenly Parent, sinful against his God. "And Jehovah God also laid this command upon the man: 'From every tree of the garden you may eat to satisfaction. But as for the tree of the knowledge of good and bad you must not eat from it, for in the day you eat from it you will positively die.'" (Genesis 2:9, 16, 17) There the Lawgiver Jehovah God declared the penalty for sin to be, not everlasting living torment of the human soul, but a positive death, a ceasing to live and exist. Adam, in God's image and likeness, understood both his heavenly Father's command and also the punishment that would be given him for breaking that command. After his heavenly Father gave him the perfect woman Eve as his wife, Adam told her about their Father's command, because, as Adam said, "this is at last bone of my bones and flesh of my flesh. This one will be called Woman, because from man this one was taken." —Genesis 2:23.

[8] From this commandment Satan the Devil knew

---

7. By keeping Paradise a sanctuary, what would it be possible for Adam and Eve to do, and what special command was it possible for them to break, and with what penalty?

8. Why, when and how did Satan the Devil attack the rightness of God's law to them?

the point upon which he could test the obedience of Adam and Eve to their heavenly Father and their exclusive devotion to their God. He was, of course, invisible to Eve, he being a spirit creature. But he made his presence manifest and presented his suggestions to wrongdoing and sin by means of a beast of the field, a serpent. Adam was not just then there to ask. So by the serpent, Satan the Devil asked Eve, not for gossip, but seemingly for information: "Is it really so that God said you must not eat from every tree of the garden?" Eve correctly answered: "Of the fruit of the trees of the garden we may eat. But as for eating of the fruit of the tree that is in the middle of the garden, God has said, 'You must not eat from it, no, you must not touch it for fear you may die.'" Eve had not been left ignorant of the law of the Paradise sanctuary. By the serpent, Satan the Devil now attacked the rightness of that law. "At this the serpent said to the woman: 'You positively will not die. For God knows that in the very day of your eating from it your eyes are bound to be opened and you are bound to be like God, knowing good and bad.'"—Genesis 3:1-5.

[9] That statement was slander; and it is slander that makes a devil. But Eve did not realize that this was a slander against God, her heavenly Father. She was "thoroughly deceived." What was she to do now? If God's command was unjust, based upon false propositions, was it wrong for her to rebel against injustice and take the law into her own hand? Besides, the fruit of the tree of the knowledge of good and bad was harmless, really a food. How good-looking it was! And what a wonderful thing it would be to have one's eyes opened to see into things as never before and to be like God himself in knowing good and bad for

9. (a) What was the serpent's statement to Eve? (b) In not appreciating this, how could she reason herself into lawbreaking, and how could she argue for the serpent's rightness?

oneself! Why, then, be theocratic by obeying any
further this unrighteous, foundationless law of
her God and Father? So, in a democratic way and
spirit, Eve began taking of the fruit of the forbidden tree and eating it. Ah, she did not drop
dead at the first bite! So the serpent must have
been right about that, Eve could argue, deceived.

¹⁰ Eve had let her confidence in her heavenly
Father be ruined. In her the start was made of
something that is so widespread today, disobedience to parents. After eating her first piece of
forbidden fruit Eve may have felt democratic
through this sort of "people's action." But she did
not feel like God, as the serpent had promised.
Neither did she then have her eyes morally opened
to see the badness of her disobedience. Besides,
if there was anything to it about dying for going
against God's law, then she would have her husband Adam die with her, by persuading him to
eat with her. Hence afterward she offered the
fruit to Adam, the head of our family.

¹¹ What was Adam now to do? Be theocratic
by bowing to God's rulership and sovereignty, or
be democratic and let the people on earth rule?
Would he keep God's Edenic sanctuary holy and
free from the sin of disobedience, a place where
Jehovah is worshiped as God? Or would he let
Eve's desire to be like God influence him? So
would he deny his God and Creator and show
pride and set himself up as God, in place of Jehovah? Adam decided to please Eve by eating with
her in a condoning of her sin and also to please
himself by keeping alongside her and sharing with
her the consequences of her sin, the announced
punishment of death. He knew what he was doing:
"For Adam was formed first, then Eve. Also Adam

---

10. What did Eve thus start off on earth, and how would she have
her husband die with her if the penalty of the lawbreaking was
really that?
11. Between what kinds of action did Adam now have to choose,
and why was he willful in sinning?

was not deceived, but the woman was thoroughly deceived and came to be in transgression." (1 Timothy 2:13, 14) Contrary to God-given knowledge, Adam acted against his headship over the human family. He sinned willfully.—Genesis 3:6, 7.

¹² Adam, as the responsible decider, had set up false worship in the Edenic sanctuary. It was the worship of self, the worship of the created person instead of the Creator. By breaking God's law he had in himself lifted himself up above theocratic law. He had made himself lofty, making a god of himself to decide what was good and what was bad from his own viewpoint. He made himself detestable, abominable or disgusting. Long afterward the wise man said: "Everyone that is proud in heart is something detestable to Jehovah." And Jesus Christ said: "God knows your hearts; because what is lofty among men is a disgusting thing in God's sight." (Proverbs 16:5; Luke 16:15) In King Solomon's day and in Jesus' day there were many animals, birds and insects that God's law pronounced unclean for the Israelites to eat. Eating such creatures made the Israelites unclean, abominable, loathsome or disgusting to God the Giver of the Ten Commandments and the law concerning clean foods. In the law of his covenant with Israel he commanded:

¹³ "Do not make your souls loathsome with any swarming creature that swarms, and you must not defile yourselves with them so that you actually get defiled by them. For I am Jehovah your God, and you must sanctify yourselves and you must prove yourselves holy, because I am holy." Also: "You must not make your souls loathsome with the beast and the fowl and anything that goes creeping on the ground that I have divided off for

---

12, 13. What worship did Adam thus set up in Eden, and how was he making himself to God, according to the principle of God's law to Israel?

you in declaring them unclean."—Leviticus 11:43, 44; 20:25.

¹⁴ Many of such beasts, fowls and insects were in the Edenic sanctuary. The tree of the knowledge of good and bad was also in the same garden sanctuary. That special tree was forbidden as food to Adam and Eve, just as those many animals were later declared unclean to the Israelites for food. As in the case of the Israelites under God's law to them, Adam and Eve committed an abominable, disgusting thing by eating of the forbidden fruit. By eating it they made their souls loathsome, abominable, disgusting to Jehovah God, who is holy and who desires his intelligent creatures to be holy. Did such now loathsome souls as Adam and Eve deserve to live forever? No! Could such abominable disgusting things be allowed to remain in such a holy place as that Edenic Paradise sanctuary? No! Immediately after Adam gave his approval to sin against God by eating forbidden fruit, he and his wife felt out of place in that sanctuary which God sanctified by having fellowship with them there. They felt nakedly unpresentable to him and tried to hide from him.

¹⁵ In this way Adam and Eve lost their holiness. By taking the law into their own hand and acting against God's righteous law, they had in effect set themselves up as gods, idolizing themselves by a form of greediness. Christians are warned that no "greedy person—which means being an idolater—has any inheritance in the kingdom of the Christ and of God." They are warned against "covetousness, which is idolatry." (Ephesians 5:5; Colossians 3:5) In God's Edenic sanctuary there was no room for idolaters, for false gods, for self-made gods; because idols and false gods are an

14. By eating forbidden food, how did Eve and Adam make their souls to God, did such souls deserve to live in Eden, and how did they now feel in Eden?
15. As what had they now set themselves up, and through what form of selfishness, and why was there no room for them as such in Eden?

abomination or disgusting thing to the one living
and true God, Jehovah.

¹⁶ Jehovah protests against putting idols in his
sanctuary. Concerning the ancient Jews he said:
" 'The sons of Judah have done what is bad in my
eyes,' is the utterance of Jehovah. 'They have set
their disgusting things in the house upon which
my name has been called, in order to defile it.' "
(Jeremiah 7:30; 32:34) The continued presence
of Adam and Eve was defiling to the Edenic Paradise sanctuary. They had not earned any right to
eat from the "tree of life in the middle of the
garden" and be thereby licensed to live forever on
earth. So God took action to cleanse his sanctuary.

¹⁷ On the false god Satan the Devil he pronounced the sentence of destruction. This he did
with these words to the serpent that the Devil had
used in deceiving Eve: "Because you have done
this thing, you are the cursed one out of all the
domestic animals and out of all the wild beasts of
the field. Upon your belly you will go and dust is
what you will eat all the days of your life. And
I shall put enmity between you and the woman and
between your seed and her seed. He [the woman's
seed] will bruise you in the head and you will
bruise him in the heel." (Genesis 3:14, 15) By
such words God did not mean the seed of the
literal serpent. He meant the seed of the false god
who was like the serpent, Satan the Devil. In the
same way, God did not mean the earthly children
of the literal woman, the sinner Eve. He meant the
seed or offspring of his holy universal organization, which he now, for the first time, compared
with a woman, a wife married to him in heaven.
—Isaiah 54:5.

¹⁸ The seed of God's universal organization must

16. Against doing what to his sanctuary does Jehovah protest,
and what did Jehovah have to do to his Edenic sanctuary?
17. In pronouncing sentence upon the serpent, the Devil's tool,
whom did God mean by the serpent's seed and by the woman?
18. Whom did God mean by the woman's seed?

be his first created and chief Son, who became the man Christ Jesus that he might be made the "one mediator between God and men." (1 Timothy 2:5) With him is associated his faithful congregation of 144,000 footstep followers, who are pictured in the Revelation to John as the twenty-four "elders" seated on thrones around God's heavenly throne. To these Christians who gain the victory over Satan the Devil as that old Serpent these words are written: "For his part, the God who gives peace will crush Satan under your feet shortly." (Romans 16:20) This links them with the fulfillment of God's promise, at Genesis 3:15, that the woman's seed must bruise the Serpent.

[19] God told the sinner Eve that she would not be put to death at once. She would be permitted to bring forth many children, but this with labor pains. Her husband would dominate her till death. Then God disabused Eve's mind of the lie that Satan the Serpent had told when Satan said that she and Adam would not positively die for eating the forbidden fruit. In Eve's hearing God said to Adam: "Because you listened to your wife's voice and took to eating from the tree concerning which I gave you this command: 'You must not eat from it,' cursed is the ground on your account. In pain you will eat its produce all the days of your life. And thorns and thistles it will grow for you, and you must eat the vegetation of the field. In the sweat of your face you will eat bread until you return to the ground, for out of it you were taken. For dust you are and to dust you will return."—Genesis 3:16-19.

[20] Adam was no longer to cultivate and take care of the Edenic sanctuary. He was unclean, unholy.

19. What did God directly tell Eve, and how did he then disabuse her mind of Satan's lie?
20. What food was Adam now to eat, what ground was cursed for him, where was he to return to the dust, and why did he not go to heaven at death?

He was no longer to eat Paradise food, but the "vegetation of the field," getting it with the sweat of his face. It was not the Paradise sanctuary that was cursed on Adam's account, but it was the ground outside; and this, and not the Paradise sanctuary, was the part of the earth that was to grow thorns and thistles for him. The Edenic Paradise sanctuary was not to be marred by graves of sinners, but it was to the dust of the ground outside the Paradise sanctuary to which Adam was to return. "The first man is out of the earth and made of dust; the second man [Jesus Christ] is out of heaven." (1 Corinthians 15:47) So Adam was not to go to heaven at death. Being of the earth, he went back to where he had come from, the dust. The life force that animated him then returned to God who had given it.—Ecclesiastes 12:7.

²¹ To prevent Adam from taking hold of another fruit to which he was not entitled, the fruit of the tree of life along with which the grant of eternal life went, what was done? "Jehovah God put him out of the garden of Eden to cultivate the ground from which he had been taken. And so he drove the man out and posted at the east of the garden of Eden the cherubs and the flaming blade of a sword that was turning itself continually to guard the way to the tree of life."—Genesis 3:22-24.

²² In any attempt to get back into the Paradise sanctuary Adam would have been blocked by those cherubs. Since he could not make his way back into the earthly Paradise because of those cherubs, much less could he make his way into the greater sanctuary of heaven, where many more cherubs would be ready to block him. Any trying to make

21. To what other fruit was Adam now not entitled, and what did God do to prevent his trying to eat it?
22. What would trying to get back into the Paradise sanctuary have meant, and what shows whether there was anything that happened to remove the sentence from Adam and Eve?

his way to the tree of life in the middle of the garden to gain life on earth forever would have meant walking into destruction by the flaming blade of that revolving sword. Yet even outside the sanctuary Adam lived for hundreds of years. During all those centuries was there anything that happened that removed the death sentence from Adam and Eve? No; there was no change in the estrangement from God. "So all the days of Adam that he lived amounted to nine hundred and thirty years and he died." (Genesis 5:5) Adam earned the wages that sin pays—death.—Romans 6:23.

²³ Sin, together with its condemnation to death, passed on to Adam's children born outside the sanctuary of Paradise. This fact is plain from what happened to his very first son, Cain. This son became a cultivator of the cursed ground outside the Edenic sanctuary. His younger brother Abel became a shepherd. Cain and Abel brought offerings to God. Close to the sanctuary of Eden, to the east entrance by which the posted cherubs kept guard, was reasonably the proper place to bring the offerings. Each one brought some of the products of his own type of work. Cain offered field products. Abel sacrificed the lives of some of his sheep, firstlings, and poured their blood upon the ground and presented fatty pieces of them to God.

²⁴ Then God indicated that there must be a sacrifice of life and that this life must be presented to him in order for sinful humankind to get back into his favor and be forgiven and redeemed from sin and the penalty of death. God looked with favor upon Abel's animal victims; he rejected Cain's bloodless offering. In jealousy Cain now shed blood, but it was the blood of his righteous brother Abel, who had pleased God by his sacrifice

offered in faith in God. By such bloodshed Cain
defiled the ground. Though not put to death at
once as a murderer, Cain came under God's special
curse. (Genesis 4:1-23; Hebrews 11:4) He was a
murderer in two respects, by his hatred of his
innocent brother and by his act of actually putting
him to death. He showed that he originated with
the Devil and was a child of the Devil. (1 John
3:8-12) In due time Cain died under God's curse.
All his offspring were also wiped out by the global
flood of Noah's day.—Genesis 4:16-24; 6:5-13.

[25] Down to the Noachian flood not one of Adam's
descendants proved able to invade the Edenic sanctuary and get to that tree of life there. That was
not now God's way for human creatures to gain
eternal life in a Paradise on earth. In God's due
time the Flood swept away every trace of that
Paradise sanctuary of Eden somewhere near the
Middle East. Thus it was that death carried on in
the human race even through Noah and his family,
who survived the flood, all the way down to this
day. All mystery about death and its cause is
brushed aside in this brief statement: "Through
one man sin entered into the world and death
through sin, and thus death spread to all men because they had all sinned." (Romans 5:12) Wise
King Solomon said: "There is no man that does
not sin." (1 Kings 8:46) That is why all men receive the wages that sin pays, which is death.
(Romans 6:23) God's acceptance of Abel's sacrifice of sheep with the shedding of blood sets a
pattern. It shows the way in which humankind
are to be freed from the condemnation of death
and delivered from death. It must be by the sacrifice of an acceptable life here on earth. Abel was
not authorized to eat any of the sacrificed firstlings of his flock in communion with God, much

---

25. How is it that death carried on through Noah and his family
down through the flood to today, and what pattern was set by
God's acceptance of Abel's sacrifice?

less to drink their blood. Why, then, did Abel's sacrifice please God?

²⁶ He had not learned it from Adam, but he learned it by faith in God. It therefore lined up with God's laws stated long afterward: "Only flesh with its soul—its blood—you must not eat." (Genesis 9:4) "For the soul of the flesh is in the blood, and I myself have put it upon the altar for you to make atonement for your souls, because it is the blood that makes atonement by the soul in it." (Leviticus 17:11) "Yes, nearly all things are cleansed with blood according to the Law, and unless blood is poured out no forgiveness takes place." (Hebrews 9:22) Jehovah, who saw that justice toward dying, sinful mankind could be turned in favor of mankind only by a sacrifice of sufficient value and power, was also loving enough to provide the needed sacrifice. He did this in his heavenly Son, his first and chief creation, whom he sent from heaven to earth to become the perfect man Jesus Christ. Jesus' sacrifice can do what the first sacrifice by man, Abel's sacrifice, could not do. It can give us deliverance from inherited sin and condemnation and from the resulting death and the grave. For this reason the Holy Bible points us to "Jesus the mediator of a new covenant, and the blood of sprinkling which speaks in a better way than Abel's blood." (Hebrews 12: 24) Abel's blood cried out to God from the ground for vengeance against the murderous brother-hater, Cain. Jesus' blood cries out from God's altar for divine mercy upon men and women of faith and obedience.—Genesis 4:10; Hebrews 13: 10-12.

A TEMPORARY MATERIAL SANCTUARY

²⁷ From Abel onward men of faith who won

26. With what divine law did Abel's sacrifice line up, and how was a sacrifice better than that of Abel's provided for mankind?
27. Why did men of faith, from Noah to Job, offer sacrifices, and what did Abraham's attempted sacrifice of Isaac foreshadow?

God's good pleasure offered sacrifices. This meant the shedding of blood and hence the pouring out of the life of a victim. Noah, Abraham, Isaac, Jacob and Job did not think Jehovah a blood-thirsty God, but displayed their clear discernment of the need of a sacrifice. So they regularly drew near to God with a sacrifice. These men of faith were the priests of God for their families and households. Abraham was even willing to offer up the human sacrifice of his son Isaac on an altar on Mount Moriah, where today the Mohammedan mosque, the Dome of the Rock, stands, in Jerusalem. This he was willing to do with faith in God and with belief in the resurrection out of death for his sacrificed son. So he acted out a prophetic drama of how the heavenly Father would sacrifice his own Son Jesus Christ in order that the believers out of all the families and nations of the earth might bless themselves in the heavenly Father and in his sacrificed Son, the promised Seed. —Genesis 12:1-3; 22:1-18.

[28] Abraham received a blessing from a man who was both a king and a priest, named Melchizedek. "And Melchizedek king of Salem [ancient Jerusalem] brought out bread and wine, and he was priest of the Most High God. Then he blessed him and said: 'Blessed be Abram of the Most High God, Producer of heaven and earth, and blessed be the Most High God, who has delivered your oppressors into your hand!'" (Genesis 14:18-20) However, there is no Bible record that the king-priest Melchizedek had a temple building as a sanctuary at which he offered sacrifices to the Most High God. Consequently none of those ancient men of faith had temple sanctuaries.

[29] When Moses the descendant of Abraham was

---

28. From what man did Abraham receive a blessing, and did he or the other men of faith have temple sanctuaries?
29. Under what circumstances was it that Jehovah gave instructions for building him a sanctuary, and why was that original one not to be sneered at?

born in Egypt, it was a land full of temples to
many gods. Still up to that time Jehovah's own
people had no temple sanctuary to him. Egypt
was not the place for any temple to Jehovah. The
land to which God led Abraham out of Mesopotamia and which God promised to give to his descendants was the place for such a sanctuary.
When Moses and his people had left slavery in
Egypt far behind and were on their way to the
Promised Land, Jehovah God led them to the foot
of Mount Sinai for a halt of almost a year. There
he instructed Moses to have the people build him
a sanctuary. As they were on the move to the
Promised Land, it was to be a portable sanctuary,
a tent of two compartments with a courtyard sur-
rounding it. Said Jehovah to Moses after having
given him the Ten Commandments: "And they
must make a sanctuary for me, as I must tent in
the midst of them. According to all that I am
showing you as the pattern of the tabernacle and
pattern of all its furnishings, that is the way you
are to make it." (Exodus 25:8, 9) Let no one
sneer at that small tent or sanctuary in the wilderness, for it was a picture of heavenly things of
tremendous value and importance to us today.
So says the inspired writer, when he quotes those
very instructions of Jehovah to Moses and makes
remarks upon them.—Hebrews 8:1-6.

[30] Erected in the spring of 1512 before the Christian era, that sanctuary tent continued to be Jehovah's place of meeting with the nation of ancient
Israel for centuries after he had settled them in
the Promised Land, in the vital Middle East. In
that bridgeland between Europe, Asia and Africa
the nation of Israel became a kingdom. Their
second king was faithful David. In 1069 B.C. David
captured Mount Zion, the citadel of Jerusalem,

---

30. How long did that sanctuary tent serve its purpose, and how
was the godly thought of building a stationary sanctuary conceived?

and made it his capital. There near his palace he
had the sacred ark of the covenant containing the
tablets of the Ten Commandments lodged under a
tent in charge of faithful Levites, who were assistants to the priests. It was now that King David
conceived the godly thought of building to Jehovah a stationary temple of wood and stone and
precious metals. He submitted the matter to God.

³¹ King David was a warrior king, whom Jehovah God had used as his executioner in shedding
the blood of his enemies. So God did not favor
David with the privilege of building the temple at
Jerusalem. Yet God honored David with something far grander than building a sanctuary of
perishable materials to his holy name.

³² David had been lovingly concerned with building a worldly material house to honor God; so
Jehovah covenanted with David to build him a
house. No, not a palace, but a royal house or line
of kings, all successors of him, all descendants of
him, until the everlasting King of the house of
David should come. God said:

³³ "Jehovah has told you that a house is what
Jehovah will make for you. When your days come
to the full and you must lie down with your forefathers, then I shall certainly raise up your seed
after you, which will come out of your inward
parts, and I shall indeed firmly establish his kingdom. He is the one that will build a house for my
name, and I shall certainly establish the throne
of his kingdom firmly forever.... And your house
and your kingdom will certainly be steadfast forever before you; your very throne will become
one firmly established forever."—2 Samuel 7:1-16.

³⁴ That was the covenant with David for the
kingdom. Jehovah swore to that covenant. Can

31. Why was David not honored with building the sanctuary proposed?
32, 33. What covenant did Jehovah now make with David in appreciation?
34. Why cannot this Davidic covenant pass away unfulfilled?

the sun and the moon pass away, ceasing to give light to men on this earth? No more can this Davidic covenant for the kingdom pass away. God cannot break his holy oath. He will never profane his covenant with David. To his vindication it is mightily being fulfilled in our own day.—Psalm 89:26-37.

[35] Encouraging his subjects to back up his successor Solomon in building a magnificent temple to Jehovah on Mount Moriah, David said: "Now set your heart and your soul to inquire after Jehovah your God, and rise and build the sanctuary of Jehovah The true God, to bring the ark of the covenant of Jehovah and the holy utensils of The true God to the house built to the name of Jehovah." (1 Chronicles 22:19) The materials being all prepared, King Solomon began building in the fourth year of his reign. In the eleventh year of his peaceful reign he completed this awe-inspiring temple, which, at present money values, would cost into the billions of American dollars. After the sacred ark of his covenant had been brought into the Most Holy of this temple, Jehovah manifested that he accepted this sanctuary for his worship. He filled the temple sanctuary with a miraculous cloud of glory. Then he sent down a miraculous fire from heaven to light the temple altar in the courtyard and to consume the first animal sacrifices upon it. The onlooking worshipers, awestruck, bowed down to the temple pavement and "prostrated themselves and thanked Jehovah, 'for he is good, for his loving-kindness is forever.'" —2 Chronicles 5:4-14; 7:1-3.

[36] In prayer at this temple dedication King Solomon reminded everyone within hearing that this

---

35. To what work, therefore, did David encourage his subjects, and how did God show his acceptance of the new temple for his worship?

36, 37. (a) What decree and what permission of pagan conduct shows whether this temple was Jehovah's real sanctuary? (b) How did Jeremiah lament over the holy city at its desolation?

spacious temple so glorious was not the real sanctuary of the God of heaven: "But will God truly dwell with mankind upon the earth? Look! Heaven, yes, the heaven of the heavens themselves, cannot contain you; how much less, then, this house that I have built?" (2 Chronicles 6:18) Had that been his true sanctuary, why would Jehovah later have decreed for it to be destroyed because the unfaithful, renegade Israelites profaned it, filling it with their abominable, loathsome, disgusting things? Why would he, with a seeming loss of his own prestige among the nations of the world, permit the pagan worshipers of the false gods of Babylon to storm into the land like roaring lions, to show no respect for those who worshiped formally at the temple, to kill the priests, to strip the temple of everything of value, and to burn it to the ground? In 607 B.C. the armies of Babylon, under King Nebuchadnezzar, destroyed the famed holy city of Jerusalem and destroyed the temple that Jehovah had once sanctified. They carried off its treasures and sacred vessels, except the sacred ark of the covenant that had disappeared and eluded greedy pagan hands. (2 Kings 25:8-21; 2 Chronicles 36:17-21) Jeremiah, whom Jehovah had used to prophesy of all this, sat mournfully and lamented to God over the holy city, the daughter of Jerusalem (Zion):

[37] "The adversary has spread out his own hand against all her desirable things. For she has seen nations that have come into her sanctuary, whom you commanded that they should not come into the congregation belonging to you. Jehovah has rejected his altar. He has spurned his sanctuary. Into the hand of the enemy he has surrendered the walls of her dwelling towers. In the house of Jehovah they have let out their own voice, as in the day of a festival. Jehovah has thought of bringing the wall of the daughter of Zion to ruin.

. . . See, O Jehovah, and do look to the one to whom you have dealt severely in this manner. Should the women keep eating their own fruitage, the children born fully formed, or in the sanctuary of Jehovah should priest and prophet be killed? O how the gold that shines becomes dim, the good gold! O how the holy stones [stones of the sanctuary] are poured out at the head of all the streets!"—Lamentations 1:10; 2:7, 8, 20; 4:1, *margin.*

EARTHLY SANCTUARY RESTORED

[38] Just as Jeremiah had prophesied, the site of Solomon's temple lay desolate for seventy years. Meanwhile those thousands of Jews who had survived the overthrow of Jerusalem and her temple were mostly captive in Babylon, prisoners whom heartless Babylon gave no other hope than that of dying far from home. But Jehovah was in his heavenly sanctuary. He was watching what was going on, with full consideration for his name and his worship. "For he has looked down from his holy height, from the very heavens Jehovah himself has looked even at the earth, to hear the sighing of the prisoner, to loosen those appointed to death." (Psalm 102:19, 20) He was timing all his movements toward his own people and their oppressors. He raised up the very conqueror whom he had foretold through Isaiah, King Cyrus of Persia: "I, Jehovah, am doing everything, . . . the One saying of Cyrus: 'He is my shepherd, and all that I delight in he will completely carry out'; even in my saying of Jerusalem: 'She will be rebuilt,' and of the temple: 'You will have your foundation laid.' " (Isaiah 44:24, 28; 45:1-5, 11-13) In 539 B.C., to the surprise of all the nations, mighty Babylon fell before the Medes and Per-

---

38, 39. (a) How long did Jehovah time it for the temple site to lie desolate? (b) According to Isaiah's prophecy, whom did Jehovah raise up, and what decree did this one issue?

sians, drinking the cup of shame that she had
made the nation of Jehovah's people drink. In the
seventieth year of Jerusalem's desolation, in 537
B.C., the king of the Persian Empire issued the
decree for the rebuilding of Jehovah's sanctuary.

[39] Said Cyrus' decree: "All the kingdoms of the
earth Jehovah the God of the heavens has given
me and he himself has commissioned me to build
him a house in Jerusalem, which is in Judah.
Whoever there is among you of all his people,
may his God prove to be with him. So let him go
up to Jerusalem, which is in Judah, and rebuild
the house of Jehovah the God of Israel—he is
The true God—which was in Jerusalem."—Ezra
1:2, 3; 2 Chronicles 36:22, 23.

[40] A remnant of about 50,000 faithful Israelites
and slaves responded to the decree and eagerly
journeyed back to Jerusalem. By the end of that
seventieth year of Jerusalem's desolation they
were back on the sites of their former cities, re-
establishing themselves. This was in absolute fulfillment of Jehovah's prophecy through Jeremiah.
On the first day of their seventh month, Ethanim,
the month in which they were to celebrate the
day of atonement and the festival of booths, they
assembled with their Jewish governor, Zerubbabel, and they joined with their high priest, Jeshua,
in rebuilding the altar of Jehovah in the courtyard space on Mount Moriah. "So they established
the altar firmly upon its own site." Then the sacrifices to Jehovah were renewed, according to what
was due each day. They even held their week-long
festival of booths, the first in seventy years. Besides this there was the "constant burnt offering,"
or the "continual burnt offering," the burnt offering that was made daily, morning and evening.
(Ezra 3:1-5; Exodus 29:38-42; Numbers 28:3-10)

40, 41. (a) How were the sacrifices to Jehovah renewed at the
right place? (b) When was the temple foundation laid, to make
whose word come true?

Thus a start was made in the renewing of the worship of Jehovah at the very place where he had put his name. What a joyous time that was for the liberated remnant of his people! The temple foundation had not yet been laid, but that followed seven months later, in 536 B.C., during the reign of Cyrus the Great.

[41] Again Jehovah's word had marvelously come true. About 185 years after Isaiah's prophecy concerning Cyrus, the temple of Jehovah was having its foundation laid, and the sanctuary of the God of ancient Israel was being rebuilt. Yet even more wonderful fulfillments of Jehovah's prophecies are we beholding today!

[42] Jehovah's sanctuary is a key target of attack, down to our own day. In the days of the Jewish rebuilders of his temple according to Cyrus' decree, the people of the lands round about resented the restoration of this remnant of Jehovah's people and the re-establishment of his temple and worship. They did everything they could, locally and at the court of the Persian rulers, to hinder the rebuilding of Jehovah's sanctuary, to "frustrate their purpose all the days of Cyrus the king of Persia down till the reign of Darius the king of Persia." (Ezra 4:1-5) The work on this second temple to Jehovah had actually been stopped under decree of a misinformed Persian king and by force of arms of the heathen opposers of Jehovah's sanctuary. During this stoppage of temple building the Jews grew materialistic and Jehovah withheld his blessings. Then, to urge on his remnant of worshipers to carry through the main purpose for which he had brought about their release from Babylon, Jehovah raised up his prophets Haggai and Zechariah to point out their neglect and to build up their faith in Almighty God. Courageously, in the second year of Darius I, they resumed

---

42. What effect did enemy interference have upon temple building, and how did Jehovah take hold of the situation that resulted?

building Jehovah's sanctuary. They refused to stop because of the objections of the enemy, and referred them to Jehovah's decree through King Cyrus the Great. The sanctuary enemies appealed to King Darius I. The Persian king made investigation, proved the actuality of Cyrus' decree for the Jews to rebuild Jehovah's temple, and loyally ordered Cyrus' decree to be enforced. So lay off from interfering, you foes of Jehovah's house, or else be impaled on a stake and have your houses turned into public privies! In fact, lend Jehovah's temple builders supplies in order to complete his house!—Ezra 6:6-12.

[43] Thus with Jehovah's power and spirit, with even the imperial backing of Persia's ruler, the temple building went forward. In a little more than four years it was completed. "They completed this house by the third day of the lunar month Adar [February-March], that is, in the sixth year of the reign of Darius the king." (Ezra 6:15) That was in the year 516 B.C. With joy Jehovah's worshipers inaugurated his completed sanctuary. The next month, Nisan 14, they held the Passover. Temple services went forward in this sanctuary constructed by Governor Zerubbabel, as they had gone forward in the temple built by Solomon. Once again the daily sacrifice, or the "constant [continual] burnt offering," was rendered up to Jehovah mornings and evenings. In 468 B.C., which was the seventh year of the Persian King Artaxerxes, the Jewish priest named Ezra, who was also a copyist of the law of God, went up from Babylon at the order of the king to this temple at Jerusalem for the purpose of bringing a large contribution that was made to the support of Jehovah's sanctuary. (Ezra 7:1 to 8:36)

43. (a) When was the rebuilt temple inaugurated and the temple services renewed? (b) What was the purpose of Ezra's visit to this temple, and what distinguished visitor was there in 332 B.C.?

In the following century, according to report, there was a visit of another historical character to this sanctuary at Jerusalem. This was the visit of the Macedonian or Grecian king, Alexander the Great, in 332 B.C., as he was on his expedition of conquest over Persia,* in fulfillment of prophecy.

⁴⁴ About two centuries later this second temple experienced a rededication. The Syrian king, Antíochus IV Epíphanes, made a vicious attempt to stamp out the worship of Jehovah. In the year 168 B.C. he profaned Jehovah's sanctuary by building an altar over the great altar of Jehovah and offering upon this an abominable sacrifice to the false god whom he worshiped, the Olympian Zeus (or Jupiter). This was on the 25th day of the Jewish month Chislev (November-December). He put a stop to the daily sacrifice or constant burnt offering at the temple. He ferociously persecuted the uncompromising worshipers of Jehovah. (1 Maccabees 1:20-64) This was what started the uprising of the Maccabees, the sons of the faithful priest Mattathias. Judas, the third son, being chosen leader, led his small forces to the defeat of the enemy, recaptured Jerusalem, and rededicated the temple on Chislev 25, 165 B.C., on the same day on which it had been desecrated by the Syrian king. Ever since then Jews have celebrated the feast of dedication, Hanukkah, on its anniversary. (1 Maccabees 4:36-59; 2 Maccabees 10:1-9; Josephus' *Antiquities of the Jews,* Book 12, Chapter 7, paragraph 7) This is referred to in John 10:22: "At that time the feast of dedication took place in Jerusalem. It was wintertime, and Jesus was walking in the temple in the colonnade of Solomon." In Jesus' days the Jews them-

---

* Josephus' *Antiquities of the Jews,* Book 11, Chapter 8, paragraphs 3-6.

44. How did this temple come to be rededicated in 165 B.C., and what festival did Jesus attend in celebration of this?

selves were profaning this temple by their practices.

45 The world scene changed, and Rome became the world power. In the year 63 B.C. the Roman General Pompey captured the hill upon which Jehovah's temple stood and made bold to enter the Most Holy of this sanctuary. He saw no sacred ark of Jehovah's covenant there, for it had not been restored to the Most Holy.* General Pompey did not touch any of the temple treasures.† So he took possession of the city of Jerusalem, and Judea became a Roman province.

46 Years later, General Crassus carried off everything of value that he could find in the temple.‡ Now the Jews rose in rebellion, but Rome came off victorious. The year 40 B.C. saw the Roman Senate nominating the Edomite or Idumean, Herod the Great, to be the king of Judea. It was first in 37 B.C. that he stormed and took possession of Jerusalem and became king *de facto*. It is from this year that Herod's kingship should be dated and counted. It is then found to overlap the birth of Jesus at Bethlehem about October 1, in 2 B.C. This wicked King Herod was the one that tried to murder the babe Jesus to prevent his growing up and becoming king.—Matthew 2:1-19.

---

* The Jewish *Mishnah* (*Yoma*, 21,2) says that the temple built by Governor Zerubbabel lacked five things that marked Solomon's temple, namely, (1) the ark of the covenant, (2) the sacred fire that had been started from heaven, (3) the Shekinah light in the Most Holy, (4) the holy spirit of Jehovah, and (5) the high priest's Urim and Thummim, the equipment for learning divine decisions.

† Josephus' *Antiquities of the Jews,* Book 14, Chapter 4, paragraph 4.

‡ *Ibidem,* Book 14, Chapter 7, paragraph 1.

45. Who is reported to have invaded the Most Holy of this sanctuary, and what did Judea become in 63 B.C.?
46. How did Herod the Great become king of Judea, and what did he try to do to Jesus?

⁴⁷ Herod, who came to be called Great, reigned for thirty-seven years. Toward the middle of his reign he laid plans to rebuild the temple that had stood from the time of Governor Zerubbabel. To please the Jews, he wanted to rebuild it on a much grander scale. In 20-19 B.C. he got the building work started, and the work continued without interrupting the regular temple service. In a year and a half the temple sanctuary or *náos* was finished. It took eight years to finish the temple courts and the covered walks round about. The complete reconstruction of the temple took much longer. In fact, this was not realized by Herod the Great. At the Passover feast of 30 (A.D.) the Jews told Jesus that the temple work had been going on forty-six years; and so could he raise it up in three days of time? (John 2:13-22) Actually the temple was not completed in its reconstruction till A.D. 64. This was just six years before the Roman army under General Titus destroyed both temple and city, in fulfillment of Jesus' prophecy spoken in the spring of 33 (A.D.). (Matthew 24: 1, 2) Those who had worshiped there were scattered to the ends of the earth.

⁴⁸ The earthly sanctuary of Jehovah has never been rebuilt. This has been in full harmony with his will. The day for such a lifeless material sanctuary has long passed. Jehovah has turned his attention to a far more important sanctuary, a living sanctuary, and to it he has transferred his name and his holy spirit. When completed in the near future, it will stand to his everlasting universal glory. Through this unusual sanctuary he will pour out his blessings upon people out of all families and nations of mankind who do his will on earth. As the sanctuary on Mount Moriah in Jerusalem was associated with his kingdom over the

---

47. To please the Jews, what did King Herod proceed to do, but how was all this brought to nothing in fulfillment of Jesus' words?
48. What has made out of order the rebuilding of that earthly sanctuary, and with what promised government is this associated?

nation of Israel, so his everlasting spiritual sanctuary is inseparably linked with his promised government, the kingdom of the heavens. It is built by One greater than King Solomon and Governor Zerubbabel, not to mention King Herod.

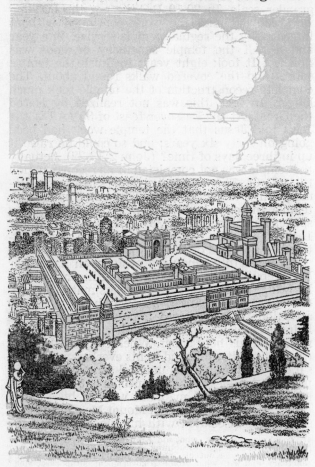

CHAPTER 4

Foregleams Of God's Kingdom

UNTIL sin made its outbreak, Jehovah God was the accepted Ruler over man in the sanctuary of Eden. When man broke the law of his rightful Ruler and man thus chose to have a new ruler and lawgiver, Jehovah God held court. He pronounced sentence upon man's newly chosen ruler, Satan the Devil, who had now become a rival god symbolized by the serpent of deception. Judge Jehovah said: "I shall put enmity between you and the woman and between your seed and her seed. He will bruise you in the head and you will bruise him in the heel." (Genesis 3:15) Many men have been bitten in the heel by a literal serpent, and many men have crushed the head of a serpent under the heel; but the brood of serpents has continued on down to this day. This has been no fulfillment of the divine judgment in Eden, for in his judgment God had really decreed that the "original serpent, the one called Devil and Satan," should be bruised in the head.—Revelation 12:9.

[2] The deadly wound was to be inflicted upon the Serpent by the promised "seed" or offspring of God's woman, that is to say, his holy universal organization. It is as a wife to him and is able to provide children for his service. His prophetic judgment in Eden at once raised the question, not merely, Who will the Seed of God's woman be? but, further, When will this Seed bruise the hated Serpent in the head and destroy him and his brood? When will this great act of deliverance come for mankind, the victims of the Serpent's lie? Even the angels of heaven who make up the wifely organization which is God's woman were interested to know.—1 Peter 1:12.

[3] The bruising of the old Serpent in the head meant a battle of rulers. Satan the Devil had established himself as ruler over man by maneuvering man into obeying him rather than Jehovah God. It would require another mighty ruler to de-

1. Why did Jehovah God hold court in the sanctuary of Eden, and whose bruising in the head did he decree?
2. What questions did God's prophetic judgment there raise?
3. What did that bruising call for, and why was this not accomplished at the Flood?

feat and destroy Satan as a ruler. The flood of Noah's day did not put Satan out of his rulership. It did wipe out the "ancient world," the "world of ungodly people," but it left Satan still in control over his demonic seed, the invisible spirits or fallen angels.—2 Peter 2:5.

[4] In the postflood world Satan the Devil soon lured the greater number of Noah's descendants into outright rebellion against Jehovah God, who had saved their ancestors, Noah's family, through that world-destroying flood. This first flare-up of rebellion took place notably at the ancient city of Babylon on the banks of the Euphrates River, in the Mesopotamian land now known as Iraq. "Noah continued to live three hundred and fifty years after the deluge." (Genesis 9:28) Yet in all that time he did not claim to be the promised Seed of God's woman just because he had built the ark of salvation; neither did he set himself up as a king over his descendants, all mankind. Had he done so, he would have set up a world government, with himself as ruler of all humankind. But Noah's great-grandson Nimrod did not follow his godly forefather's example. Nimrod parted company with Noah. Though Noah still lived, Nimrod broke the rainbow covenant made by God with Noah to safeguard the sanctity of animal blood. Nimrod became a sports and military hunter and set himself up as king in opposition to Jehovah. We read:

[5] "This is the history of Noah's sons, Shem, Ham and Japheth. And the sons of Ham were Cush and Mizraim and Put and Canaan. And Cush became father to Nimrod. He made the start in becoming a mighty one in the earth. He displayed himself a mighty hunter in opposition to Jehovah. That is why there is a saying, 'Just like Nimrod

---

4, 5. (a) Where did rebellion begin after the Flood? (b) What had Noah not made himself toward his descendants, but how did Nimrod not follow his example?

a mighty hunter in opposition to Jehovah.' And
the beginning of his kingdom came to be Babel
and Erech and Accad and Calneh, in the land of
Shinar. Out of that land he went forth into Assyria
and set himself to building Nineveh and Rehoboth-
Ir and Calah and Resen between Nineveh and
Calah."—Genesis 10:1, 6, 8-12.

⁶ Thus by more than sixteen hundred years Nimrod was the original forerunner of the great king
Nebuchadnezzar, the emperor of the Babylonian
Empire. In Noah's day, when the rebels against
Jehovah planned to make Babel (or Babylon) the
world capital and to erect a heaven-high sanctuary
to false religion, Jehovah broke up their ungodly
scheme. How? By confusing the language of the
builders and so forcing them to scatter, each language group to its own self.

⁷ By this miracle Jehovah God showed that he
rules supreme and that his will cannot be blocked
on earth. Non-Jewish religions report that Nimrod
died a violent death. Despite all his hunting and
building and conquering he did not prove to be the
promised Seed of God's woman. But his violent
death, which is understood to have come as a judgment against Nimrod, did not frighten away the
king movement. In the days of Abraham, who was
born two years after the death of Noah, there
were a number of kings in the Middle East, yes,
in the very regions where Nimrod had ruled as
first human king. Abraham had now moved from
Ur of the Chaldeans. Under God's guidance he had
come into the promised land to the west.

⁸ Amid all those kings of this world, did not
God have a king to represent him on earth? He
did; and Abraham had the privilege of meeting

---

6. Thus whose forerunner did Nimrod become, and how did God
break up the original Babylonian scheme?
7. What movement did Nimrod's death not frighten away, and
what fact shows this?
8. Whom did God then have on earth as king to represent him, and
what did Abraham give to him?

him in the Promised Land. This was Melchizedek "king of Salem" and "priest of the Most High God." Melchizedek as God's king and priest was superior to Abraham and blessed him; and Abraham gave Melchizedek a tenth of all the spoils that he had brought back from his God-given victory over four invading kings from the north.

[9] Significant were Melchizedek's words of blessing: "Blessed be Abram of the Most High God, Producer of heaven and earth, and blessed be the Most High God, who has delivered your oppressors into your hand!" (Genesis 14:1-20) The city of Melchizedek's kingdom was Salem, this being the original part of the later city of Jerusalem. Here, then, was a typical kingdom of God on earth, and Melchizedek ruled as a righteous king in the name and by the appointment of the Most High God, "the King of eternity." He sat on Jehovah's throne in a typical way. He had the authority not only to reign but also to offer sacrifice to God and to bless those whom God approved, such as Abraham. What became of his theocratic government the Bible does not say. But Melchizedek had no successor in that kingdom of God at Salem. That was why hundreds of years had to pass before a typical kingdom of God was again on our earth. For this reason Melchizedek was not the promised Seed who must bruise the old Serpent, Satan the Devil, in the head and deliver the dying, oppressed human race. However, Melchizedek was used as a type of the royal Seed of God's woman, who would be higher than any human king, higher even than King David and King Solomon.

[10] God himself swore with an oath that this promised Seed of his woman would be a king-priest like Melchizedek and would sit on God's

9. With what words did Melchizedek bless Abraham, and why was it first hundreds of years after Melchizedek before a typical kingdom of God was again on earth?
10. Who was to be a king-priest like Melchizedek, and by what oath?

throne, not a material throne on earth like Melchizedek's and David's and Solomon's, but God's
own heavenly throne. More than a thousand years
before the birth of Jesus Christ, Jehovah God inspired King David to sing this melody: "The utterance of Jehovah to my Lord is: 'Sit at my right
hand until I place your enemies as a stool for your
feet.' Jehovah has sworn (and he will not feel
sorry): 'You are a priest to time indefinite according to the manner of Melchizedek!' Jehovah himself at your right hand will certainly break kings
to pieces on the day of his anger.'"—Psalm 110:
1, 4, 5.

¹¹ In being without a successor in office, Melchizedek was a prophetic prefigurement of Jesus
Christ, who will be Jehovah's priest-king perpetually. "For this Melchizedek, king of Salem, priest
of the Most High God, who met Abraham return-
ing from the slaughter of the kings and blessed
him and to whom Abraham apportioned a tenth
from all things, is first of all, by translation, 'King
of righteousness,' and is then also king of Salem,
that is, 'King of peace.' In being fatherless, mother-
less, without genealogy, having neither a beginning of days nor an end of life, but having been
made like the Son of God, he remains a priest
perpetually." (Hebrews 7:1-3) Jesus Christ the
Son of God is the one to serve in connection with
Jehovah's true sanctuary. Being King-Priest for
all time by reason of his immortality since his
resurrection from the dead, he needs no successor
in office. Priesthood and kingship toward the Most
High God end up in him. How different King
Melchizedek of Salem was from King Nimrod of
Babylon!

¹² The fact stands out unmistakably: The one

---

11. In being without successor, how did Melchizedek well picture
Jesus Christ, and with what sanctuary does the latter serve?
12. (a) By whom must the true Seed of God's woman be sworn
into office? (b) How did Abraham set the proper pattern for his
great-grandchildren, the Israelites, and when and how did Moses
sing forth the relationship of God to his people?

who is the true Seed of God's woman must be sworn into his kingship and priesthood by the Most High God, Jehovah. In view of the presence of King Melchizedek in the Promised Land, Abraham had no reason for wanting to make himself king over his household or over the land. Abraham set the proper pattern for his great-grandchildren, the sons of Jacob or Israel, the Israelites. Jehovah delivered his people of ancient Israel from slave-driving Egypt. He brought them miraculously through the Red Sea to safety and destroyed the pursuing Egyptians behind them, burying them beneath the collapsing walls of water. Then Moses jubilantly sang out the true relationship of Jehovah toward his people, saying: "Jehovah will rule as king forever and ever." (Exodus 15:18) He was Israel's heavenly King!

[13] On being brought into the Promised Land of Canaan the Israelites were ruled over by judges, without family successors. Judge Gideon, although Israel's visible deliverer, refused to set up a ruling dynasty or line of kings in his family. He said: "I myself shall not rule over you, nor will my son rule over you. Jehovah is the one who will rule over you." (Judges 8:23) Only at the faithless people's demand did Jehovah God proceed to give the twelve tribes of Israel a visible human king. When aged Judge Samuel prayed to God in grief, Jehovah comforted Samuel, saying: "It is not you whom they have rejected but it is I whom they have rejected from being king over them." (1 Samuel 8:7) The first king given to them, Saul of the tribe of Benjamin, ended up disastrously under God's disapproval. Concerning Saul, Jehovah said to Israel: "I have given thee a king in mine anger, and have taken him away in my wrath." (Hosea 13:11, AS) During King Saul's reign Jehovah

13, 14. (a) How, then, did Israel come to have a human king, and how did the first one end up? (b) Whom did Jehovah find to be a man agreeable to his heart for king, and to whom did Jehovah liken him?

found in the tribe of Judah a man who was agreeable to His heart. He had the prophet Samuel anoint this shepherd lad, David of Bethlehem, to become king after Saul. In this way David was the anointed one of Jehovah, or the christ of Jehovah. (1 Samuel 13:13, 14; 16:3-13) However, David was not Jesus Christ, or Jesus the Anointed One. He was, like Melchizedek, only a prophetic prefiguration of Jesus Christ the Son of God. In prophecy Jesus Christ was even spoken of as David, which means "Beloved," in words like the following:

¹⁴ "I will set up one shepherd over them, and he shall feed them, even my servant David; he shall feed them, and he shall be their shepherd. And I, Jehovah, will be their God, and my servant David prince among them; I, Jehovah, have spoken it."—Ezekiel 34:23, 24, AS.

¹⁵ King Saul died in battle. The Israelites came to appreciate that Jehovah had anointed David to be Saul's successor, and they anointed him as Jehovah's anointed. Firmly established in his kingdom at Jerusalem, David desired to build a sanctuary to Jehovah to take the place of the tent or tabernacle that Moses had built in the wilderness. Jehovah denied the warrior David this privilege. But in appreciation of David's godly desire Jehovah of his own accord made a covenant with David for a kingdom that was never to be removed from David's family. At David's death, then, what was to happen? Jehovah's kingdom covenant with David said: "I shall certainly raise up your seed after you that will come to be one of your sons and I shall indeed firmly establish his kingship. He is the one that will build me a house and I shall certainly establish his throne firmly forever. I myself shall become his father and he himself will become my son, and my loving-kindness I

15. Whom did Israel then anoint to be king, and what was to happen to the kingdom after this one died?

shall not remove from him the way I removed it
from the one [Saul] that happened to be prior to
you. And I will cause him to stand in my house
and in my kingship to everlastingness and his
throne will itself become one lasting forever."
—1 Chronicles 17:11-14.

¹⁶ No king, from King Constantine of Rome
down to any kings or political rulers in Christendom today, has come under this Kingdom covenant of Jehovah with David. Hundreds of years
before Christendom came into existence and had
kings, that Kingdom covenant began applying and
operating toward Jesus Christ the Son of God.

¹⁷ In his position as Jehovah's anointed, King
David sat on Jehovah's throne. He did not sit on
Jehovah's throne in the way that David's Lord,
Jesus Christ, now sits at God's right hand. David
sat merely as Jehovah's representative on a visible
throne on Mount Zion in Jerusalem. He acknowledged Jehovah as Israel's real King. In Psalm
59:13 he wrote under inspiration: "God is ruling
in Jacob [Israel] to the ends of the earth." Near
the end of his life, when David was rejoicing over
the generous contributions that the leading men
of Israel had made toward the building of Jehovah's sanctuary by his son Solomon, David blessed
God and said: "Yours, O Jehovah, are the greatness and the mightiness and the beauty and the
eminence and the dignity, for everything in the
heavens and in the earth is yours. Yours is the
kingdom, O Jehovah, even the One lifting yourself up as head over all." (1 Chronicles 29:10, 11)
But David also said: "Jehovah . . . went on to
choose Solomon my son to sit upon the throne of
the kingship of Jehovah over Israel."—1 Chronicles 28:5; 2 Chronicles 9:8.

16. Why have no kings of Christendom come under that Kingdom
covenant?
17. On whose throne did King David sit, and whom did he acknowledge as Israel's real king?

¹⁸ So David's successor was said to represent Jehovah on the throne of Israel: "Solomon began to sit upon Jehovah's throne as king in place of David his father and to make a success of it." (1 Chronicles 29:23) Likewise all the other descendants of David who succeeded him according to Jehovah's kingdom covenant sat on the "throne of Jehovah." The kingdom was His. It was a typical kingdom of God on earth. The house of David provided the visible kings.

¹⁹ What, then, happened to that everlasting covenant of the kingdom when Nebuchadnezzar king of Babylon destroyed the capital city of Jerusalem and its sanctuary and overthrew the throne of King Zedekiah and carried him into exile in Babylon, to die there? Did the kingdom covenant then cease to exist? No; that kingdom covenant was to continue until the Seed of God's woman would come, concerning whom Jehovah said: "I will cause him to stand in my house and in my kingship to everlastingness and his throne will itself become one lasting forever." It was just that the typical kingdom of God on earth was reduced to a ruin and ceased to exist. Zedekiah's royal sons were slaughtered by the king of Babylon; but there were other descendants of King David through whom the legal and the natural heir to David's throne might come. Jehovah made sure of this when he condemned King Zedekiah and said:

²⁰ "And you, O unhallowed wicked one, prince of Israel, whose day has come, the time of your final punishment, thus says the Lord GOD: Remove the turban, and take off the crown; things shall not remain as they are; exalt that which is low, and abase that which is high. A ruin, ruin, ruin I will make it; there shall not be even a trace

---

18. On whose throne did David's successors sit, and so what did Israel's kingdom typify?
19, 20. (a) What happened, then, to the kingdom covenant after King Zedekiah was dethroned and his sons were slaughtered? (b) What did Ezekiel tell King Zedekiah concerning the kingdom?

of it until he comes whose right it is; and to him I will give it."—Ezekiel 21:25-27, RS.

²¹ Those in David's line of descent did not sit on an earthly throne at Jerusalem after its first destruction in 607 B.C. However, they could pass along the claim according to the kingdom covenant until the final one came who had the right to the throne and crown. Then God would enthrone and crown that rightful heir. Then that one, as the foretold Seed of God's woman, would be authorized to bruise the "original serpent," Satan the Devil, in the head.

²² How long, then, would it be until the ruined kingdom would be restored and God's kingdom would be given to the Seed of God's woman, who has the right to it? When the remnant of repentant Jews were restored to their homeland after it had lain desolate of man and domestic beast for seventy years, the typical kingdom of God in the line of David was not re-established. They were subject to a non-Jewish ruler, King Cyrus of Persia. They merely had a local governor who was from the royal house of David to direct their affairs. In 167 B.C. the Maccabean revolt against the Syrian king, Antíochus IV Epíphanes, took place and the Maccabees established their own government. In 104 B.C. Judas Hyrcanus Aristobulus took the title "King of the Jews." But that was a kingdom of a Levite priest. It was not a restoration of God's kingdom in the line of King David of the royal tribe of Judah.—Genesis 49: 8-10.

²³ In the spring of 33 (A.D.), when Jesus rode triumphally on an ass into Jerusalem, as Solomon

---

21. After 607 B.C., what could those in David's line of descent do concerning the Kingdom covenant?
22. On the return of the remnant from Babylon to Jerusalem, why was God's typical kingdom not re-established, and why was the kingdom established by the Maccabean Judas Hyrcanus Aristobulus not the kingdom?
23. Was the kingdom of God established after Jesus rode triumphally into Jerusalem, or after his being resurrected, or on the day of Pentecost?

had done to his coronation many centuries before, the kingdom of God by the rightful heir of King David failed to be established anew. After Jesus' resurrection from the dead and just before he ascended to heaven to sit down at his Father's right hand, Jesus' disciples plainly asked him: "Master, are you restoring the kingdom to Israel at this time?" Jesus, in effect, answered them No! He said: "It does not belong to you to get knowledge of the times or seasons which the Father has placed in his own jurisdiction; but you will receive power when the holy spirit arrives upon you, and you will be witnesses of me both in Jerusalem and in all Judea and Samaria and to the most distant part of the earth." (Acts 1:6-8) Ten days afterward, on the festival day of Pentecost, the holy spirit of God was poured out upon them and they did receive power. But the kingdom of Israel was not set up again there at Jerusalem, the capital of Israel.

[24] The faithful disciples of Christ did not stay in Jerusalem waiting for the kingdom of God to be restored there to Israel. They knew that the rightful Heir to God's kingdom then sat at Jehovah's right hand in heaven. So they went out witnessing to Christ, going out from Jerusalem. In the year 70 (A.D.) the Roman armies under General Titus destroyed Jerusalem and its temple of Herod; but in good time before the horrible destruction the Christians yet in Jerusalem fled from the doomed city and escaped perishing with it. They acted on Jesus' instructions, in Luke 21: 20-24. The apostle Paul had written before that to the Christian congregation in Rome: "The God who gives peace will crush Satan under your feet shortly." (Romans 16:20) But that crushing of God's great adversary under their feet did not

---

24. Why did Christ's disciples not wait in Jerusalem for God's kingdom to be established, and how does Revelation 12:17 show that Satan was not crushed under their feet at Jerusalem's destruction?

occur at the destruction of unfaithful Jerusalem A.D. 70. More than twenty-five years afterward the Revelation to John concerning the "things that must shortly take place" warned Christians that the original Serpent would persecute God's "woman" ferociously and would make war upon her spiritual children on earth, the spiritual brothers of the Lord Jesus Christ.—Revelation 12:17.

[25] In the Revelation John heard the souls of faithful Christians who had been slaughtered because of God's Word and because of the witness work that they used to do cry out: "Until when, Sovereign Lord holy and true, are you refraining from judging and avenging our blood upon those who dwell on the earth?" (Revelation 6:9, 10) And even today we ask, When will the Seed of God's woman bruise the wicked Serpent in the head? How long was it to be from the ruin of the typical kingdom of God in 607 B.C. until God's heavenly kingdom is established by giving it to the Serpent-Bruiser, the Seed of God's woman, who has the right to it?

[26] At its ruin in 607 B.C. the capital city of the typical kingdom of God began to be trodden down, trampled upon by the non-Jewish nations, King Nebuchadnezzar of Babylon starting off this trampling. Jerusalem was founded anew in 537 B.C. by the faithful remnant that returned from exile in Babylon to their desolated land. But the trampling of Jerusalem under foot by the non-Jewish nations continued. Jesus predicted the destruction of the rebuilt Jerusalem within the days of his apostles. The Roman armies in the Middle East did this destructive work in a few months in 70 (A.D.) But Jesus said that the trampling would continue on beyond that. For how long? Hear his

---

25. What question do we today ask concerning the bruising of the Serpent and concerning the kingdom of the Serpent-Bruiser?
26. When did the trampling down of the capital city of the typical kingdom of God begin, and how do we know that the trampling had not ceased even in Jesus' own days on earth?

words: "There will be great necessity upon the land and wrath on this people, and they will fall by the edge of the sword and be led captive into all the nations, and Jerusalem will be trampled on by the nations, until the appointed times of the nations are fulfilled."—Luke 21:23, 24.

[27] Back in 607 B.C. the Jerusalem that was overthrown stood for the kingdom of God because it had the typical throne of Jehovah on which the anointed one of Jehovah sat as his king. Likewise, the Jerusalem that is trampled upon by worldly nations stands for the kingdom of God. In his own days on earth Jesus said these words as a part of his Sermon on the Mount: "Do not swear at all, neither by heaven, because it is God's throne; nor by earth, because it is the footstool of his feet; nor by Jerusalem, because it is the city of the great King." (Matthew 5:34, 35) So the end of the trampling down of Jerusalem at the complete fulfillment of the "appointed times of the nations" would mean the rising again of symbolic Jerusalem, namely, the kingdom of God. It would mean the giving of the kingdom of God to the great Heir of King David, who used to sit on Jehovah's throne in Jerusalem of old. It would mean that this Heir would begin to reign because he has the right to do so in harmony with the Kingdom covenant that Jehovah God made with King David.

"THE APPOINTED TIMES OF THE NATIONS"

[28] It is vital, then, to know the length of these "appointed times of the nations." How many times are there? How long does each time last? In the Holy Scriptures the number seven is used as a symbol of spiritual completeness or perfection. Did not seven days make up God's complete crea-

---

27. What did the Jerusalem that began to be trampled in 607 B.C. stand for, and so what would the end of the trampling at God's appointed time mean?
28. How many are the "times" during which Jerusalem was to be trampled down, and through whose dream do we know?

tive week? So, through the apocalyptic book of Daniel, God informs us that the appointed times of the nations for trampling Jerusalem under foot are seven, a complete number. He sent to King Nebuchadnezzar a dream that none of the scientists, wise men and religious leaders of Babylon could interpret. Finally Daniel the prophet of Jehovah was called. Frightened King Nebuchadnezzar told Daniel the details of the dream and encouraged him not to be afraid of telling the straight truth about the meaning. Daniel, whom the king had named Belteshazzar, said:

²⁹ "My lord, may the dream be for those who hate you and its interpretation for your enemies! The tree you saw, which grew and became strong, so that its top reached to heaven, and it was visible to the end of the whole earth; whose leaves were fair and its fruit abundant, and in which was food for all; under which beasts of the field found shade, and in whose branches the birds of the air dwelt—it is you, O king, who have grown and become strong. Your greatness has grown and reaches to heaven, and your dominion to the ends of the earth."—Daniel 4:19-22, *RS.*

³⁰ The dream tree had a personal application to the dreamer, in the first place. But Nebuchadnezzar had been permitted by Jehovah God the Almighty to establish Babylon as a world power. It was a successor to the first and second world powers, namely, Egypt and Assyria. This Babylonian world power commanded world-wide attention and respect. So Nebuchadnezzar was a symbol of something greater than just himself. He stood as a symbol of world dominance, which, at the moment, he was exercising by permission and according to the purpose of the Most High God.

29. With what identification did Daniel start off interpreting the dream?
30. Of what was King Nebuchadnezzar a symbol at that time, and why did he then and the other nations to follow not have interference from the kingdom of God?

Jehovah God had used him in executing divine vengeance upon the unfaithful nation of Judah, overthrowing its kingdom, and thus beginning the "appointed times of the nations," during which Jerusalem must be trampled on by such worldly nations. On this account Babylon and the other nations that were to follow during the "appointed times" did not have the interference of the kingdom of Jehovah God even in a typical way. As a national power the typical kingdom of God was cut off.

[31] Daniel continued: "And whereas the king saw a watcher, a holy one, coming down from heaven and saying, 'Hew down the tree and destroy it, but leave the stump of its roots in the earth, bound with a band of iron and bronze, in the tender grass of the field; and let him be wet with the dew of heaven; and let his lot be with the beasts of the field, till seven times pass over him;' this is the interpretation, O king."—Daniel 4:23, 24, *RS*.

[32] In the simplest meaning, this pictured that Nebuchadnezzar himself would be toppled from his position of world dominance but would not be destroyed to the point of never getting back into power. The "stump" of him would remain in the earth, but would be banded from growth or expansion for the duration of "seven times." Meanwhile the governmental organization of Babylon kept on working, only not with Nebuchadnezzar active in the throne. His son Evil-meródach may have carried on for him as acting government head.

[33] In the larger meaning of the chopped-down tree, world dominance by the rightful one was cut down. Only the kingdom of God has the right to world domination. Only the anointed king of Jehovah has the God-given right to rule the entire

---

31. What was to be done with the symbolic tree, and how much time was to pass in connection with it?
32. In simplest meaning, what did that picture, and what happened to Babylon's governmental organization in the meantime?
33. What was the real world domination that was cut down, and who went up into the domination?

earth, even as the kingdom of Israel had ruled all the Promised Land during the years of its faithfulness to God. But that typical kingdom of God went down in 607 B.C. and world-conquering Nebuchadnezzar went up into domination over all the Promised Land. In this international change the low-spreading vine, King Zedekiah of Judah, was pulled up by the roots and stripped of

fruit, his sons being killed. (Ezekiel 17:5-10, 20, 21, AS) God's kingdom covenant then turned to someone else as heir.

³⁴ Daniel's interpretation continued: "It is a decree of the Most High, which has come upon my lord the king, that you shall be driven from among men, and your dwelling shall be with the beasts of the field; you shall be made to eat grass like an ox, and you shall be wet with the dew of heaven, and seven times shall pass over you, till you know that the Most High rules the kingdom of men, and gives it to whom he will. And as it was commanded to leave the stump of the roots of the tree, your kingdom shall be sure for you from the time that you know that Heaven rules." —Daniel 4:24-26, RS.

³⁵ Nebuchadnezzar was to make a personal exhibition of God's handling of governmental matters respecting the earth. During this personal exhibition, however, Nebuchadnezzar's world-dominating position, like the tree stump, was to be kept safe for him till he came to his senses after the passing of seven times over him. Likewise, in 607 B.C. the kingdom of Jehovah as represented typically by the kingdom of Jerusalem was to be abased, cut down. It was then to continue in this lowly state, not carrying on governmental functions, for the period of "seven times." During all this period, however, the kingdom covenant made by Jehovah with King David for an everlasting kingdom was to continue binding upon Jehovah God and awaiting complete fulfillment with the rightful Heir.

³⁶ Twelve months after Daniel's interpretation Nebuchadnezzar was bragging about Babylon as a world power. Then a heavenly voice said: "O

34. What did Daniel's interpretation then say concerning King Nebuchadnezzar?
35. During the seven times upon King Nebuchadnezzar, what was to be kept safe for him, and during the corresponding abasement of Jerusalem's kingdom, what was to continue in force?
36. A year later, how was the dream as interpreted literally fulfilled upon Nebuchadnezzar personally?

King Nebuchadnezzar, to you it is spoken: The kingdom has departed from you, and you shall be driven from among men, and your dwelling shall be with the beasts of the field; and you shall be made to eat grass like an ox; and seven times shall pass over you, until you have learned that the Most High rules the kingdom of men and gives it to whom he will." At once the mightiest ruler on earth in that day lost his reason and imagined he was a beast, possibly an ox. "He was driven from among men, and ate grass like an ox, and his body was wet with the dew of heaven till his hair grew as long as eagles' feathers, and his nails were like birds' claws." His bragging about himself and exalting Babylon above the kingdom of God deserved to be corrected, and Nebuchadnezzar's false god Merodach or Marduk was helpless to prevent it. While the "seven times" were passing over him in this condition, he was acting like a dumb beast of the field; but iniquities and oppressions continued to be practiced by Babylon's acting government.—Daniel 4:28-33, *RS*.

[37] In like manner, while government of mankind has been continued by worldly political systems during the larger "seven times" since the ruin of God's typical kingdom of Judah in 607 B.C., the rulers not in God's covenant for the kingdom have acted like crazed Nebuchadnezzar. They have not acted like man made in God's image. Hence all peoples, not merely Jehovah's witnesses, have suffered.

[38] What happened at the end of Nebuchadnezzar's "seven times"? He tells us: "At the end of the days I, Nebuchadnezzar, lifted my eyes to heaven, and my reason returned to me, and I blessed the Most High, and praised and honored

---

37. During the larger "seven times," how have worldly rulers acted like Nebuchadnezzar, and with what effect upon the people?
38. What did Nebuchadnezzar say happened at the end of the "seven times" for him?

him who lives for ever; for his dominion is an everlasting dominion, and his kingdom endures from generation to generation; all the inhabitants of the earth are accounted as nothing; and he does according to his will [where?] in the host of heaven and among the inhabitants of the earth; and none can stay his hand or say to him, 'What doest thou?' At the same time my reason returned to me; and for the glory of my kingdom, my majesty and splendor returned to me. My counselors and my lords sought me, and I was established in my kingdom, and still more greatness was added to me. Now I, Nebuchadnezzar, praise and extol and honor the King of heaven; for all his works are right and his ways are just; and those who walk in pride he is able to abase." (Daniel 4:34-37, *RS*) Nebuchadnezzar made this acknowledgment, not of the false god Marduk, but of Daniel's God, Jehovah.

[39] Nebuchadnezzar is reported to have reigned for forty-three years. So these "seven times" of insanity in between must have been seven years at the most, in his personal case. In the Holy Bible a "time" is used in places to stand for a literal year. (Daniel 7:25; 12:7, *AV;* Revelation 12:6, 14; 11:2, 3) But here Nebuchadnezzar was acting out a prophetic drama, in which a year of time would stand for a much longer period. This must be so, for the trampling down of Jerusalem as representing Jehovah's kingdom did not end at the end of Nebuchadnezzar's insanity; and six centuries later Jesus Christ said that Jerusalem would continue being trodden down or trampled on by the nations till the appointed times of the Gentile nations should be fulfilled. How long, then, are these "seven times"?

---

39. In Nebuchadnezzar's personal case, how long, at most, were those "seven times," but why could not this be the case as regards the trampling down of Jerusalem?

⁴⁰ The Bible measures by lunar time when speaking of months and years. In Nebuchadnezzar's case a "time" stood for a lunar year, the average of which was reckoned as 360 days. Actually, a twelve-month lunar year was eleven days shorter than the average solar year. This required the lunar calendar to add a thirteenth month of twenty-nine days to certain years, in order to bring the calendar in agreement with the solar calendar. Addition of a thirteenth month was done seven times in every nineteen years. When speaking of longer periods of time, God said that a day should stand for a whole year. On this basis, then, a lunar year of 360 days would stand for 360 years, "a day for a year, a day for a year." (Numbers 14:34; Ezekiel 4:6, *AV*) Therefore a symbolic "time" would amount to 360 years. "Seven times," symbolically speaking, would amount to 2,520 literal years. The "seven times" or seven years of Nebuchadnezzar's madness thus predicted a period of 2,520 years. Since the Holy Bible shows that these "seven times" or 2,520 years began in the early fall of the year 607 B.C., then the "appointed times of the nations" would end in the early fall of the year 1914 (A.D.).

⁴¹ During all those years since 607 B.C. the kingdom of Jehovah God had not been operating by means of an anointed descendant of King David according to the kingdom covenant. It had been like a cut-down tree, with no creatures under it or in its branches. The kingdom covenant was like that tree stump left in the earth. It was double-banded by Jehovah's restraining power until "seven times" should have passed over it. Like-

wise, Nebuchadnezzar could not regain his sanity
and come back in fit condition to his throne in
the Babylonian Empire to dominate the world until the decreed "seven times" or seven years had
ended. Then it was a ruler who acknowledged the
King of heaven, Daniel's God, that returned to
the throne and was established in the kingdom
with glory, majesty and splendor and "still more
greatness." In like fashion the Kingdom covenant
could not get final and complete fulfillment until
the "seven times" of 2,520 years had passed over
it. Then the time would come for God to remove
his bands of restraint. Then the time would come
for him to re-establish the kingdom with a descendant of the anointed King David. Then the
kingdom should be given to the one who had the
right to it by Jehovah's kingdom covenant.

⁴² What did all this mean regarding world domination at the end of the "seven times" in the fall
of the year 1914 (A.D.)? Nothing less grand and
wonderful than this, that the domination should
pass into the control of the restored kingdom of
God, because then had come the "times of restoration of all things of which God spoke through the
mouth of his holy prophets of old time." (Acts
3:21) The beginning of the "appointed times of
the nations" was marked by the ruining of the
typical kingdom of God in Judah and by trampling down its capital, Jerusalem, under the Gentile nations. The ending of those "seven times" of
2,520 years had to mark an end to such kingdom
ruin and to trampling down its symbolical capital.
How? By the re-establishment of God's kingdom
according to the kingdom covenant with David,
beyond the power of the worldly nations to trample it down. Then, to show that he rules the
kingdom of men, Jehovah the Most High God

---

42. Why would all this mean that in 1914 (A.D.) the domination
had to pass into the control of God's kingdom restored, and what
would this show about God?

must give it to whom He wills. He must set over it the lowliest of men.—Daniel 4:14, *RS*.

[43] That means He must give it to the anointed Son of David, Jesus Christ, who was considered the basest of men, so base, in fact, that he was wrongly called sacrilegious, a blasphemer, a seditionist, a winebibber and a glutton, and was impaled upon a torture stake like a criminal slave. He lowered himself from heaven to earth by emptying himself of heavenly power and glory and taking a slave's form and coming to be in the likeness of men. On earth he took God's yoke upon himself and invited others to take his yoke upon themselves, because, said he: "I am mild-tempered and lowly in heart." Then "he humbled himself and became obedient as far as death, yes, death on a torture stake."—Philippians 2:5-8.

[44] Because of such lowliness God must highly exalt Jesus, higher than King David, who reigned on earthly Mount Zion. The Most High God must exalt him to become David's "Lord" by seating this anointed Son of David at His own right hand, next to himself in the universe. The restored kingdom of God over humankind must therefore be established in heaven, as it were, on a heavenly Mount Zion, not on the earthly Mount Zion in the Middle East. Then Jehovah God must send the rod of his anointed King's strength out of this heavenly Zion and command him: "Go subduing in the midst of your enemies." (Psalm 110:1, 2; Revelation 14:1) Then at Jehovah's orders Jesus Christ must proceed to the bruising of that "original serpent," Satan, in the head. That event approaches. This kingdom of David's Son must bless the Most High God, just as restored Nebuchadnezzar did. It must bless all men of good will.

---

43. How was the one to whom Jehovah gave the kingdom the "lowliest of men"?
44. Because of such manifest lowliness, what did Jehovah have to do to Jesus according to the Kingdom covenant, and now what event approaches?

CHAPTER 5

The March Of World Powers

DURING the passing of the 2,520 years of the "appointed times of the nations" men and angels have witnessed the march of world powers in grand parade on earth. The march began in 607 B.C., when the 2,520 years began to count. But long before then the all-wise King of heaven, Jehovah God, foresaw the march and the successive world powers in the line of procession. In impressive proof of his unerring foresight he foretold the march and marchers, even names and characteristics of the marchers, that we might identify them. Marvelously he has had their history written down long ahead of time. Hence his sacred Word, the Holy Bible, contains much history written in advance, history which the later histories written by men concerning past events now astoundingly confirm.

[2] It is only from the standpoint of Jehovah's prophetic Word that we can understand and appreciate what has been taking place on earth since the close of the "appointed times of the nations" in the fall of 1914 (A.D.). The long march of the world powers is nearing its end. World-shattering events are just before us. Jehovah's history written in advance makes certain of this to us.

[3] The march during the "appointed times of the nations" began with Babylon. Long before this, Babylon had been established in the valley of Mesopotamia by Nimrod, the great-grandson of Noah, about 2,239 years before the Christian era. But before becoming a world power that had to do with the witnesses of Jehovah God it was preceded by two other world powers; first, Egypt, and second, Assyria. Only by subduing these rivals to world domination, and then by desolating the kingdom of Jehovah's people with capital at ancient Jerusalem, did Babylon become a world power, the third world power listed in Biblical history. Assyria conquered Egypt and even tried

---

1. What march began in 607 B.C., and how do we know that Jehovah God foresaw the march and marchers?
2. From what standpoint only can we understand what has taken place since A.D. 1914, and hence what is just before us?
3. When did the march of world powers begin with Babylon, and by what line of action on Babylon's part?

to prevent the rise of Babylon to dominance by destroying the city. But Babylon was rebuilt and strove for the ascendancy. It destroyed the Assyrian capital, Nineveh, about 633 B.C. It reached the zenith of its power in the days of King Nebuchadnezzar, who destroyed Jerusalem and its sanctuary to Jehovah God.

⁴ It was particularly by his prophet Daniel that Jehovah God foretold the line of march of the world powers. The record is to be found in the prophetic book of Daniel. Thirteen years before Jerusalem and its temple were destroyed Nebuchadnezzar came up against Jerusalem and compelled King Jehoiakim of Judah to take an oath of allegiance to him as overlord. That was after Jehoiakim had reigned for eight years on the "throne of Jehovah" at Jerusalem. But Jehoiakim continued reigning as Nebuchadnezzar's servant for only three years. (2 Kings 24:1) In this third and last year of his reign as subject to Babylon, King Jehoiakim broke his oath and rebelled.

⁵ In this last year of Jehoiakim's rebellion the book of Daniel begins its historical account in these words: "In the third year of the reign of Jehoiakim king of Judah, Nebuchadnezzar king of Babylon came to Jerusalem and besieged it. And the Lord [Jehovah]* gave Jehoiakim king of Judah into his hand, with some of the vessels of the house of God." (Daniel 1:1, 2, RS) Rebellious Jehoiakim did not go out in self-surrender to the king of Babylon. He died inside Jerusalem, just as Jehovah had foretold.—Jeremiah 22:18, 19.

---

* This is one of 134 places where the Jewish copyists or Sopherim say they changed the primitive Hebrew text to read *Adonay* ("the Lord") instead of *Yehowah* or *Yahweh* ("Jehovah").

4, 5. (a) By whom particularly did Jehovah foretell the line of march? (b) With what year of the reign of King Jehoiakim does the book of Daniel begin?

⁶ His son Jehoiachin (or Jeconiah) succeeded him to the "throne of Jehovah" in Jerusalem, up to which King Nebuchadnezzar had come. Jehoiakim's body was dragged and cast dead outside the gates of Jerusalem and buried, unlamented; but it was his son Jehoiachin that went out alive to the besieger, Nebuchadnezzar, after reigning merely three months. According to Jehovah's purpose, Nebuchadnezzar spared eighteen-year-old Jehoiachin's life and took him along with his household and officials to Babylon. There Jehoiachin had offspring and kept up the legal line according to Jehovah's covenant with King David for the everlasting kingdom. (2 Kings 25:27-30; Matthew 1:11-17) As for the vessels of Jehovah's sanctuary at Jerusalem, Nebuchadnezzar "brought them to the land of Shinar, to the house of his god, and placed the vessels in the treasury of his god." Nebuchadnezzar made Jehoiachin's uncle, Zedekiah, king in place of him, but took other members of the royal family and of the nobility to Babylon. This included the youth Daniel and three close companions, Hananiah, Mishael and Azariah of the tribe of Judah. This was eleven years before Jerusalem and its sanctuary were destroyed, or in 618 B.C.—Daniel 1:2-7, RS.

⁷ In Babylon Daniel and his three companions were given special education and proved to be wiser than the professional wise men of Babylon. Daniel became Jehovah's prophet in Babylon and continued as such until the third year of the reign of King Cyrus of Persia. (Daniel 1:8-21; 10:1) Meanwhile King Zedekiah broke the oath of allegiance that he had given in Jehovah's name and began to rebel against Nebuchadnezzar. (Ezekiel

6. (a) How was the legal line of King David according to the kingdom covenant continued through King Jehoiachin? (b) When and how were Daniel and three close companions taken to Babylon?

7. (a) What did Daniel become in Babylon? (b) How did King Zedekiah come to have none of his children sit upon the throne of Jerusalem?

17:13-21) So in the ninth year of this rebel, the king of Babylon came for the third time against Jerusalem. About eighteen months the city withstood the siege. Then the Babylonian armies broke through the walls of the famine-stricken city. King Zedekiah escaped from the doomed city but was overtaken by an enemy military force. Blinded after King Nebuchadnezzar had slaughtered his sons before his eyes, Zedekiah was taken in chains to Babylon to die there. This was in the eleventh year of his reign, in the year 607 B.C. Neither he nor his nephew, the former king Jehoiachin (Coniah or Jeconiah), ever had any children of theirs to sit upon the throne of David and rule in Judah.—Jeremiah 22:24-30.

[8] The following month, or fifth month (Ab), the Babylonian armies burned the sanctuary of Jehovah and razed the city of Jerusalem to the dust. The sacred ark of Jehovah's covenant escaped seizure by them, but they took the rest of the sacred utensils of the temple, either whole or broken in pieces, back to Babylon. Two months later, in the seventh month (Ethanim), the poor people who were left behind in the land fled south to Egypt, and the land of Judah and Jerusalem lay desolate without man or domestic animal. There the seventy years of the desolation of the land began. Also, the "seven times" or the "appointed times of the nations" for trampling on desolated Jerusalem began.—2 Kings 25:22-26.

NEBUCHADNEZZAR'S DREAM OF THE IMAGE

[9] With the typical kingdom of Jehovah God ruined and with two of its anointed kings imprisoned at Babylon, King Nebuchadnezzar indeed

8. How did the land of Judah and Jerusalem become desolate without man or domestic animal, and when did the "seven times" begin to count?
9. (a) When did Nebuchadnezzar begin to reign as visible dominator of the world? (b) When did he have his first prophetic dream, and who proved unable to interpret it for him?

began to reign as visible dominator of the world, as head of the third world power of Bible history, without interference of Jehovah the God of Israel. There, in the fall of the year 607 B.C., Nebuchadnezzar started off the "seven times," which were to run for 2,520 years till the rightful government over mankind should be set up by the Most High God. Of this impressive fact Jehovah God notified the king of Babylon in the second year of his reign as world ruler, or in 606-605 B.C. This he did by sending a dream that the king of Babylon could not recall on awakening, but the terror of the forgotten dream stuck with him. He called for the magicians, the enchanters, the sorcerers, and the professional Chaldeans, all of them servants of Satan the Devil, the "god of this world," to interpret the dream. They requested first to know what the dream was. Unable to tell them, the infuriated king issued a decree for all the wise men of Babylon to be destroyed. This included Daniel and his three companions.—Daniel 2:1-13, *RS*.

[10] Face to face with the executioner, Daniel asked to see the king and then asked for a delay of the execution that he might learn the dream and give the king its interpretation. Then Daniel and his three companions joined in prayer to Jehovah God. The answer to prayer came, and the world-important secret was revealed to Daniel in a vision of the night. Gratefully Daniel blessed Jehovah, saying: "Blessed be the name of God for ever and ever, to whom belong wisdom and might. He changes times and seasons; he removes kings and sets up kings; he gives wisdom to the wise and knowledge to those who have understanding; he reveals deep and mysterious things; he knows what is in the darkness, and the light dwells with him." (Daniel 2:12-22, *RS*) Now to the great secret!

---

10. How did Daniel learn the dream and its interpretation, and with what words did he bless Jehovah God?

¹¹ To the salvation of all the wise men of Babylon, Daniel was taken in before the king. What he said is of the highest importance to us today, for, said he, "there is a God in heaven who reveals mysteries, and he has made known to King Nebuchadnezzar what will be in the latter days. . . . To you, O king, as you lay in bed came thoughts of what would be hereafter, and he who reveals mysteries made known to you what is to be." (Daniel 2:27-29, *RS*) We are living in the urgent times involved in the fulfillment of Nebuchadnezzar's dream!

¹² Daniel disclaimed any wisdom of his own as he now recalled this forgotten dream to the king's mind: "You saw, O king, and behold, a great image. This image, mighty and of exceeding brightness, stood before you, and its appearance was frightening. The head of this image was of fine gold, its breast and arms of silver, its belly and thighs of bronze, its legs of iron, its feet partly of iron and partly of clay. As you looked, a stone was cut out by no human hand, and it smote the image on its feet of iron and clay, and broke them in pieces; then the iron, the clay, the bronze, the silver, and the gold, all together were broken in pieces, and became like the chaff of the summer threshing floors; and the wind carried them away, so that not a trace of them could be found. But the stone that struck the image became a great mountain and filled the whole earth." (Daniel 2:31-35, *RS*) Amazed, the king of Babylon recognized the description, but what did it all mean?

¹³ "This was the dream; now we will tell the king its interpretation," said Daniel as he spoke for himself and his three companions who had joined him in prayer. "You, O king, the king of kings, to whom the God of heaven has given the

11. How did Daniel give credit to Jehovah before the king, and why is what he now said of highest importance to us?
12. What was the dream that Daniel recalled to the king's mind?
13. Whom did Daniel interpret the head of gold to be, and why?

kingdom, the power, and the might, and the glory, and into whose hand he has given, wherever they dwell, the sons of men, the beasts of the field, and the birds of the air, making you rule over them all—you are the head of gold."—Daniel 2:36-38, *RS.*

[14] Did this mean that Nebuchadnezzar was personally the head? Or was the interpreter Daniel really speaking past Nebuchadnezzar to someone else, the real head of gold, an unseen ruler represented by the king of Babylon? And did the metallic body underneath the golden head represent the organization of several levels beneath that mysterious behind-the-scenes head, or even such a several-level organization beneath Nebuchadnezzar himself? If so, was that image already all in existence except for, say, part of the iron legs and the feet of iron and clay? If so, then this dream image was mainly a static picture of something already in existence and was not prophetic except in part of the iron legs and in the feet. Furthermore, if Nebuchadnezzar as golden head represented an invisible personality behind the scenes, then the silver breast and arms must have pictured the topmost level of the organization under that invisible head; the belly and thighs of bronze must have pictured the next-lower level of the organization; and the legs of iron and the feet partly of iron and partly of clay must have represented the bottommost level or levels of that organization, this lowest or iron level being already partly developed at least. What, then?

[15] From that standpoint, Nebuchadnezzar as visible king of kings being symbolized by the golden head, the metallic body under that golden head would symbolize the visible organization under

---

14. If Nebuchadnezzar as the symbolic gold head represented an unseen ruler, what would the metal parts of the body represent, and to what extent would this be a prophetic image?
15. Since from that standpoint the golden head would picture Nebuchadnezzar, what would the other metal parts of the image picture?

Nebu-
chadnezzar,
an organiza-
tion already in
existence and op-
erating for the most
part at least. Hence the
silver breast and arms beneath the golden head would

symbolize the level of governmental organization immediately beneath Nebuchadnezzar himself; the bronze belly and thighs would symbolize the level of governmental organization subordinate to the silvery level above and not in direct contact with the head of government, Nebuchadnezzar; and the legs of iron and the feet partly of iron and partly of clay would symbolize the lowest level or levels of governmental organization and farthest removed from the governmental head. What, though, would this mean?

[16] This would mean that Daniel and his three companions, possibly along with some few other Babylonian officials, were symbolized by the silver breast and arms. Why so? Because immediately after Daniel interpreted the dream correctly, "the king gave Daniel high honors and many great gifts, and made him ruler over the whole province of Babylon, and chief prefect over all the wise men of Babylon. Daniel made request of the king, and he appointed Shadrach, Meshach, and Abednego over the affairs of the province of Babylon;

16. How, though, would this involve Daniel and his three companions with the image, and thus what part of an invisible organization would they visibly stand for?

but Daniel remained at the king's court." (Daniel 2:48, 49, *RS*) As a result, Daniel and his three Jewish companions were symbolized by the silver breast and arms of the image that was to be destroyed. In fact, they also visibly represented the topmost silvery level in the mighty organization underneath the *invisible* ruling power pictured by Nebuchadnezzar, the golden head. This could not be the right understanding or interpretation of the meaning of the metallic image, because Daniel and his three companions are no part of an organization that is doomed to suffer the destruction of the dream image.

[17] No! That symbolic image is not a static picture with prophetic properties in only its lower parts. It is progressive and prophetic from head to foot, and what happens to it is also prophetic. Nebuchadnezzar personally is not represented somewhere low down in the image, somewhere in the legs of iron. He could not be down there and at the same time be the head of the image. As king of kings in the Babylonian world power by the permission of the God of heaven, who permitted him to destroy both Jerusalem and its sanctuary, Nebuchadnezzar is the golden head of the symbolic image.

[18] He is the head of gold as he is the head of a dynasty of rulers over the Babylonian Empire. So the golden head in fact symbolizes the dynasty of the Babylonian world power beginning with Nebuchadnezzar. The Bible itself mentions two others in that dynasty, namely, Evil-meródach and Belshazzar. (2 Kings 25:27; Jeremiah 52:31; Daniel 5:1-30, *RS*) Nebuchadnezzar is reported to have reigned forty-three years from his enthronement in 625 B.C., or for twenty-five years after he destroyed Jerusalem and its sanctuary in 607

B.C. Evil-meródach began to reign in 582 B.C. as
immediate successor to Nebuchadnezzar. Belshazzar* brought to an end the dynasty of Nebuchadnezzar in 539 B.C., when he was put to death vio-
lently. (Daniel 5:30, 31, *AV*) Thus the golden
head of the symbolic image really came into
existence when Nebuchadnezzar became world
ruler at Jerusalem's destruction in 607 B.C., after
which event the "seven times" began.

¹⁹ The head of gold was not all there was to the
dream image. Underneath was a body of several
layers of metals. So the dynasty represented by
the golden head was not to last. Secular histories
list other kings in the line from Nebuchadnezzar
to Belshazzar. From Jerusalem's destruction onward the Babylonian world power lasted only till
539 B.C., or less than seventy years. Pointing to

---

* It is Daniel who has introduced Belshazzar to this
modern world long before modern archaeology routed
the "higher critics" of the Bible and gave worldly proof
of his historicalness. For example, in 1929 the *Yale
Oriental Series · Researches ·* Volume XV, said:
"Cuneiform allusions to Belshazzar have thrown so
much light upon the role which he played that his place
in history stands clearly revealed. There are many texts
which indicate that Belshazzar almost equalled Nabonidus in position and prestige. Dual rulership during most
of the last Neo-Babylonian reign is an established fact.
Nabonidus exercised supreme authority from his court
at Têmâ in Arabia, while Belshazzar acted as co-regent
in the homeland with Babylon as his center of influence.
It is evident that Belshazzar was not a feeble viceroy;
he was entrusted with 'the kingship.' "—See page 186
of Chapter XIV, entitled "The Meaning of Non-Cunei-
form Allusions to Belshazzar," of Volume XV of the
above series under the title "Nabonidus and Belshazzar
—A Study of the Closing Events of the Neo-Babylonian
Empire," by Raymond Philip Dougherty, William M.
Laffan Professor of Assyriology and Babylonian Literature and Curator of the Babylonian Collection, Yale
University, New Haven, Connecticut, U.S.A.

---

19. How did the metallic image show that the Babylonian world
power was not to last, and how did Daniel's interpretation state
this?

this termination of Babylonian world power, Daniel said further in interpretation: "After you [that is, your dynasty] shall arise another kingdom inferior to you." (Daniel 2:39, *RS*) This kingdom was foreshadowed by the breast and arms of silver. What kingdom, then, does this part of the image symbolize?

²⁰ This was the "kingdom" or world power of the Medes and Persians. The expression "After you" refers to time, and reminds Nebuchadnezzar that another rulership will succeed his dynasty to the world's domination. It was yet to come. The expression "inferior to you" refers to the level of the new world power or its quality as compared with the Babylonian world power. It was lower than the head of gold and was of a metal less precious, silver. This world power of the Medes and Persians developed a civilization of brilliant worldly splendor, which was not secondary to that of Babylon. But it did not have the eminent distinction before Jehovah God of overturning his typical kingdom at Jerusalem. Before Medo-Persia became a world power, the fourth world power in Bible history, King Cyrus the Persian succeeded in uniting Media and Persia, after which he conquered the powerful kingdom of Lydia in western Asia Minor. Jehovah's prophetic Word foretold that Cyrus would come against Babylon and topple it from its heaven-high position. After that he would be used as an instrument in doing a restoration work that Jehovah purposed for this Persian conqueror to do.—Isaiah 44:28.

²¹ In proof that it was really the Most High God that delivered the world-powerful Babylon into the hands of Cyrus the Great, the prophet Isaiah declared about two hundred years in advance:

20. In what way was this silverlike "kingdom" after, and in what way inferior to the golden head kingdom, and what was foretold about Babylon's conqueror?

21, 22. In proof that it was Jehovah who delivered Babylon into Cyrus' hands, what did Isaiah declare long in advance?

[22] "This is what Jehovah has said to his anointed one, to Cyrus, whose right hand I have taken hold of, to subdue before him nations, so that I may ungird even the hips of kings; to open before him the two-leaved doors, so that even the gates will not be shut: 'Before you I myself shall go, and the swells of land I shall straighten out. The copper doors I shall break in pieces, and the iron bars I shall cut off. And I will give you the treasures in the darkness and the hidden treasures in the concealment places, in order that you may know that I am Jehovah, the One calling you by your name, the God of Israel. For the sake of my servant Jacob and of Israel my chosen one, I even proceeded to call you by your name; I proceeded to give you a name of honor, although you did not know me. I am Jehovah, and there is no one else. With the exception of me there is no God. I shall closely gird you, although you have not known me, in order that people may know from the rising of the sun and from its setting that there is none besides me. I am Jehovah, and there is no one else.' 'I myself have roused up someone in righteousness, and all his ways I shall straighten out. He is the one that will build my city, and those of mine in exile he will let go, not because of hire nor because of bribery,' Jehovah of armies has said."—Isaiah 45:1-6, 13.

[23] Because the gates of Babylon were strangely left open on the night of October 29, 539 B.C., the conquering troops marched down the dried-up bed of the Euphrates River and over the river quays and were able to get inside the towering walls of Babylon. Jehovah's prophecies through Isaiah foretold that warriors of Elam and Media would be associated with Cyrus in conquering Babylon. (Isaiah 13:17-22; 21:2, 9) In harmony

---

23. (a) How did Cyrus' forces get inside the walls of Babylon, and who was associated with the Persians in its capture? (b) How did a message turn Belshazzar's feasting to dismay?

with this, Cyrus' uncle, Darius the Mede, joined forces in this victorious action against Babylon. The prophet Daniel was in the city at the time. He was a student of God's prophecies, including that through Jeremiah, who had likewise foretold the fall of Babylon or Sheshach. (Daniel 9:1, 2, *AV;* Jeremiah 25:12-26; 50:1 to 51:64) On the night that mighty Babylon fell and its last king, Belshazzar, was killed, Belshazzar and his many lords were feasting, feeling quite secure behind the city walls. Feasting turned to dismay when Jehovah caused the appearance of a man's hand to write in strange alphabetic characters on the wall of Belshazzar's dining room. Finally the prophet Daniel had to be called in to read and interpret the handwriting on the wall. Under inspiration Daniel found the miraculous message to confirm what Jehovah's prophets Isaiah and Jeremiah had said long previous. Daniel declared that his God, the God of Israel, had written the message. He said:

²⁴ "Then from his presence the hand was sent, and this writing was inscribed. And this is the writing that was inscribed: MENE, MENE, TEKEL, and PARSIN [the plural number of the word PERES]. This is the interpretation of the matter: MENE, God has numbered the days of your kingdom and brought it to an end; TEKEL, you have been weighed in the balances and found wanting; PERES, your kingdom is divided and given to the Medes and Persians."

²⁵ Before that night had passed, the handwritten prophecy on the wall came true, in vindication of Jehovah's word and of his prophet Daniel. "That very night Belshazzar the Chaldean king was slain. And Darius the Mede received the kingdom, being about sixty-two years old." (Daniel 5:24-

24. What did Daniel read and interpret that message to say?
25. How did the message come true that night, and what change of world domination took place?

28, 30, 31, *RS*) At this death of the last king in Nebuchadnezzar's dynasty over Babylon, the golden head of his dream image ceased to exist as a world power. Medo-Persia, as the symbolic breast and arms of silver, came into the control as the fourth world power of Bible history. That was in 539 B.C.

²⁶ Evidently at the death of his uncle, Darius the Mede, Cyrus the Persian became the sole head of the Persian Empire. He did the work of restoration foretold by Isaiah. In 537 B.C.* Cyrus' decree went into effect toward the captive Jews then exiles in Babylon, and the faithful Jewish remnant were released to go back to their homeland and rebuild the sanctuary of Jehovah and the holy city of Jerusalem. The conquered city of Babylon did not at once go to ruin in fulfillment of Jehovah's prophecy concerning its lasting desolation, but King Cyrus ruled from this city.

²⁷ The silver breast and arms about which Nebuchadnezzar had dreamed pictured a "kingdom," the line of kings beginning with Cyrus the Great, who reigned jointly for a time with his uncle, Darius the Mede, and continuing for more than two hundred years. In this line of Persian kings there were more than the few whom the Bible names. Cyrus was the first Aryan or the first of the Japhetic branch of the human family to become world ruler. As world ruler, Cyrus the Great reigned for nine years and was succeeded in 529 B.C. by King Cambyses, who extended the Persian Empire by conquering Egypt in 525 B.C. A usurper followed him, in 522 B.C., a Magian named Gaumata who pretended to be Smerdis. He reigned

* See *The Bible as History,* by Werner Keller (1956), page 300.

26. When and how was the prophecy of the Jewish restoration fulfilled, and did Babylon's desolation begin at once?
27, 28. (a) What did the silver breast and arms of Nebuchadnezzar's dream image picture? (b) How did Cambyses enlarge the Persian Empire, and what connection did Xerxes I and Artaxerxes I have with two noted Bible characters?

for less than eight months, and was put to death
by the first Persian king named Darius, who thus
became king in 521 B.C.

[28] This Persian Darius I launched a campaign
against Greece but met a signal defeat at the
battle of Marathon. He was followed, in 486/485
B.C., by Xerxes I or Ahasuerus, the husband of
the Biblical Queen Esther. (Esther 1:1-3; 3:7) He
too set out to conquer Greece but failed, meeting
with military disaster at Thermopylae and with
a naval disaster in the battle of Salamis in 480
B.C. He was succeeded by Artaxerxes I, surnamed
Longimanus because his right hand was longer
than the left. It was in the twentieth year of this
Artaxerxes, or in 455 B.C., that he commissioned
his Jewish cupbearer Nehemiah to be governor of
the province of Judea and to go to Jerusalem and
rebuild its walls. At Nehemiah's rebuilding of
Jerusalem's walls the count began of the "seventy
weeks" of years, of Daniel 9:24-27, which set the
dates for the appearance and the death of the
Messiah or Christ, Jesus of Nazareth.—Nehemiah
1:1; 2:1-18.

[29] Then, in order, came King Xerxes II; Darius II
(the Persian); Artaxerxes II, surnamed Mnemon;
Artaxerxes III, surnamed Ochus; Arses, who
reigned two years (338-336 B.C.); and finally
Darius III, surnamed Codomannus, whose reign
was abruptly terminated in 331 B.C. With him
the Persian world power, symbolized by the silver
breast and arms of Nebuchadnezzar's dream image, ended. This was by his defeat that year in
the battle of Gaugamela, near where Nineveh,
capital of the Assyrian Empire, had once stood.
By whom was he defeated? By the Macedonian
who established the next world power, the Macedonian or Grecian Empire, the fifth world power,
namely, by Alexander the Great.

29. With the reign of what king did the Persian world power
end, and by whom was the next world power established?

FIFTH, SIXTH AND SEVENTH WORLD POWERS

[30] Now in our study of the metallic image of Nebuchadnezzar's dream we come to "its belly and thighs of bronze [or copper]." The prophet Daniel told Nebuchadnezzar that this part of the image represented a kingdom or line of kings. Said Daniel: "After you shall arise another kingdom inferior to you, and yet a third kingdom of bronze, which shall rule over all the earth." (Daniel 2:39, *RS*) Alexander was the son of King Philip II of Macedon, who imposed his power upon all Greece to the south and put an end to the city-state system of the Greeks. Alexander carried out the ambition of his father and proceeded to the conquest of the Persian Empire to the east, in Asia. This Alexander the Great was therefore foretold in the prophecy of Daniel, as we shall see. He gained one victory after the other over the Persian king, Darius III, and in 331 B.C. took from him the city of Babylon and defeated him at the battle of Gaugamela. With that the Persian world power collapsed, and Alexander of Macedon became world ruler, establishing the fifth world power of Bible history. In 327 B.C. he extended his conquests into the western parts of India. His empire was greater than any of those that preceded his. From this standpoint this bronze or copper kingdom was one "which shall rule over all the earth."

[31] As world ruler, Alexander the Great lived only eight years, dying in Babylon in 323 B.C. During his military expeditions the so-called *koiné* or common Greek was developed, in which language the Christian Greek Scriptures of the Holy Bible were written. Because of the great sweep of Alexander's empire and the Grecian colonies that he established, the *koiné* Greek became the

30. How did Daniel in his interpretation foretell this Macedonian or Grecian Empire, and how did it become one to "rule over all the earth"?
31. Because of Alexander's empire-building expeditions, what became the international language, and for what good news did this become the proper medium to spread the news to all parts?

international language. Hence it was the proper language medium by which to spread the good news of God's kingdom under Christ to all parts of the then known world in the days of Christ's apostles.

³² When Alexander died in 323 B.C. the "kingdom" pictured by the belly and thighs of bronze (copper) did not come to an end and give way to the iron part of the symbolic image. Alexander's two sons and his brother, who were in line to succeed him, were murdered within fourteen years. Alexander's empire became broken up, four of his generals taking power, each one over a section of Alexander's empire. Within less than half a century after Alexander's death three distinct Hellenic or Grecian empires had established themselves, each one with its own line of kings. One of these Hellenic empires was based in Macedon, another in Syria and the third in Egypt. The latter two made it their effort to Hellenize or Grecize Egypt and the Middle East and Asia as far east as India. It was during this period that the Hebrew Scriptures of Jehovah's prophets were translated into the common Greek of that time, to form what is called the Greek *Septuagint* used by the early Christians. In the course of time the rising power of Rome, Italy, swallowed up these Hellenic empires, first that of Macedonia, then that of Syria, and finally that of Egypt in 30 B.C.

³³ In that year the Hellenic empire of Egypt was subjected to Rome, and Egypt became a Roman province ruled by a Roman governor. By that year (30 B.C.) at the latest, Rome became the dominant world power, the sixth world power. The march of world powers, as marked out by the metallic image of Nebuchadnezzar's dream,

32. Why did the kingdom pictured by the belly and thighs of bronze not come to an end at Alexander's death, and by whom was there a gradual swallowing up of his empire?
33. How was this next world power foretold by Daniel in interpretation, and why should not the two iron legs suggest division?

had now descended to the legs of iron. Daniel, interpreting Nebuchadnezzar's dream, foretold this to him, saying: "And there shall be a fourth kingdom, strong as iron, because iron breaks to pieces and shatters all things; and like iron which crushes, it shall break and crush all these." (Daniel 2:40, *RS*) The fact that there were two legs of iron did not mean that the world power symbolized by the legs was divided into an East and a West or a North and a South, any more than the fact that there were two silver arms meant that the Persian world power was divided politically into two opposite parts. The Roman world power, the sixth world power in Biblical history, went through changes and proved stronger than the golden, silver and bronze (copper) empires prior to it. For strength and ability to crush, it was indeed like iron.

[34] The sixth world power, the Roman, was not the only world power symbolized by the iron legs. Within the centuries of existence of the ironlike system of world power there arose the greatest and mightiest in all the line of march. This was the seventh world power, which was foretold in Bible prophecy. It was the British Empire, the mightiness of which was increased in course of time by the co-operation of the United States of America in the North American continent. This resulted in a dual world power, the strongest and most far-reaching of all history down till A.D. 1914.

[35] But there was a final or completing part of the symbolic image, namely, "its feet partly of iron and partly of clay." On this the prophet Daniel made the following inspired comment: "And whereas thou sawest the feet and toes, part of potters' clay, and part of iron, it shall be a

---

34. Why was the Roman not the only world power symbolized by the iron legs?
35. What was the completing part of Nebuchadnezzar's dream image, and what interpretation did Daniel place on this final part?

divided kingdom; but there shall be in it of the strength of the iron, forasmuch as thou sawest the iron mixed with miry clay. And as the toes of the feet were part of iron, and part of clay, so the kingdom shall be partly strong, and partly broken [brittle]. And whereas thou sawest the iron mixed with miry clay, they shall mingle themselves with [by] the seed of men; but they shall not cleave one to another, even as iron doth not mingle with clay."—Daniel 2:41-44, *AS*, margin.

[36] As the iron section of the symbolic image started off with the Roman Empire and led on to the Anglo-American dual world power, the firmness and strength of the iron would represent the hardness and toughness of their world control and rule. But what of the ten toes in which the symbolic image terminated? This feature showed that at the time of the end of this symbolic image the remnant of the Roman or sixth world power would vie with the Anglo-American or seventh world power and that there would be other independent political governments associated with those competing powers. The number ten being a Biblical number symbolizing earthly completeness, the ten toes picture all such coexisting powers and governments.

[37] But how did these symbolic ten toes come to be part of iron and part of miry clay? It came to be that way because "they shall mingle themselves with [by] the seed of men." It is true that the pagan Roman Empire was partly converted into the Holy Roman Empire, anointed by the religious pontiffs of the Roman Catholic Church. The Roman Catholic Hierarchy tried to dominate this Holy Roman Empire, and a struggle for power arose between the political rulers of this empire

36. What would the iron of the image suggest, and what is pictured by the ten toes of the image?
37. What part did the Roman Catholic Church play in a section of the Roman Empire?

and the pope and his religious clergy. There was a marriage of Church and State, except in the United States of America.

[38] However, a mingling of rulers or political heads with the "seed of men" would mean a combining with one another and producing a political offspring; or it would mean a popularizing, a democratizing or a socializing of the forms of government. In the nineteenth century the socialist movement made great strides in Christendom. In the year 1848 the Communist Manifesto, giving a brief, clear statement of scientific socialism, was issued by Karl Marx and Friedrich Engels, and revolutionary movements swept through Europe. Even Pope Pius IX was obliged to flee from Rome, not to return till 1850. The socialist element, when sharing to any extent in government, has aimed at weakening and overthrowing so-called capitalistic government; whereas democratic elements in government have weakened the power of imperial, absolute monarchs. There has been no cleaving together in love or kindredness between these more modern, radical elements and the older imperial types of world domination. It has been like trying to mix iron with clay.

INDESTRUCTIBLE KINGDOM WITHOUT SUCCESSORS

[39] At this stage comes the dramatic climax of the dream of Nebuchadnezzar and its fulfillment! The prophet Daniel continued his interpretation: "In the days of those kings the God of the heavens shall set up a kingdom which shall never be destroyed, nor shall the kingdom be left to another people; it shall break in pieces and annihilate all these kingdoms, but it shall stand forever, as you saw how a stone was hewn from a mountain with-

---

38. On the part of the political rulers, what mingling of themselves with or by the seed of men has there been in a strictly political way, and with what result?

39. How did Daniel interpret the climax of Nebuchadnezzar's dream?

out hands, which broke in pieces the iron, the bronze, the clay, the silver, and the gold. A great God makes known to the king what shall be in the future; the dream is certain, and its interpretation sure."—Daniel 2:44, 45, *AT*.

[40] A.D. 1914 the "seven times" or the "appointed times of the nations" ended. In the fall of that year, according to the Bible's time schedule, the God of the heavens set up his promised kingdom, enthroning and crowning his anointed Son, the glorified Jesus Christ, to be the King of kings and Lord of lords. (Revelation 12:1-5; 17:14; 19:16) Thus this establishment of God's kingdom was by no human hands. It was as if a stone had been cut out of a mountain without human hands. Jehovah God's universal sovereignty is symbolized by the mountain; and this kingdom in the hands of his anointed King who fulfills the kingdom covenant with David is simply an expression of Jehovah's universal sovereignty. It is the "kingdom of our Lord [God] and of his Christ."—Revelation 11:15.

[41] This birth of the Kingdom occurred "in the days of those kings," not merely the kings pictured by the ten toes but also those pictured by the iron, bronze (copper), silver and gold parts of the image. Although the Babylonian, the Persian, the Grecian and the Roman Empires had long ago passed away as world powers, yet there were the basic remnants of those previous world powers still in existence in 1914 (A.D.), the Turkish Ottoman Empire occupying the territory of ancient Babylonia, whereas national governments operated in Persia (now Iran) and in Greece and in Rome, Italy.

[42] This heavenly kingdom set up by the God of the heavens will never be destroyed. It will there-

40. How was the symbolic stone cut out without hands, and what is the mountain out of which it was thus cut?
41. In what way was it "in the days of those kings" that God's kingdom was thus born?
42. Why will the power of that kingdom not be left to another people, and when will it strike the symbolic image?

fore not leave its sovereignty to any new world power as a successor, nor will it ever be trodden down or trampled on by any worldly nation. There will be no nation or worldly power on earth to which to leave such sovereignty, for God's kingdom by his anointed King will break all these kingdoms pictured in the metallic image to pieces and bring them to an everlasting end. That heavenly kingdom, brought forth like a newborn babe from God's universal organization over which he exercises sovereignty, is now speeding on its mission to strike the symbolic image on its feet of iron and clay. At the time for the final Armageddon war, "the war of the great day of God the Almighty," that symbolic Stone will strike the symbolic image with crushing impact.

[43] The literal destruction of the symbolic image will rapidly go forward, without a hand being raised by any of Jehovah's witnesses on earth. The symbolic image of world domination by rulers of this old world will be ground to powder, and the wind of God's storm will sweep the powder away like the chaff of the threshing floor, never to be brought together again on earth. Like the image-smashing stone that grew to mountain size to fill our entire earth, God's kingdom will become the governmental mountain that will fill the whole earth and dominate all human affairs forever. "They will not do any harm or cause any ruin in all my holy mountain; because the earth will certainly be filled with the knowledge of Jehovah as the waters are covering the very sea." (Isaiah 11:9) The will of the great God will then be done on earth as well as in heaven. The long march of ungodly world powers will have ended forever.

---

43. How thoroughly will the symbolic image be disposed of, and how will the stone become a mountain filling all the earth?

CHAPTER 6

*The King
For Enforcing
The Supreme Will*

WHEN the Roman Empire was holding sway as the sixth world power of Biblical history, the heir to the long-promised kingdom of

God was born among men, about October 1 in the year 2 B.C. This heir of the heavenly kingdom really came down from heaven. What events in heaven preceded his birth on earth have not been made known to us, but there were important preliminaries to his birth here on earth. Quite fittingly for a king, he was to have a forerunner to introduce him among men. About fifteen months before the birth of the promised King of the family line of David, the angel Gabriel appeared to the father of the future forerunner. He appeared inside the first holy compartment of Jehovah's sanctuary in Jerusalem, or in so-called Herod's temple, where priest Zechariah was offering incense to Jehovah while the worshipers were praying outside in the courtyard. Gabriel said:

[2] "Have no fear, Zechariah, because your supplication has had acceptance, and your wife Elizabeth will be the mother of a son to you, and you are to call his name John. And you will have joy and great gladness, and many will rejoice over his birth; for he will be great before Jehovah.* But he must drink no wine and strong drink at all, and he will be filled with holy spirit right from his mother's womb, and many of the sons of Israel will he turn back to Jehovah* their God. Also he will go before him with Elijah's spirit and power, to turn back the hearts of fathers to children and the disobedient ones to the practical wisdom of righteous ones, to get ready for Jehovah* a prepared people."—Luke 1:13-17.

[3] After his week of temple service was up, old Zechariah went home and his aged wife Elizabeth conceived the child to be named John. During the

---

* "Jehovah," in at least nine printed Hebrew translations of the Biblical account of Luke.

1, 2. During the sway of what world power was the heir of the promised kingdom born, and according to Gabriel's announcement what was he to have precede him?
3. When did Gabriel appear to Mary, and what were her circumstances?

sixth month of her pregnancy the angel Gabriel
was sent about sixty miles north of Jerusalem,
to the city of Nazareth in the province of Galilee.
He appeared to a virgin Jewess named Mary, the
daughter of Heli, of the family line of King David.
(Luke 3:23-31) She was engaged to marry a carpenter named Joseph, who also was of the family
line of King David but through the second-last
king of Jerusalem, Jeconiah or Jehoiachin. But before finally merging in King David, the ancestral
lines of Joseph and Mary meet in Zerubbabel and
his father Shealtiel, descendants of David. Thus
Mary's coming offspring would have fleshly descent from King David through both his son King
Solomon and his other son Nathan. Luke 3:34-38
gives that part of Mary's ancestry that reaches
back from Abraham to "Adam, the son of God,"
as follows: 1. Adam. 2. Seth. 3. Enos. 4. Cainan.
5. Mahalaleel. 6. Jared. 7. Enoch. 8. Methuselah.
9. Lamech. 10. Noah. 11. Shem. 12. Arphaxad.
13. Cainan. 14. Shelah. 15. Eber. 16. Peleg. 17. Reu.
18. Serug. 19. Nahor. 20. Terah. 21. Abraham.
From Abraham Joseph's ancestry and Mary's run
as follows:

Joseph's Matthew 1:2-16	*Mary's* Luke 3:23-34	Matthew 1:2-16	Luke 3:23-34
21. Abraham	Abraham	38.	Melea
22. Isaac	Isaac	39. Abijah	Eliakim
23. Jacob	Jacob	40. Asa	Jonam
24. Judah	Judah	41. Jehoshaphat	Joseph
25. Perez	Perez	42. Jehoram	Judas
26. Hezron	Hezron	43. [Ahaziah]	Symeon
27. Ram	Arni	44. [Jehoash]	Levi
28. Amminadab	Amminadab	45. [Amaziah]	Matthat
29. Nahshon	Nahshon	46. Uzziah	Jorim
30. Salmon	Salmon	47. Jotham	Eliezer
31. Boaz	Boaz	48. Ahaz	Jesus
32. Obed	Obed	49. Hezekiah	Er
33. Jesse	Jesse	50. Manasseh	Elmadam
34. David	David	51. Amon	Cosam
35. Solomon	Nathan	52. Josiah	Addi
36. Rehoboam	Mattatha	53. [Jehoiakim]	Melchi
37.	Menna	54. Jechoniah	Neri

Matthew 1:2-16	Luke 3:23-34	Matthew 1:2-16	Luke 3:23-34
55. SHEALTIEL	SHEALTIEL	68.	Amos
56. ZERUBBABEL	ZERUBBABEL	69. Zadok	Mattathias
57. [Hananiah, according to 1 Chronicles 3:19, 21]		70. Achim	Joseph
		71. Eliud	Jannai
58.	Rhesa	72. Eleazar	Melchi
59.	Joanan	73. Matthan	Levi
60. Abiud	Joda	74. Jacob	Matthat
61. Eliakim	Josech	75.	Heli (Mary's father)
62.	Semein		
63.	Mattathias	76. Joseph	Joseph (son-in-law of Heli)
64.	Maath		
65.	Naggai	77. JESUS (foster son)	JESUS (Mary's son)
66. Azor	Esli		
67.	Nahum		

⁴ Oh what news Gabriel brought King David's distant granddaughter Mary! "Have no fear, Mary, for you have found favor with God; and, look! you will conceive in your womb and give birth to a son, and you are to call his name Jesus. This one will be great and will be called Son of the Most High, and Jehovah God will give him the throne of David his father, and he will be king over the house of Jacob forever, and there will be no end of his kingdom." Mary, not yet united to the carpenter Joseph, asked how this birth could be without a human father. Gabriel answered: "Holy spirit will come upon you, and power of the Most High will overshadow you. For that reason also what is born will be called holy, God's Son." Submissively Mary said: "Look! Jehovah's slave girl! May it take place with me according to your declaration."—Luke 1:26-38.

⁵ Mary immediately conceived God's Son Jesus, because holy spirit now came upon her and power of the Most High overshadowed her. She hastened to tell her pregnant relative, Elizabeth the wife of priest Zechariah, who Gabriel said was pregnant with John. As soon as Mary greeted her,

---

4. What was the information that Gabriel gave to Mary, and how did she respond to it?
5. What took place when Mary visited and greeted Elizabeth?

John in her womb leaped and Elizabeth became "filled with holy spirit." She said to Mary: "Blessed are you among women, and blessed is the fruit of your womb! So how is it that this privilege is mine, to have the mother of my Lord come to me? For, look! as the sound of your greeting fell upon my ears, the infant in my womb leaped with great gladness."—Luke 1:39-44.

⁶ Here Elizabeth under the spirit's operation acknowledged that Mary's child was to be her "Lord." Under impulse of the same holy spirit, Elizabeth's yet unborn son John likewise acknowledged Mary's child to be his "Lord." Centuries previously, King David had made the same acknowledgment, in Psalm 110:1. Mary herself, under inspiration, magnified Jehovah God, the heavenly Father of her unborn son. She stayed with Elizabeth nearly till the birth of John and then returned to Nazareth.—Luke 1:46-56.

⁷ Elizabeth's son was now born. Her husband called the boy's name John and then, filled with holy spirit, he prophesied this about his son John: "But as for you, young child, you will be called a prophet of the Most High, for you will pioneer before Jehovah to make his ways ready, to give knowledge of salvation to his people by forgiveness of their sins, because of the tender compassion of our God." (Luke 1:57-78) In the meantime the carpenter Joseph found out that Mary was pregnant. Thinking that she had committed immorality, he was inclined to cancel the marriage engagement rather than make a public charge of fornication against her and have her stoned to death. But one night a dream came to Joseph, and with it an angel who said that Joseph should marry Mary. Why? "For that which has been

6. What acknowledgment did Elizabeth and unborn John thus make, and how was this in harmony with Psalm 110:1?
7. What prophecy did Zechariah make at his son John's birth, and how was the carpenter Joseph encouraged to marry the pregnant Mary?

begotten in her is by holy spirit. She will give birth to a son, and you must call his name 'Jesus', for he will save his people from their sins." After waking up, Joseph obeyed and took Mary to his home.—Matthew 1:18-25.

[8] Jesus, the Son of God, was not born there at Nazareth. Before he could be born, Joseph and Mary had to go more than sixty miles to the south to Bethlehem, the birthplace of King David in the province of Judah or Judea. Caesar Augustus, the first emperor of the Roman Empire, decreed that all the inhabited earth under the empire should be registered at the place where each one's family originated. So, about the middle of the Jews' seventh lunar month called Ethanim, or about our October 1, in the year 2 B.C., Jesus the Son of God was born in Bethlehem. The winter rains had not yet begun and shepherds were still keeping their flocks out nights in the open fields around Bethlehem. There was a miraculous burst of light, in the midst of which an angel appeared and said: "Have no fear, for, look! I am declaring to you good news of a great joy that all the people will have, because there was born to you today a Savior, who is Christ the Lord, in David's city. And this is a sign for you: you will find an infant bound in cloth bands and lying in a manger." Then suddenly the shepherds saw with that angel a "multitude of the heavenly host, praising God and saying: 'Glory in the heights above to God, and upon earth peace among men of good-will.'" The shepherds found the newborn babe and became witnesses to the birth of God's Son. Then they bore witness of this to others, but not to wicked King Herod of Judea.—Luke 2:1-20.

[9] After being taken down south to Egypt till after King Herod the Great died, Jesus was brought

8. What happened so that Jesus was not born at Nazareth, and how did shepherds become witnesses of the birth of God's Son?
9. Where, however, did Jesus grow up, and what work did John the son of Zechariah undertake, and why?

back north to Nazareth. Here he grew and became a carpenter apprentice to his foster father Joseph. During this time John's parents died, and according to God's purposes John took up living in the wilderness of Judea. Here he grew to thirty years of age, living on insect locusts and honey. Then God sent John to begin baptizing and acting as the forerunner of the Son of God, Jesus, the Heir to the kingdom of David. (John 1:33, 34) So in the spring of the year 29 (A.D.), or in the "fifteenth year of the reign of Tiberius Caesar," the successor of Caesar Augustus,* John began preaching in the wilderness of Judea and baptizing in the river Jordan the Jews who repented of their sins. John's father, priest Zechariah, had prophesied concerning him: "You will pioneer before Jehovah to make his ways ready, to give knowledge of salvation to his people by forgiveness of their sins." It was therefore appropriate for John to tell the Jews under the Ten Commandments to repent of their sins and to be baptized in symbol of their repentance. —Matthew 3:1-11; Luke 3:1-6.

¹⁰ John also began announcing the coming of God's kingdom. Did he say: 'Repent, for the kingdom of David has drawn near'? Had John preached that message, the Roman emperor and also Pontius Pilate, the Roman governor of Judea, would have got after John for stirring up insurrection and violating the law of *laesa majestas* ("injured majesty"). But what did John preach? This: "Repent, for the kingdom of the heavens has drawn near." (Matthew 3:1, 2) God had told

---

* Caesar Augustus had died August 19, A.D. 14. Hence the "fifteenth year of the reign of Tiberius Caesar" ended August 18, A.D. 29. Before that date John the Baptist, about thirty years of age, began preaching.

---

10. The announcement of the coming of what did John make, and how did John know and show that he was the forerunner of God's Son?

John that he was the forerunner of the Son of God and that he would have the privilege of identifying the Son of God, if not also baptizing him. John's father, if not also his mother Elizabeth, had told John what the angel Gabriel had said inside the temple sanctuary, that John was to be a forerunner and, like the prophet Elijah, "get ready for Jehovah a prepared people." Hence John was expecting Jehovah's Son to come to him for identification. He told the repentant Jews: "I, on the one hand, baptize you with water because of your repentance; but the one coming after me is stronger than I am, whose sandals I am not fit to take off. That one will baptize you people with holy spirit and with fire."—Matthew 3:11; Luke 1:17.

[11] Jesus was still carpentering with his mother and his half brothers and half sisters up in Nazareth. But Jesus knew that he was not to keep carpentering always. His mother had told him how he was God's Son by means of God's holy spirit that had come upon her for her to conceive him. Joseph his foster father had also told him that he, Joseph, was not Jesus' father but that he had been begotten in Mary by holy spirit. Mary had also told him that the angel Gabriel had said that Jehovah God would give Jesus the throne of his earthly forefather David and he would be king over the house of Jacob (or Israel) forever and his kingdom would never end. So Jesus knew he was the royal heir of the covenant that Jehovah had made with David for the everlasting kingdom.

[12] But when was he to enter in upon his kingdom career? He was now in his thirtieth year of human life. He could not start out on his own accord. He had been told that the angel Gabriel

---

11. How did Jesus come to know his true relationship to Joseph and that he was the royal heir of the kingdom covenant with David?
12. How did Jesus know when to make his appearance as kingdom heir?

said that John the son of priest Zechariah was to be his forerunner. So he must let the forerunner first appear and run on his mission for about six months, announcing the coming one. Then one day the news did come to Jesus at Nazareth that John had begun baptizing repentant Jews and that John was proclaiming: "The kingdom of the heavens has drawn near." At that, Jesus must have been stirred to the depths of his soul. Ah, now, the time had drawn near for him to appear as kingdom heir!

[13] He was now reaching thirty years of age, the age of a fully mature man. The sixty-ninth week of years, foretold by Daniel 9:24-26, was also coming to an end and the seventieth week of years counting from Nehemiah's rebuilding of the walls of Jerusalem was about to begin. Jesus here realized it was the due time for him to appear as the Messiah, the Christ, about whom the angel had made announcement at his birth in Bethlehem. Jesus laid down his carpenter tools. He left his shop and home. He headed southeast to his forerunner John, who was announcing there at the banks of the Jordan River the approach of the kingdom of the heavens. He would go, not to Jerusalem, the city of the great King Jehovah, not to the temple of Herod to be anointed as king of the Jews by the high priest, Annas. He would go to his forerunner, this priest's son, not to be anointed with holy anointing oil as king over earthly Israel, but to be baptized in water.—Matthew 3:13; Mark 1:9.

[14] John the Baptist was glad to see Jesus. But why should Jesus ask to be baptized in water? John knew he was baptizing Jews who were sinners and who were repentant over their sins against the law of Jehovah God given to the na-

---

13. What prophetic week was then to begin, and where did Jesus go, and to have what done to him?
14. Why was John backward about baptizing Jesus in water?

tion of Israel through Moses. Jesus was no such repentant sinner. John knew that Jesus was holy, for
he was God's Son conceived in Mary by holy spirit.
Why, John knew that when he was yet unborn in
his mother's womb he had leaped in her womb
in acknowledgment of the then unborn Jesus as
his "Lord." So John tried to prevent Jesus from
being baptized, saying: "I am the one needing to
be baptized by you, and are you coming to me?"

[15] How did Jesus overcome John's objections?
Jesus said: "Let it be, this time, for in that way
it is suitable for us to carry out all that is righteous." Submissively John joined in doing what was
suitable for them at that time. He baptized Jesus
the Heir of the kingdom covenant, Jesus praying
during this procedure, not confessing any sins.
Then John had the identity of the Son of God
confirmed to him, not an identification of him
merely in a human sense but one of him in a
spiritual sense, in a sense different from his being
begotten in a human womb. What happened?

[16] "After being baptized Jesus immediately came
up from the water; and, look! the heavens were
opened up, and he saw descending like a dove
God's spirit coming upon him. Look! also, there
was a voice from the heavens that said: 'This
is my Son, the beloved, whom I have approved.' "
(Matthew 3:13-17; Luke 3:21-23) This was the
miraculous event that John later told his disciples
he had been awaiting: "I viewed the spirit coming down as a dove out of heaven, and it remained
upon him. Even I did not know him, but the very
One who sent me to baptize in water said to me,
'Whoever it is upon whom you see the spirit coming down and remaining, this is the one that
baptizes in holy spirit.' And I have seen it and

---

15. How were John's objections overcome, and after baptizing Jesus what confirmation did John have made to him?
16. How did this confirmation come to John, and how did he know
in what way to understand it?

have borne witness that this one is the Son of
God."—John 1:32-34.

¹⁷ By this divine act Jesus had been begotten
by means of God's spirit, apart from Mary's womb,
to become a spiritual Son of God, a "new creation" with spirit life in the invisible heavens in
view. By this act also he had been anointed, not
by Israel's high priest with a horn of oil, but by
Jehovah God and with holy spirit. By his human
birth into the family of King David and by being
adopted by the carpenter Joseph who was in the
royal line, Jesus had become the heir of King
David, naturally and legally, according to Jehovah's covenant for the kingdom. But now by his
being begotten from heaven and being declared
to be God's Son and by his being anointed with
God's holy spirit, Jesus became God's Anointed
One or Christ. He became the anointed Heir to
a kingdom grander and higher than that of King
David's earthly Israelitish kingdom in the Promised Land of Palestine. Jesus became the Heir of
the heavenly Kingdom. Truly in him Messiah, "the
anointed one, the prince," had come in that year
of 29 (A.D.), at the end of the sixty-nine weeks
of years, in accurately timed fulfillment of Daniel
9:25 (AS). Truly in him as Kingdom Heir the
"kingdom of the heavens" had drawn near; in
fact, it was in the midst of the Jews.—Luke 17:21.

¹⁸ What, then, had the water baptism of Jesus
signified? Not that he was a repentant sinner, for
he had kept God's law perfectly. He did this in
a way far better than the Jew did who wanted
to inherit everlasting life and who told Jesus:
"Teacher, all these things I have kept from my
youth on." (Mark 10:17-20) Recognizing Jesus
as the holy human Son of God, John did not
baptize Jesus in symbol of Jesus' repentance over

17. (a) To what was Jesus thus begotten, and of what did he become the Heir? (b) In him what was now found in the midst of
the Jews?
18, 19. Why did John not baptize Jesus in a symbol of repentance,
and why, then, did Jesus come to be baptized in water?

sins. What form of words, if any, John used when submerging Jesus beneath Jordan's waters the Bible does not tell us. But Jesus knew why he had come to be baptized. It was to do his heavenly Father's will on earth as well as in heaven.

[19] Paul the apostle explains it, saying concerning his Master Jesus: "It is not possible for the blood of bulls and of goats to take sins away. Hence when he comes into the world he says: ' "You did not desire sacrifice and offering, but you prepared a body for me. You did not approve of whole burnt-offerings and sin offering." Then I said, "Look! I am come (in the roll of the book it is written about me) to do your will, O God." ' After first saying, 'You did not desire nor did you approve of sacrifices and offerings and whole burnt-offerings and sin offering'—sacrifices which are offered according to the Law—then he actually says, 'Look! I am come to do your will.' . . . By the said 'will' we have been sanctified through the offering of the body of Jesus Christ once for all time." (Hebrews 10:4-10) The apostle Paul was here applying to Jesus at his baptism prophetic Psalm 40:6-8.

[20] By Jesus' water baptism he was symbolizing his dedication of himself, body and all, to do Jehovah's will in a way more than the law given through Moses demanded. At his water baptism, at his being buried by John under the waters, Jesus symbolically died to his past situation in earthly life. His will did not die, for when he was lifted out of the Jordan he still had his power of will. He said after that: "My food is for me to do the will of him that sent me and to finish his work." "I seek not my own will but the will of him that sent me." "I have come down from heaven to do, not my will, but the will of him that sent me. This is the will of him that sent me, that

20. What, then, did Jesus there symbolize, and what shows whether, at his baptism, his will died?

I should lose nothing out of all that he has given me but that I should resurrect it at the last day. For this is the will of my Father, that everyone that beholds the Son and exercises faith in him should have everlasting life, and I should resurrect him at the last day." And in prayer to God just before he was betrayed by unfaithful Judas, Jesus said: "My Father, if it is not possible for this to pass away except I drink it, let your will take place." "Nevertheless, let, not my will, but yours take place."—John 4:34; 5:30; 6:38-40; Matthew 26:42; Luke 22:42; see also 1 Corinthians 7:37.

[21] Till the day that Jesus was actually baptized into literal death by impalement on a torture stake, he continually had to exercise his power of will in harmony with God his Father's will. (John 21:22) He was not a hypocrite when he taught his disciples to pray to God: "Let your kingdom come. Let your will come to pass, as in heaven, also upon earth."—Matthew 6:9, 10.

[22] This soul-stirring fact must be held in our mind: The water baptism that God began by John was a sign that the kingdom of the heavens had drawn near! John's baptism of Jesus was an indication that the kingdom of God had drawn near; in fact, that kingdom came into the midst of the Jews at the descent of God's spirit upon Jesus after his water baptism. There God himself baptized his Son with holy spirit. Jesus' coming to the baptismal spot to do God's will and his symbolizing that dedication of himself by a water baptism was a step of Jesus toward God's kingdom. He had turned his back on carpentering in Nazareth. He had now come to serve the interests of the kingdom of the heavens, which John was pro-

---

21. Why was Jesus not a hypocrite when he taught his disciples to pray: "Let your will come to pass"?
22. A sign of what was John's baptism generally, but of Jesus' particularly, and so in behalf of what was Jesus dedicating himself to God?

claiming. He had dedicated himself to the interests of God's universal sovereignty which was represented in that kingdom.

[23] The baptism that was begun in Jesus' case was different from John's baptism for the repentance of Jewish sinners against the Mosaic law. The water baptism that was begun in Jesus is the baptism of all believers in him and in his heavenly Father, believers who come in Christlike dedication to do the will of God. It is a baptism in recognition of or "in the name of the Father and of the Son and of the holy spirit." (Matthew 28: 19) It is a baptism symbolizing the believer's dedication of himself to the Universal Sovereign Jehovah God, to do his will as revealed in connection with his kingdom. It is therefore not out of the right course of things that Jehovah God should now revive among his witnesses on earth the full water baptism, with the dipping of the believer's whole person under the water, as a symbol of his dedication irrevocably to do the will of God in imitation of his anointed King Jesus Christ.

[24] From his water baptism and his spirit anointing onward Jesus, now Christ, lived for God's kingdom of the heavens. Under temptation out in the Judean wilderness, Jesus refused the offer of Satan the Devil to give him all the kingdoms of this world and their glory if Jesus would fall down and do an act of worship to him as the "god of this system of things." Jesus well knew he was the heir of the kingdom according to God's covenant with David. He knew that he had just been anointed with God's spirit to be the Heir of the kingdom of the heavens. So he turned down Satan's cheap offer and commanded: "Go away, Satan! For it is written, 'It is Jehovah your God

23. In what way was the baptism that was begun in Jesus' case different from John's baptism for repentant Jews?
24. With what knowledge, and under the enlightenment of what, did Jesus turn down Satan's offer of the kingdoms of this world?

you must worship, and it is to him alone you must render sacred service.' " (Matthew 4:8-10) Jesus knew also, under the enlightenment of holy spirit, that he had been anointed to preach good news to the meek ones.—Isaiah 61:1-3; Luke 4:16-21.

[25] After John the Baptist had been imprisoned and restrained from preaching and baptizing, Jesus Christ began preaching openly the Kingdom, saying: "Repent, for the kingdom of the heavens has drawn near." (Matthew 4:12-17) He chose for himself twelve apostles whom he taught how to preach and whom he sent forth in twos to preach the good news of the Kingdom. He foretold the end of Satan's world and the establishment of God's kingdom, and foretold this as one of the evidences of its establishment in heaven: "This good news of the kingdom will be preached in all the inhabited earth for the purpose of a witness to all the nations, and then the accomplished end will come."—Matthew 24:14.

[26] Finally Jesus Christ died as a martyr, a witness to God's kingdom, faithful to his dedication to God's will, faithful to his anointing to preach the Kingdom. Before the Roman governor Pontius Pilate many Jewish priests at the head of a mob had rejected Jesus, saying: "We have no king but Caesar." And when Jesus died on the torture stake, there was posted above his head the notice: "Jesus the Nazarene the King of the Jews." (John 19:15, 19) This occurred on Friday, Nisan 14, A.D. 33, in the middle of the seventieth week of years that had been foretold in Daniel 9:26, 27. At the moment of his death there occurred an earthquake and the heavy double curtain of the temple sanctuary in Jerusalem was rent in two, from top to bottom.—Matthew 27:51.

25. After John's imprisonment, what did Jesus begin preaching, and what did he foretell as an evidence of the setting up of God's kingdom?
26. How was the kingdom issue made prominent at Jesus' execution, and what occurred when he died?

²⁷ That "original serpent," Satan the Devil, had bruised the Seed of God's woman in the heel; but in vain! Jehovah God could not break his covenant with David's Heir, Jesus Christ, for the kingdom. He could not let his promise fail, that the Seed of His woman should bruise the Serpent in the head. He had also started Jesus toward spiritual life in the heavens by begetting him with holy spirit after his water baptism. He must yet bring his anointed Son to full birth in the heavens. Under no circumstances could God's Son be held fast by death. At the exact foretold time, on the third day after his death, the heavenly Father raised him to life in heaven, "the firstborn from the dead," so declaring him God's divine immortal heavenly Son. "His Son, who sprang from the seed of David according to the flesh, but who with power was declared God's Son according to the spirit of holiness by means of resurrection from the dead—yes, Jesus Christ."—Colossians 1:18; Romans 1:3, 4.

²⁸ By God's irresistible power Jesus was lifted up out of his baptism into death in order to be able to do his Father's further will for him in heaven. He became a "new creation" in every sense. He arose as a spirit person, with a spirit body, "he being put to death in the flesh, but being made alive in the spirit." (1 Peter 3:18) Because of this spiritual resurrection he could ascend into heaven on the fortieth day after his resurrection to appear in the presence of God in behalf of all his believers and to sit down at the right hand of God as David's "Lord."—Hebrews 9:24; 10:12.

27. Why was it in vain that Satan thus bruised Jesus in the heel, and how was Jesus now declared to be God's Son?
28. To be what was Jesus made alive from the dead, and what did he then do?

CHAPTER 7

The Holy Ones Who Will Govern

J ESUS Christ gathered his first disciples from among men and women whom John the Baptist had prepared for him. The angel Gabriel had said that John was to "get ready for Jehovah a prepared people." (Luke 1:13-17) When the baptized Jesus came back from his forty days of fasting, studying and being tempted in the wilderness of Judea, John saw him coming and exclaimed: "See, the Lamb of God that takes away the sin of the world!" (John 1:29) The next day two of John's disciples, Andrew and John the son of Zebedee, began to follow Jesus. Andrew found his brother Simon Peter and "said to him: 'We have found the Messiah' (which means, when translated, Christ)." Simon Peter learned this to be true and began following the promised Messiah or Christ. Later Jesus found Philip of Bethsaida and said to him: "Be my follower." Eager to spread the good news, Philip found Nathanael. Jesus showed miraculous foreknowledge of this Nathanael, who then said: "Rabbi, you are the Son of God, you are King of Israel."—John 1:35-49.

[2] It is evident that Jesus was recognized as the promised Christ or Messiah and as the Son of God by his disciples from the first. In fact, John the Baptist told his disciples there at the Jordan River that he had baptized Jesus and had seen God's spirit descend in a visible manifestation upon Jesus, and he had thus been a witness to the fact that "this one is the Son of God." (John 1:29-34) John's disciples were believing this fact when John directed them to Jesus the "Lamb of God." However, Jesus did not publicly announce himself to the people as being the Messiah or Christ, although he did speak of himself as the Son of God, with continual references to his heavenly Father who had sent him. Among the Jews who heard Jesus preach and saw his miracles, opinions differed as to who he was. But did his first disciples carry the same conviction concerning him as at the beginning? In the third year of his ministry,

1. How did Jesus get his first disciples, and what confessions did they make concerning him then?
2. What confession showed that Jesus' apostles were of the same conviction toward the close of his ministry, and what did Jesus then say to Peter?

when up near Caesarea Philippi, Jesus asked
them: "You, though, who do you say I am?"
Simon Peter answered: "You are the Christ, the
Son of the living God." Jesus called Peter happy
and told him that the heavenly Father had revealed it to him. Then Jesus added: "Also I say
to you, You are Peter [*Petros,* Greek], and on
this rock-mass [*petra,* Greek] I will build my
congregation, and the gates of Ha'des will not
overpower it."—Matthew 16:13-18.

[3] Peter does not agree with Roman religionists
who claim that Jesus here said that Peter was
the "rock-mass" on which the spiritual house, the
congregation, is built. In his first letter Peter dis-
claims being the rock-mass (*petra*) by referring
to Jesus Christ and writing: "Coming to him as
to a living stone, rejected, it is true, by men, but
chosen, precious, with God, you yourselves also
as living stones are being built up a spiritual house
for the purpose of a holy priesthood, to offer up
spiritual sacrifices acceptable to God through
Jesus Christ." (1 Peter 2:4, 5) Peter was just a
living stone in that spiritual house built on Jesus
Christ. In this fact Paul agreed with Peter, saying:
"All ate the same spiritual food and all drank the
same spiritual drink. For they used to drink from
the spiritual rock-mass [*petra*] which followed
them, and that rock-mass [*petra*] meant the
Christ." (1 Corinthians 10:3, 4) So Jesus Christ
referred to himself as the "rock-mass" or *petra;*
and it is upon himself as the "Christ, the Son of
the living God," that he builds his congregation,
whom the gates of Ha'des cannot overpower.
Ha'des, which is the common grave of mankind,
did not overpower Jesus Christ himself, because,
on the third day after dying and being buried,
Almighty God raised him up to life.

---

3. Who is the rock-mass here mentioned as confessed by Peter
himself?

⁴ Jesus did not overthrow the Jewish synagogue in order to found the Christian congregation upon himself as the symbolic rock-mass. He taught in many a Jewish synagogue. (Matthew 4:23; 9:35; 12:9; 13:54) After being betrayed to his enemies and when standing before the Jewish Supreme Court of Jerusalem under the charge of heresy and blasphemy, Jesus said to the chief priest Annas: "I have spoken to the world publicly. I always taught in a synagogue and in the temple, where all the Jews come together, and I spoke nothing in secret." (John 18:19, 20) Consequently, before his impalement and resurrection from the dead, Jesus did not organize his followers as a congregation, as a spiritual house or sanctuary of God.

"THE LORD'S EVENING MEAL"

⁵ It was Thursday night, Passover night, the night of Nisan 14 of 33 (A.D.), the anniversary of the original Passover of the Israelites under Moses down in Egypt just before their deliverance. Jesus gathered his twelve apostles to himself into a large upper room in Jerusalem to celebrate. At the table he said: "I have greatly desired to eat this passover with you before I suffer; for I tell you, I will not eat it again until it becomes fulfilled in the kingdom of God." (Luke 22:14-16) That meant that this was the last literal Passover that he would eat as a natural Jew. In the course of this festival meal Jesus dismissed Judas from the room, thus freeing Judas to betray him that night.—John 13:21-31.

⁶ They finished eating the Passover lamb with

4. What shows whether Jesus overthrew the synagogue in order to establish the Christian congregation upon himself?
5. Where and when did Jesus celebrate his last Passover supper, and why did he dismiss Judas Iscariot from it?
6. What new thing did Jesus start for his disciples to celebrate on Nisan 14 of each year, and how does Matthew describe it?

loaves of unleavened bread and with wine, according to the requirements of Jehovah's Law covenant with ancient Israel. Jesus now indicated that a new arrangement was to begin with Jehovah's faithful worshipers. Jesus here mentioned to them a new covenant and a covenant for the kingdom, and he accordingly set up a new evening meal for celebration on Nisan 14 each year, Mosaic calendar. The apostle Matthew was then present and partook of this model meal, and he tells us what took place: "As they continued eating, Jesus took a loaf and, after saying a blessing, he broke it and, giving it to the disciples, he said: 'Take, eat. This means my body.' Also he took a cup and, having given thanks, he gave it to them, saying: 'Drink out of it, all of you; for this means my "blood of the covenant" which is to be poured out in behalf of many for forgiveness of sins. But I tell you, I will by no means drink henceforth any of this product of the vine until that day when I drink it new with you in the kingdom of my Father.' Finally, after singing praises, they went out to the mount of Olives."—Matthew 26:26-30.

⁷ When Jesus told those remaining eleven apostles that the loaf was or meant his body, the apostles correctly understood that it meant Jesus' own personal body of flesh and bone. Jesus had never told them that the congregation that he was going to build upon himself as a rock-mass would be his spiritual "body," over which he would be the heavenly Head. In the four life-accounts of Jesus written by Matthew, Mark, Luke and John, Jesus is reported using the word "congregation" or "church" only in Matthew 16:18; 18:17; but not saying that it was to be a spiritual body under him as Head. So in his words, "This means my body," he did not refer to the coming spiritual body which is the Christian congregation under

7. To what body did Jesus refer by his words over the loaf of bread?

him as its Head. He referred to his own body that he had got through the virgin Jewess Mary and that God had miraculously prepared for him.

[8] What was to be done with this body? According to Luke 22:19, Jesus said: "This means my body which is to be given in your behalf. Keep doing this in remembrance of me." This meant that his human body was to be given in an unrecallable, unrepeatable sacrifice in their behalf and in behalf of all humankind that should believe on him and accept his sacrifice. In proof, Hebrews 10:10 states: "By the said 'will' [of God] we have been sanctified through the offering of the body of Jesus Christ once for all time." His human body was acceptable in sacrifice to God because it was perfect, sinless, it being symbolized by the bread loaf with no leaven in it, as leaven was a Bible symbol of sin. (1 Corinthians 5:8; Hebrews 7:26-28) In his own body Jesus acted as a sin bearer for those of imperfect, sinful mankind who should believe in the value and power of his sacrifice. Peter reminds Christians: "Christ suffered for you, leaving you a model for you to follow his steps closely. He committed no sin, nor was deceit found in his mouth. . . . He himself by imputation bore our sins in his own body upon the stake, in order that we might be done with sins and live to righteousness. And 'by his stripes you were healed'."—1 Peter 2:21-24.

[9] This simple meaning of the unleavened loaf is upheld by the meaning that Jesus placed upon the cup of wine, the "product of the vine." He handed it to them to drink, with these words: "This means my 'blood of the covenant' which is to be poured out in behalf of many for forgiveness of sins." The wine thus was an emblem of his blood. While it was in the blood vessels of his

---

8. What was to be done with his human body, and for what purpose?
9. What was to be done with Jesus' blood, and why this?

human body it spelled earthly human life to him in its perfection. The Creator of Jesus' body had said long ago: "The soul of the flesh is in the blood, and I myself have put it upon the altar for you to make atonement for your souls, because it is the blood that makes atonement by the soul in it." (Leviticus 17:11) Jesus' blood being poured out would mean his death as a man. It was human sins that were here involved, and it was therefore necessary for the blood of a perfect human sacrifice to be splashed upon God's altar, "for it is not possible for the blood of bulls and of goats to take sins away." (Hebrews 10:4) Jesus knew what he had to do with his blood, for he knew God's rule: "Unless blood is poured out no forgiveness takes place."—Hebrews 9:22.

[10] The covenant that Jesus here brought to the apostles' attention required this blood. But which covenant was this? Not the old Law covenant with God that had been mediated by the prophet Moses at Mount Sinai. By the time of the Lord's evening meal that Law covenant had been operating for over fifteen hundred years, for it had been put in force by the shedding of blood of animal victims. On this the apostle Paul says: "Neither was the former covenant inaugurated without blood. For when every commandment according to the Law had been spoken by Moses to all the people, he took the blood of the young bulls and of the goats with water and scarlet wool and hyssop and sprinkled the book itself and all the people, saying: 'This is the blood of the covenant which God has laid as a charge upon you.' And he sprinkled the tent and all the vessels of the public service likewise with the blood. Yes, nearly all things are cleansed with blood according to the Law, and unless blood is poured out no forgiveness takes place." (Hebrews 9:18-22) Hence, Jesus in speak-

---

10. What was the covenant to which Jesus referred in connection with his blood, and what did he thus indicate was just ahead?

ing of his own lifeblood as the "blood of the covenant" meant that a new and grander covenant resting upon his perfect human blood was immediately ahead. According to Luke 22:20, Jesus said: "This cup means the new covenant by virtue of my blood, which is to be poured out in your behalf."

[11] In introducing this "new covenant" Jesus used the same form of words that Moses had used when inaugurating the old Law covenant with natural Israel, namely, "the blood of the covenant." At Jesus' mention of a new covenant the apostles must have remembered Jehovah's promise, in Jeremiah 31:31-34: " 'Look! There are days coming,' is the utterance of Jehovah, 'and I will conclude with the house of Israel and with the house of Judah a new covenant; . . . I will put my law into the midst of them, and in their heart I shall write it. And I will become their God, and they themselves will become my people.' 'And they will no more teach each one his companion and each one his brother, saying, "Know Jehovah!" for they will all of them know me, from the least one of them even to the greatest one of them,' is the utterance of Jehovah. 'For I shall forgive their error, and their sin I shall remember no more.' " This new covenant could provide no basis for Jehovah God to forgive human sins and error and remember them no more unless it rested on the poured-out blood of a perfect human victim, equal to the perfect man Adam in the Edenic sanctuary. The perfect man Jesus, in letting his sinless blood be poured out in death, was acting as the mediator of this new covenant between God and man.

[12] The people who had been taken into the old

11. At Jesus' mention of the new covenant, of whose prophecy must his apostles have been reminded, and upon what basis must this covenant rest in order to provide for forgiving sins?
12. In contrast with those in the old Law covenant, who are those taken into the new covenant, and in what way are their unity and their likeness of privilege shown?

Law covenant through Moses were Israelites, natural Jews according to the flesh. Those taken into the new covenant must be spiritual Israelites, Jews inwardly whose circumcision is that of the heart and not of the fleshly foreskin, being thus of the house of spiritual Israel and of the house of spiritual Judah. (Romans 2:28, 29) Such Israelites or Jews according to the spirit make up the congregation that Jesus Christ said he would build upon himself as the "rock-mass" or *petra*. Being one congregation in the new covenant, such spiritual Israelites or Jews show their unity and their likeness of privilege by eating and drinking the same special things, just as the people of Jehovah under Moses "all ate the same spiritual food and all drank the same spiritual drink." —1 Corinthians 10:3.

[13] Using this fact as an argument for the unity of spiritual Israelites with one another and with their God Jehovah, Paul goes on to say concerning the celebrating of the Lord's evening meal: "The cup of blessing which we bless, is it not a sharing in the blood of the Christ? The loaf which we break, is it not a sharing in the body of the Christ? Because there is one loaf, we, although many, are one body, for we are all partaking of that one loaf." (1 Corinthians 10:16, 17) Although the congregation of spiritual Israel is made up of many members, eventually 144,000 members, yet they are one integrated, unified body. This oneness as a body they display by partaking or eating of the one loaf of unleavened bread served at the yearly celebration of the Lord's evening meal. That one loaf is an emblem of the sacrificed body of Jesus Christ, upon which they feed in common participation by their active, fruitful faith every day of the year. That emblematic cup for which

---

13. At celebrating the Lord's evening meal, how does the congregation, although made of many members, show its oneness, as stated by the apostle Paul?

they bless God likewise stands for something they share in common, and that is the precious lifeblood of Jesus Christ. By faith in his blood they gain forgiveness of sins and justification or a righteous standing with Jehovah God. "While we were yet sinners, Christ died for us. Much more, therefore, since we have been declared righteous now by his blood, shall we be saved through him from wrath." (Romans 5:8, 9) Race, color, earthly nationality, language, social position do not disunite this one congregation.—Galatians 3:28, 29.

¹⁴ The Lord's evening meal powerfully calls attention to the sacrifice of Jesus Christ, especially in behalf of his congregation of spiritual Israelites. Because of this perfect human sacrifice which was offered to Jehovah God and of which they partake by faith, they cannot engage in any idolatry but must render exclusive devotion to God. The table of the Lord's evening meal with its wine cup is symbolically the "table of Jehovah" with the "cup of Jehovah." Its cup pictured Jesus' blood of the covenant. His blood was foreshadowed by the blood of the animal victims with which Moses inaugurated the old Law covenant long previous. According to the account in Exodus 24:3-8, the blood that was used to put that old covenant in force included the blood of peace offerings or "communion offerings to Jehovah." Now when a peace or communion offering was presented, the blood, fat and vital organs of the victim were offered to Jehovah; the priest officiating at the altar got a prescribed portion, and the offerer and persons with him ate the remainder. (Leviticus 3:1-17; 7:11-15, 28-34) In this way by their communion sacrifices the ancient Israelites ate in communion with Jehovah God at his altar table. In like manner the

14. To what do the loaf of bread and the cup really call attention, and with whom do the partakers really have communion, and why may they therefore not commit idolatry?

spiritual Israelites, when celebrating the Lord's evening meal, are holding communion not only with one another but, most importantly, with God. They cannot at the same time practice idolatry and so have communion with demons. Paul says:

[15] "Look at that which is Israel in a fleshly way: Are not those who eat the sacrifices sharers with the altar? What, then, am I to say? That what is sacrificed to an idol is anything, or that an idol is anything? No; but I say that the things which the nations sacrifice they sacrifice to demons, and not to God, and I do not want you to become sharers with the demons. You cannot be drinking the cup of Jehovah and the cup of demons; you cannot be partaking of 'the table of Jehovah' and the table of demons."—1 Corinthians 10:18-21; Malachi 1:6-8, 12, *AS*.

[16] The celebrating of the Lord's evening meal each year on the fourteenth day of Nisan, lunar calendar, should strengthen the partakers to refrain from every form of idolatry and to yield exclusive devotion to the only living and true God, Jehovah, who provided his Lamb Jesus Christ for us. Jesus did not tell his followers to celebrate his birthday, the exact date of which is not given in the Bible, as human birthday celebrations were pagan. However, he did enjoin upon his faithful congregation of spiritual Israelites a celebration. This was the "Lord's evening meal" that he instituted in Jerusalem that Passover night. He "took a loaf and, after giving thanks, he broke it and said: 'This means my body which is in your behalf. Keep doing this in remembrance of me.' He did likewise respecting the cup also, after he had the evening meal, saying: 'This cup means the new covenant by virtue of my blood. Keep doing

---

15. How does Paul point this out to celebrators of the Lord's evening meal?
16. What, therefore, should this yearly evening meal help the celebrators to refrain from, and in remembrance of what do they celebrate?

this, as often as you drink it, in remembrance of me.' " And the apostle Paul comments on this, saying: "For as often as you eat this loaf and drink this cup, you keep proclaiming the death of the Lord, until he arrives." (1 Corinthians 11:23-26) In this way Jesus told us to celebrate his death, not his birth.

[17] In obedience to this arrangement and command of the Lord Jesus Christ, Jehovah's dedicated, spirit-begotten people, whom he has brought into his new covenant, have celebrated the Lord's evening meal yearly on the anniversary of when Jesus introduced it, on Nisan 14, since the 1870's according to published reports.*

[18] In the unleavened bread and the wine used on that occasion they have discerned the perfect human body and the blood of the Lord Jesus, with heartfelt gratitude. They have endeavored to show the proper respect and appreciation toward these precious provisions for salvation, that they might not partake of the emblems in a manner that undervalued these things. They have had in mind the apostle Paul's warning: "Consequently, whoever eats the loaf and drinks the cup of the Lord unworthily will be guilty respecting the body and the blood of the Lord. First let a man approve himself after scrutiny, and thus let him eat of the loaf and drink of the cup. For he that eats and drinks eats and drinks judgment against himself if he does not discern the body. That is why many among you are weak and sickly and quite a few are sleeping in death. But if we would discern what we ourselves are, we would not be judged. How-

---

* See *Zion's Watch Tower*, the issue of April, 1880, page 8, under the title "Christ Our Passover," paragraph 3.

17. When and how often have Jehovah's modern witnesses celebrated the Lord's evening meal, and since what date, according to reports?
18. How have they tried to partake of the emblems without bringing judgment upon themselves?

ever, when we are judged, we are disciplined by
Jehovah, that we may not become condemned
with the world."—1 Corinthians 11:27-32, 20, 21.

[19] Particularly since celebrating the Lord's evening meal on Sunday, March 20, 1932, after sundown, multitudes of sheeplike persons, the "other
sheep" of the Right Shepherd Jesus Christ, have
been attending the yearly celebration, not to partake of the emblems, but to observe. For example,
at the celebration on Thursday, April 3, 1958,
after sundown, there was a reported attendance
of 1,150,000 at meeting places of Jehovah's witnesses world-wide. Of this total number merely
15,000 partook of the loaf and cup. The "great
crowd" of other sheep did not partake, for they
appreciated that they are not of the congregation
of spiritual Israelites in the new covenant that
was validated by Jesus' blood. They know, too,
that Jesus set up this evening meal with those
who were to be taken into the covenant for the
Kingdom. In his table discussion following the new
evening meal, Jesus said to the eleven faithful
apostles: "You are the ones that have stuck with
me in my trials; and I make a covenant with you,
just as my Father has made a covenant with me,
for a kingdom, that you may eat and drink at my
table in my kingdom, and sit on thrones to judge
the twelve tribes of Israel." (Luke 22:28-30) The
observing "other sheep" have personal Scripture
evidence that they are not in that Kingdom covenant.

[20] True, these eleven apostles did flee and leave
Jesus when he was arrested later that night in
the garden of Gethsemane. But after he was raised
from the dead on the morning of Nisan 16, Jesus
appeared to his fearful disciples, who were assem-

---

19. Since 1932 in particular, what great crowd has been attending
the Lord's evening meal celebration, and why?
20. What did Jesus do to the eleven apostles who fled from him at
his betrayal, and when were they brought into the nation of
spiritual Israel?

bling underground. Forty days later he made his final appearance to them. He told them that God's kingdom would not be restored to the earthly nation of Israel and instructed them to remain in Jerusalem until God's holy spirit arrived upon them. Then, before their eyes, he ascended heavenward out of their sight. Two angels that then appeared said to them: "This Jesus who was received up from you into heaven will come thus in the same manner as you have beheld him going into heaven." (Acts 1:1-11) Ten days later, on the festival day of Pentecost at Jerusalem, Jesus Christ at his Father's right hand in heaven began baptizing with the holy spirit. With a miraculous demonstration he poured it upon the 120 gathered disciples. They were thus begotten by the spirit to be God's spiritual children and were brought into the newborn nation of spiritual Israel.

[21] As spiritual Israelites they were taken into the new covenant through the poured-out blood of the Mediator Jesus Christ and were made the people for the name of Jehovah, His witnesses. They were anointed to be heirs of the Kingdom with Jesus Christ and were thus taken into the covenant for the Kingdom with him, the Heir and Lord of King David. By this anointing with the spirit they were also commissioned or ordained to preach the good news of the Kingdom to all nations. By the sanctifying power of the holy spirit they were made "saints" or holy ones, "a holy nation."—Acts 2:1-38; Romans 8:15-17; 1 John 2:20, 27; 1 Peter 2:9.

ORGANIZING THE CONGREGATION ON THE ROCK-MASS

[22] On that Pentecostal day of baptizing his followers on earth with holy spirit Jesus began building his congregation on himself as the rock-mass

21. Into what covenant were they taken through Jesus' blood, and for what purpose were they anointed and sanctified?
22. When did Jesus begin building his congregation upon the rock-mass, and whom did he use as secondary foundations?

(*petra*). Long before then Jehovah had used the twelve sons of Jacob (Israel) to be the foundations of the nation of Israel, composed of twelve tribes. (Genesis 49:1, 2, 28) Copying that as a type, Jesus Christ used his twelve faithful apostles as secondary foundations built upon himself. He pictured his congregation as a city with twelve foundations: "The wall of the city also had twelve foundation stones, and on them the twelve names of the twelve apostles of the Lamb." (Revelation 21:14) But to show that the glorified Jesus in heaven is the all-supporting foundation, the apostle Paul said to the congregation: "You are fellow citizens of the holy ones and are members of the household of God, and you have been built up upon the foundation of the apostles and [Christian] prophets, while Christ Jesus himself is the foundation cornerstone. In union with him the whole building, being harmoniously joined together, is growing into a holy temple for Jehovah. In union with him you, too, are being built up together into a place for God to inhabit by spirit." —Ephesians 2:19-22.

[23] In building the congregation upon himself as the rock-mass Jesus did so, not only in piling up upon himself "living stones," his dedicated baptized followers, but also in organizing them for Jehovah's service as the temple or sanctuary of God. This called for the appointing of numerous special servants and the assigning of them to their duties inside the congregation. The apostle Paul explains this in these words concerning the organizing work done by Jesus in heaven:

[24] "The very one that descended [to earth] is also the one that ascended far above all the heavens that he might give fullness to all things. And he gave some as apostles, some as prophets, some as missionaries, some as shepherds and teachers,

23, 24. What did Jesus' building the congregation upon himself include, and how did Paul explain this in Ephesians 4:10-14?

with a view to the training of the holy ones for ministerial work, for the building up of the body of the Christ, until we all attain to the oneness in the faith and in the accurate knowledge of the Son of God, to a full-grown man, to the measure of growth that belongs to the fullness of the Christ; in order that we should no longer be babes."—Ephesians 4:10-14.

[25] Jesus' purpose in organizing the congregation and appointing special servants was that the holy ones might all receive full training for ministerial work and might not remain spiritual babes but become full-grown persons in union with Christ. They must all become "persons of advanced age" in a Christian spiritual sense, all of them "elders" or elderly persons, as pictured by the twenty-four "elders" seen in the vision to John, seated on thrones round about God's heavenly throne.—Revelation 4:4, 10, RS.*

[26] The first local Christian congregation was established in Jerusalem. There the visible governing body of the "holy nation" of spiritual Israel had its headquarters until shortly before the city of Jerusalem was destroyed A.D. 70. But due to the great witness that was given at Jerusalem on and after Pentecost to thousands of visitors who became believers, congregations were established in many other cities, towns and communities. The number of these increased still more after the good news of the Kingdom was authorized to be preached to the non-Jewish peoples from A.D. 36 onward. All these congregations had their local organization for meetings and for preaching out in the field. Where such special servants were available, each congregation had overseers and

---

* See chapter 1, pages 14-17.

25. What was Jesus' purpose in organizing the congregation and appointing special servants for it?
26. How were many congregations established outside Jerusalem, and, where competent ones were available, what did such congregations have?

their assistants, ministerial servants. For example, to whom did Paul write at the city of Philippi in Macedonia? Here is the introduction of his letter to the Philippians: "Paul and Timothy, slaves of Christ Jesus, to all the holy ones in union with Christ Jesus who are in Philippi, along with overseers and ministerial servants." (Philippians 1:1) Paul also called attention to the overseers of the congregation of Ephesus, Asia Minor.—Acts 20: 17-28.

[27] Timothy and Titus were general overseers over congregations in certain assigned areas. Hence Paul's two letters to Timothy and his one letter to Titus are really instructions to overseers. However, in 1 Timothy 3:1-12 and in Titus 1:5-9 the apostle Paul sets out the qualifications required of those suitable to be appointed by Timothy and Titus to be overseers and ministerial servants in local Christian congregations. Of course, all these special servants had to be Christian "elders" or older men spiritually. This had to be true of the twelve apostles; and Peter speaks of himself as an "elder" or "presbyter" (according to the Greek) when he writes: "To the older men among you I give this exhortation, for I, too, am an older man [*presbýteros,* Greek] like them and a witness of the sufferings of the Christ, a sharer even of the glory that is destined to be revealed."—1 Peter 5:1.

[28] The governing body at Jerusalem necessarily consisted of none but "elders" or "presbyters" or "older men." These were not only the "twelve apostles of the Lamb" but also other servants in the congregation there. Acts 15:1, 2, 6, 22, 23 records that, when the congregation in Antioch, Syria, referred a disputed matter to the governing

27. Why were Paul's letters to Timothy and Titus of a special kind, and what first were all special servants in congregations required to be before appointment?
28. Necessarily, then, of what was the governing body at Jerusalem composed, and what shows it included more than the twelve apostles?

body in Jerusalem, "the apostles and the older men [presbyters] gathered together to see about this affair." After deciding the disputed matter, "the apostles and the older men" determined to send certain men with a letter stating their decision. They began the letter in this way: "The apostles and the older [presbyters] brothers to those brothers in Antioch and Syria and Cilicia who are from the nations." But how did all these become "elders"?

²⁹ In the congregations of Christendom the term "elder" has become a title and "eldership" has become a position or office to which men are appointed. In support of this, the religious organizations having such elders and elderships appeal to Acts 14:23 (*AS*), which tells of Paul and Barnabas as founders of congregations: "And when they had appointed for them elders in every church, and had prayed with fasting, they commended them to the Lord, on whom they had believed." Also Titus 1:5 (*RS*): "This is why I left you in Crete, that you might amend what was defective, and appoint elders in every town as I directed you." However, does this mean appointing men to eldership as an office, or appointing men who were already elders in the required sense to offices or service positions in the congregations? Is "eldership" appointive?

³⁰ In the ancient days of the prophet Moses the congregation of natural Israel was reported as having "elders." Jehovah God specially sent Moses to these "elders" or older men of Israel. (Exodus 3:16, 18) But were those elders appointed to eldership or did they grow into being elders physically and mentally? *The Jewish Encyclopedia,* Volume V (of 1910), page 92, under "Elder," says:

---

29. In Christendom, what have "elder" and "eldership" become, and what questions do we raise about their supporting texts, Acts 14:23 and Titus 1:5?
30. To whom in Israel did Jehovah specifically send Moses, and what does *The Jewish Encyclopedia* say about "elders"?

In primitive times age was a necessary condition of authority. Not only among the ancient Jews, but also among other nations of antiquity, the elders of the nation or of the clan constituted the official class. The institution of elders existed among the Egyptians (Gen.l.7), among the Midianites (Num.xxii.7), and later among the Greeks (*gérontes* or *presbýteroi*) and Romans ("patres" or "senatus"). . . . the elders occupied an important position in the communal as well as in the political affairs of the Jewish people. It is not certain that they were elected by the people, although they were considered their representatives, . . . The position and function of the elder are nowhere clearly defined.

[31] Now as to the Christian congregation or congregation of spiritual Israel, one fact is clear from Ephesians 4:13, 14 and 1 Corinthians 3:1-3 and Hebrews 5:11-14: A man becomes a Christian "elder" or "presbyter" by spiritual growth and development, not by mere physical age or by appointment. According to the qualifications set out by Paul at 1 Timothy 3:1-12 and Titus 1:5-9, it is from men who are "elders" by spiritual growth that overseers and ministerial assistants are appointed. It is in this sense, then, that those with appointive power appoint elders, not to be elders, but to be responsible servants in or over congregations.

[32] However, who is it that has the appointive power to appoint or ordain elders to service positions for the congregations? In the latter half of the nineteenth century it was argued that the congregations themselves are authorized by the Holy Scriptures to ordain or appoint their own "elders."* It was pointed out that in Acts 14:23 concerning the appointing or ordaining of elders in every church the word in the original Greek

---

* See the book *The New Creation*, by C. T. Russell, copyrighted 1904, pages 276-282.

31. How does one become a Christian "elder," and in what way is it, then, that "elders" are appointed?
32. During the last half of the nineteenth century, who was it argued had the authority to appoint elders, and by what method?

THE HOLY ONES WHO WILL GOVERN

text is *kheirotoneîn* and that this Greek verb "means, '*to elect by stretching out the hand,*' still the usual form of voting. This definition is given in Prof. Young's Analytical Bible Concordance. As that may be considered a Presbyterian authority, we will give also the definition set forth in 'Strong's Exhaustive Concordance,' which may be considered a Methodist authority. The latter defines the root of the word—'A hand-reacher, or voter (by raising the hand).'"*

[33] Those definitions, though, take note of only the primitive or early meaning of the Greek verb *kheirotoneîn*. With the development of the Greek language the meaning enlarged in course of history.

[34] *A Greek-English Lexicon,* by Liddell and Scott, in a new edition by Jones and McKenzie, reprinted in 1948, defines *kheirotoneîn* as follows: "*stretch out the hand,* for the purpose of giving one's vote in the assembly, . . . II. with accusative of person, *elect,* properly *by show of hands,* . . . b. later, generally, *appoint,* . . . *appoint to an office* in the Church, *presbytérous* Acts of the Apostles 14:23, compare 2 Epistle to the Corinthians 8:19 (Passive)."

[35] Agreement with this is found in *A Greek and English Lexicon to the New Testament,* by John Parkhurst, in a new edition (1845) by J. R. Major, page 673, which says: "III. *To choose by vote* or *suffrage,* however expressed. Occurs 2 Corinthians 8:19. IV. With an accusative following, *to appoint* or *constitute to an office,* though without suffrages or votes. Occurs Acts 14:23."

[36] In proof of this latter meaning of appointing

---

* *The New Creation,* page 276, paragraph 2. See also *Zion's Watch Tower* as of March 15, 1906, page 91, paragraphs 7, 8.

33-35. Of what meaning only did the definitions give of *kheirotonein* take note, and what other later meaning do two Greek-English authorities give as applicable?
36. As proved by Josephus' *Antiquities of the Jews,* what meaning did this Greek verb have in the apostles' days?

without votes by others in the congregation, the
Jewish historian Josephus wrote his *Antiquities
of the Jews* in the common Greek in the days of
Christ's apostles, in the last half of the first century. In Book 6 and in Chapters 4 and 13, Josephus
uses the Greek verb *kheirotonein* when saying
that King Saul of Israel was ordained by God. The
Bible does not show that the congregation of Israel
stretched forth their hands and voted King Saul
into office. The prophet Samuel anointed Saul to
be king and he became the anointed one ordained
(*kheirotonein*) by Jehovah God.* Consequently, in
the apostles' days, the Greek verb used in Acts
14:23 and in 2 Corinthians 8:19 had come to mean
ordain or *appoint* by even an individual without
any supporting or guiding votes of others by hand-
stretching.

[37] Whereas Acts 14:23 says "they appointed
older men to office for them in the congregation"

---

* Josephus' *Antiquities of the Jews*, Book 6, Chapter
4, paragraph 2, reads: "Accordingly Saul sent away his
servant that followed him. Then the prophet took a
vessel of oil, and poured it upon the head of the young
man, and kissed him, and said, 'Be thou a king, by the
ordination of God [*basileùs hypò toû Theoû kheirotonē-
theìs*] against the Philistines, and for avenging the Hebrews for what they have suffered by them.' " *Antiquities*, Book 6, Chapter 13, paragraph 9, reads: "Hereupon
David entered into the king's tent, but he did neither
kill Saul, though he knew where he lay, by the spear
that was stuck down by him, nor did he give leave to
Abishai, who would have killed him, and was strongly
inclined so to do. For he said it was a horrid crime to
kill one that was ordained [*kheirotonein*] king by God,
although he were a wicked man: for that he who gave
him the dominion, would in time inflict punishment
upon him; so he restrained his eagerness." See the
translation by William Whiston, M.A., Boston, Mass., of
1849, pages 188, 189, 217. Compare also 1 Samuel 10:1,
20-24; 26:5-12.

---

37. As having a bearing on the meaning of Acts 14:23, what did
Paul tell an individual to do, in Titus 1:5, and by what method,
and hence how may Acts 14:23 not rightly be interpreted?

and uses the Greek verb *kheirotonein,* the apostle Paul instructed an individual, Titus the overseer, to "make appointments of older men in city after city, as I gave you orders." There was no election of those older men to office by having Titus get the majority vote of any congregation by resorting to their stretching out the hands for or against candidates. That was the democratic method. But the appointment according to orders from Paul, who was an inspired member of the Christian governing body, was the theocratic method. (Titus 1:5) Hence the Greek text of Acts 14:23 may not be rightly interpreted in support of the democratic or congregational method as against theocratic appointments.

[38] The spiritual Israelites, who are in the new covenant to be a people for Jehovah's name, are his "holy ones." They form a living sanctuary for him to dwell in by his spirit. They must be organized upon Jesus Christ the "rock-mass" and his twelve apostles, in harmony with the theocratic arrangement and not the democratic method. The democratic way calls for the rule of an organization from the people up as the source of one's powers and authority. The theocratic way calls for the rule of the organization from the top down, from the Supreme Being down. It is the clean, peaceful, efficient way for Jehovah's living "sanctuary" of his holy ones. It is the blessed way for them to be organized for serving on earth as Jehovah's witnesses. Serving faithfully till death, they will reign and govern with Jesus Christ in heaven. Thus the covenant for the Kingdom into which they have been anointed by God will be fulfilled.

---

38. Why is the democratic method not the right way for Jehovah's living sanctuary on earth, but for faithfully serving on earth how will the holy ones be rewarded?

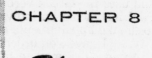

CHAPTER 8

The "Little Horn" In Opposition

FROM being mercilessly worn down to finally being given the everlasting kingdom over this entire green earth—this sums up the astounding experience of the holy ones of the Most High God, as seen in vision by the prophet Daniel. The golden glory of the Babylonian world power was about to lose its luster. The last one of its dynasty of Chaldean kings was on the throne of world government. It was the first year of Belshazzar king of Babylon. The dream and visions of Daniel's own head in that year of the time of the end of Babylon as the third world power had to do partly with that passing world power. So it was timely and suitable that the dream should be sent to Daniel before Babylon came down from its lofty throne. The remnant of Jehovah's holy ones, such as Daniel, Zerubbabel and the Jewish high priest Jeshua, were still held down as captives and slaves in Babylon. The dream and its brief angelic interpretation greatly alarmed Daniel. His color changed. But, seeing as we do the almost completed interpretation of it today by the unfolding facts of history for the past two millenniums and a half, with some highly dramatic features yet to be fulfilled, we can well appreciate why Daniel was so alarmed.

[2] Here is Daniel's description of the dream in its terribleness:

[3] "I saw in my vision by night, and behold, the four winds of heaven were stirring up the great sea. And four great beasts came up out of the sea, different from one another. The first was like a lion and had eagles' wings. Then as I looked its wings were plucked off, and it was lifted up from the ground and made to stand upon two feet like a man; and the mind of a man was given to it. And behold, another beast, a second one, like a bear. It was raised up on one side; it had three ribs in its mouth between its teeth; and it was told, 'Arise, devour much flesh.' After this I looked,

---

1. Why was the vision that Daniel had in King Belshazzar's first year timelily given in that year, and how did it affect Daniel?
2, 3. What was Daniel's description of the terrible dream?

and lo, another, like a leopard, with four wings of a bird on its back; and the beast had four heads; and dominion was given to it. After this I saw in the night visions, and behold, a fourth beast, terrible and dreadful and exceedingly strong; and it had great iron teeth; it devoured and broke in pieces, and stamped the residue with its feet. It was different from all the beasts that were before it; and it had ten horns. I considered the horns, and behold, there came up among them another horn, a little one, before which three of the first horns were plucked up by the roots; and behold, in this horn were eyes like the eyes of a man, and a mouth speaking great things."—Daniel 7:2-8, *RS*.

[4] The world of today is familiar with the British "lion," the American "eagle," the Russian "bear," the Chinese *lung* or "dragon," and the imperial German two-headed "spread eagle." But what do the four different beasts of Daniel's dream prefigure historically? In anxiety Daniel asked an angel for us that we today might know the "truth concerning all this." Daniel tells us: "So he told me, and made known to me the interpretation of the things. 'These four great beasts are four kings who shall arise out of the earth.'" Ah, then, the four beasts correspond with the four metals of the dream image that Daniel had interpreted to King Nebuchadnezzar more than fifty years previously. (Daniel 7:15-17; 2:31-45, *RS*) By means of two heaven-sent dreams the march of world powers from 607 B.C. down to modern times was to be made doubly sure, as by two witnesses.

[5] Up out of a churning sea the four beasts arose, in the same way that hundreds of years later the apostle John saw in vision the seven-headed, ten-horned wild beast ascend out of the abyss of the sea, it being like a leopard, but having the feet

---

4. What did the angel tell Daniel that the four wild beasts pictured, and with what other symbolisms do these four correspond?
5. In this vision, what does the sea picture, and what do the four winds picture?

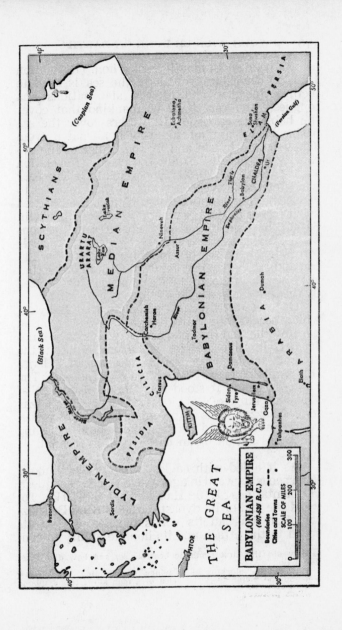

THE GREAT SEA

BABYLONIAN EMPIRE
(607-539 B.C.)

Boundaries
Cities and Towns

SCALE OF MILES
0   100   200   300

SCYTHIANS

(Caspian Sea)

(Black Sea)

MEDIAN EMPIRE

Ecbatana,
A.Hmetha

PERSIA

(Persian Gulf)

Susa,
Shushan

M.

URARTU
ARART

Lake
Urmiah

Lake
Van

Nineveh

Tigris

River

Assur

CHALDEA

Babylon

Ur

Euphrates

BABYLONIAN EMPIRE

River

Carchemish
Haran

Tadmor

Damascus

Dumah

ARABIA

LYDIAN EMPIRE

Byzantium

Sardis

CILICIA

Tarsus

PISIDIA

Mt.

KITTIM

Sidon
Tyre
Jerusalem
Gaza

Tahpanhes

Eloth

CAPHTOR

as of a bear and a mouth as of a lion. (Revelation 13:1, 2) In Bible symbology the sea is used to picture "peoples and crowds and nations and tongues," the vast body of mankind that cover the habitable earth as the waters cover the sea basins. They are all the people alienated from Jehovah God by sin and by the "ruler of the authority of the air," Satan the Devil. (Revelation 17:15; Isaiah 57:20, 21; Ephesians 2:2) The four winds of the heavens stirring up the great sea to cause the four beasts to arise picture the "wicked spirit forces in the heavenly places" together with Satan, "the spirit that now operates in the sons of disobedience," as all these together play their forces upon the sea of humanity exploited by Satan and raging against Jehovah God, in order that they may bring forth the world powers symbolized by the four vicious beasts.

[6] Genesis 10:8-10 makes it plain that Babylon, which became the third world power, symbolized here by the lion that had eagles' wings, arose, not from Jehovah's people, but from Nimrod the "mighty hunter in opposition to Jehovah." Hence this symbolic beast "came up out of the sea." The king for which it stood was the dynastic line of Chaldean kings of Babylon, from Nebuchadnezzar to Belshazzar. This Babylonian kingly power devoured nations and peoples like a lion, including Jehovah's nation of ancient Israel.—Jeremiah 4: 5:7; 50:17.

[7] As if aided with eagles' wings, this symbolic lion speeds forward in aggressive war for conquest. (Lamentations 4:19; Habakkuk 1:6-8, *AV*) Toward the end of its dynastic rule in King Belshazzar, Babylon had its wings plucked. It lost its speed to the attack and its lionlike ability to con-

---

6. How did this first symbolic beast arise, and how did it act like a lion?
7. How did the plucking of its wings, the standing of it on two feet and the giving to it the heart of a man affect this symbolic lion?

tinue as king of the beastly world powers. It became relatively weak, like a man with no more rapidity of movement than that of two legs. It was given the "mind of a man" in a beast's body and was not able to act like king "among the beasts of the forest"; it no longer had the "heart of the lion." (Micah 5:8, *AS;* 2 Samuel 17:10) It went down in defeat before the symbolic bear. It yielded world domination to Medo-Persia.

[8] The 'king' symbolized by the bear was the line of Medo-Persian rulers from Darius the Mede to Darius III the Persian, from 539 B.C. to 331 B.C. This line of world rulers was symbolized by the silver breast and arms of Nebuchadnezzar's dream image. This symbolic bear was "raised up on one side," either to attack in order to seize, spread and maintain world power or else to show that the Persian line of rulers would take the ascendancy over the Median king, Darius, who was the first and only Mede in the Medo-Persian world rulership. The symbolic bear had three ribs in its mouth between its teeth. These may denote the three directions in which the Persian world power pushed its conquests, to the north to humble Babylon in 539 B.C.; to the west through Asia Minor and across into Thrace; and to the south to conquer Egypt. The number three being also a symbol of intensity or emphasis, the three ribs may also emphasize the greed of this symbolic bear for territorial conquests.

[9] It hungrily lunged against the nations in response to the command: "Arise, devour much flesh." By devouring Babylon according to the will of Jehovah God, this fourth world power was in position through Cyrus the Great, Darius I the Persian and Artaxerxes I to let Babylon's Jewish captives go home, and to help and encourage them

---

8. What was symbolized by the bear, its being raised up on one side, and its having three ribs in its mouth?
9. What resulted from its obeying the command to arise and devour much flesh?

to rebuild the temple of Jehovah at Jerusalem and to build and repair the walls of the holy city. Like a bear, this world power became fat with "a hundred and twenty-seven jurisdictional districts," so that Ahasuerus or Xerxes I, the husband of the Jewish Queen Esther, was "king from India to Ethiopia."—Esther 1:1.

[10] Under invisible active force of the demons the agitated sea of mankind produced another symbolic beast of world domination, the four-winged, four-headed leopard. The 'king' that it symbolized was the Macedonian or Grecian line of world rulers, beginning with Alexander the Great. The speed with which Alexander conquered the Persian world power, moving through Asia Minor, then down into Egypt and finally eastward to the western borders of India, can well be likened to the speed of a leopard, what with four wings to increase its bounding agility and speed. (Habakkuk 1:8, AV) His dominion was greater than that of the symbolic bear. It included not only the domains of the Persian Empire but also Macedonia and Greece as well as Thrace. Alexander set out to conquer the Persian Empire in 334 B.C. He still had ambitious plans when he died June 13, 323 B.C., at Babylon. Daniel's prophecy was correct in saying of this symbolic leopard, "Dominion was given to it"; it "shall rule over all the earth."—Daniel 7:6; 2:39, RS.

[11] The symbolic leopard became four-headed when Alexander died and four of his military generals sought to establish themselves as successors (Diádochi) over sections of his domain. Finally, General Seleucus was holding Mesopotamia and Syria; General Ptolemy, the domains in Africa; General Lysimachus, Asia Minor and Thrace; and General Cassander, Macedonia.

---

10. What did the third wild beast symbolize, how did it have speed, and how was it true that dominion was given to it to rule over all the earth?
11. How did the symbolic leopard become four-headed?

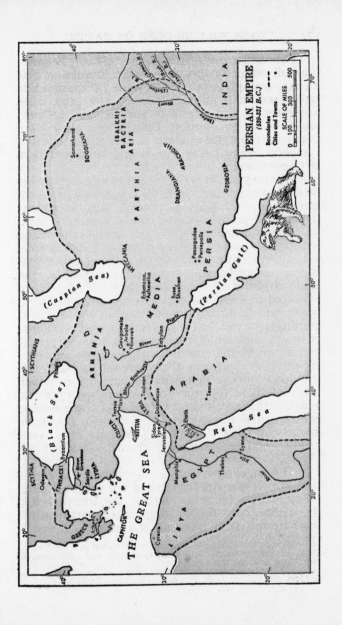

[12] Peaceful relations did not obtain between these divisions of the Macedonian Empire. A new menace arose from the west, from Rome; and this rising political, military power interfered more and more in the affairs of the Hellenic political divisions of the empire. One by one they were taken over by the western power, till at last the symbolic leopard was tamed and subjected to a stronger master.

[13] By the year 30 B.C. the symbolic fourth beast was in complete undisputable control as the sixth world power of Biblical history. This 'king' was the line of political world rulers, beginning with Emperor Caesar Augustus of Rome and ending with the dominant worldly rulers of today. Daniel was interested to know the identity of this decidedly different beast, just the same as God-fearing Bible students of today are. Said Daniel: "Then I desired to know the truth concerning the fourth beast, which was different from all the rest, exceedingly terrible, with its teeth of iron and claws of bronze; and which devoured and broke in pieces, and stamped the residue with its feet; and concerning the ten horns that were on its head, and the other horn which came up and before which three of them fell, the horn which had eyes and a mouth that spoke great things, and which seemed greater than its fellows. As I looked, this horn made war with the saints [the holy ones; *qaddishín*], and prevailed over them."—Daniel 7:19-21, *RS*.

[14] The angel gave Daniel interpretative information, which is really for guiding our understanding today. "Thus he said: 'As for the fourth beast, there shall be a fourth kingdom on earth, which shall be different from all the kingdoms, and it

---

12. How was this symbolic leopard finally tamed and subjected?
13. What did the fourth wild beast symbolize, and what features did Daniel ask the truth about?
14. What interpretative information did the angel then give Daniel?

shall devour the whole earth, and trample it down, and break it to pieces. As for the ten horns, out of this kingdom ten kings shall arise, and another shall arise after them; he shall be different from the former ones, and shall put down three kings. He shall speak words against the Most High, and shall wear out the saints of the Most High, and shall think to change the times and the law; and they shall be given into his hand for a time, two times, and half a time." (Daniel 7:23-25, *RS*) Recorded facts of history bear that prophecy out.

[15] Repeatedly it is stated that this symbolic fourth beast is different from the three before. This "beast" began with the Roman Empire, and of it H. G. Wells, in *A Short History of the World,* says:

> Now this new Roman power which arose to dominate the western world in the second and first centuries B.C. was in several respects a different thing from any of the great empires that had hitherto prevailed in the civilised world. It was not at first a monarchy, and it was not the creation of any one great conqueror. It was not indeed the first of republican empires; . . . But it was the first republican empire that escaped extinction and went on to fresh developments. . . . it was never able to maintain itself in central Asia or Persia because they were too far from its administrative centres. It . . . presently incorporated nearly all the Greek people in the world, and its population was less strongly Hamitic and Semitic than that of any preceding empire . . . So that the Roman Empire was essentially a first attempt to rule a great dominion upon mainly Aryan lines. It was so far a new pattern in history, it was an expanded Aryan republic. . . . The Roman Empire was a growth, an unplanned novel growth; the Roman people found themselves engaged almost unawares in a vast administrative experiment. . . . It was always changing. It never attained to any fixity. In a sense the [administrative] experiment failed. In a sense the experiment remains unfinished, and Europe and America to-

---

15. With what did this symbolic fourth beast begin, and in what way was its first development different from the beasts before?

day are still working out the riddles of world-wide statecraft first confronted by the Roman people.
—Chapter 33, "The Growth of the Roman Empire," pages 149-151. Published 1922.

[16] The Roman world power extended itself all around the Mediterranean Sea, to include also Morocco and Spain. It spread northwestward across Europe and leaped across the English Channel into Britain itself. In 55 B.C. the first Roman invasion of Britannia took place under Julius Caesar, the granduncle of Caesar Augustus. In 120 (A.D.) Emperor Hadrian himself visited Britain and built the Roman wall from the Tyne River to the Solway inlet. In 204 (A.D.) the Romans subdued southern Britain and divided it into two provinces. But Jehovah's prophecy marked out for this greedy, domineering sixth world power to go the way of its predecessors. It, too, was dissolved. The pieces into which it was broken up were symbolized by the ten horns on the head of the terrible and dreadful fourth beast. Their number *ten* symbolizes allness as to our earth.

[17] Daniel specially wanted to know what the other horn that came up and caused three of the horns to fall meant. Today that horn is known and identified by unerring historical records. It arose as the British Empire, notably from the seventeenth century onward. The angel explained concerning the 'king' pictured by this victorious horn: "He shall be different from the former ones." On this difference *The Encyclopædia Britannica* (eleventh edition of 1910), Volume 4, pages 606a and 610a, says as of the year 1910:

> BRITISH EMPIRE, the name now loosely given to the whole aggregate of territory, the inhabitants of which, under various forms of government, ultimately look to the British crown as the supreme head. The term "empire" is in this connexion ob-

16. How did this sixth world power expand itself, but into what was it dissolved in fulfillment of prophecy?
17. What was symbolized by the other horn that overthrew three, and how does *The Encyclopædia Britannica* describe it as different?

viously used rather for convenience than in any
sense equivalent to that of the older or despotic
empires of history.

The vast congeries of states, widely different in
character, and acquired by many different meth-
ods, holds together under the supreme headship of
the crown on a generally acknowledged triple
principle of self-government, self-support and self-
defence. The principle is more fully applied in
some parts of the empire than in others; . . .

[18] Says British historian H. G. Wells:

We may note here briefly the varied nature of
the constituents of the British Empire in 1914
which the steamship and railway had brought
together. It was and is a quite unique political
combination; nothing of the sort has ever existed
before. First and central to the whole system was
the "crowned republic" of the United British Kingdom, . . . It will be manifest, therefore, that no
single office and no single brain had ever com-
prehended the British Empire as a whole. It was
a mixture of growths and accumulations entirely
different from anything that has ever been called
an empire before. . . . Like the Athenian Empire,
it was an overseas empire; its ways were sea
ways, and its common link was the British navy.
Like all empires, its cohesion was dependent physically upon a method of communication; . . .
—Pages 365, 366, 368 of *A Short History of the
World*, Chapter 64, "The British Empire in 1914."

[19] The British Empire did "devour the whole
earth" in that it became global, so that the sun
never set upon its possessions and territories. It
embraced one fourth of the land surface of the
earth and one fourth of the earth's population.
It was the greatest empire of world history. But
more than that: In 1775 the thirteen British colonies in America revolted and established their
independence after eight years of fighting. The
kingless American republic, with a president as
chief of government, fought, expanded and spread
across the North American continent from the

---

18. How does a British historian describe that horn as different?
19. In what way did this symbolic horn "devour the whole earth,"
and what did part of it become to add further to its power?

Atlantic seaboard to the Pacific Coast. It purchased Alaska and gained possession of various islands of the sea. By force of compelling circumstances it became the ally of the Mother Country; and together Britain and America fought their painful way to victory through two world wars. From the second world conflict the American republic emerged as the dominant nation of the world, but still holding strong bonds and still co-operating in vital matters with Britain.

[20] The foretold "horn which had eyes and a mouth that spoke great things, and which seemed greater than its fellows," is identified by history as being the Anglo-American dual world power, the seventh world power foretold in Bible prophecy. The three horns or "three kings" that this mighty "horn" put down before 1914 were the naval powers of (1) Spain, (2) The Netherlands, and (3) France.*

[21] This Anglo-American seventh world power is very observing, astute, diplomatic and worldly-wise; it is the "horn which had eyes." It has a "mouth that spoke great things," dictating the policy for a great part of the world, acting also as the mouthpiece or prophet for the world. (Revelation 16:13; 19:20) Nations have pricked up their ears at what it has had to say, before shaping their course. Like the preceding world powers of Egypt, Assyria, Babylon, Medo-Persia, Greece and Rome, it has used its mouth against Jehovah

---

* See *Modern Europe to 1870*, by Carlton J. H. Hayes, of 1953, pages 330-356, in chapter 8, entitled "British Expansion." Note particularly paragraph 2 on page 356, which calls attention to two centuries of fighting by Britain with the Spanish, Dutch and French in order to come forth in 1763 as the "foremost commercial and colonial power in the world."

---

20. So, in its latest development, what did that horn symbolize, and what three horns did it cause to fall?
21. In what way does this symbolic horn have eyes, and how has its mouth spoken great things and even words against the Most High?

God and has had to do with Jehovah's faithful witnesses, his "holy ones," in the earth. "He shall speak words against the Most High, and shall wear out the saints of the Most High, and shall think to change the times and the law." (Daniel 7:25, *RS*) In spite of all this "he" claims to be Christian!

²² The Anglo-American dual world power is undeniably a part of this unchristlike world. It is a part of "all the kingdoms of the world and their glory," which Satan the Devil offered to Jesus Christ in the mountain of temptation but which Jesus refused, saying: "Go away, Satan! For it is written, 'It is Jehovah your God you must worship, and it is to him alone you must render sacred service.'" (Matthew 4:8-10) In its conscienceless striving for world domination this symbolic horn with eyes and mouth has not worked in the interests of the promised Kingdom of God. In expressing its aims for leadership in this world its talkative mouth has not been without sin or without diplomatic falsities. It has spoken against the will and purpose of the Most High and has refused to recognize that "thou, whose name alone is JEHOVAH, art the most high over all the earth." —Psalm 83:18, *Authorized Version* of 1611.

²³ To this day this symbolic horn has thought "to change the times and the law" of God. In the autumn of 1914 the "seven times," or "the appointed times of the nations," ended also for the Anglo-American dual world power. The time had then passed for the trampling down of the "Jerusalem above," which is free and which is the "mother" of God's "saints" or holy ones. The time had then come for the promised Kingdom of God and of his Christ to stand forth as the rightful ruler of the earth. It was the right time for the kingdoms of this world, particularly the kingdoms

---

22. Of what is this symbolic horn a part, and how has it not worked for God's kingdom or spoken according to God's will? 23, 24. (a) How did this symbolic horn think to change the "times" of God? (b) How did it think to change His law?

of Christendom, to bow before that newborn New
World government and hand over their sovereignty
and their control of the earth.—Psalm 2:1-12.

[24] The Anglo-American dual world power thought
differently of the "times" and scoffed at the fact
that the "appointed times of the nations" had
ended in 1914.* It launched off into world war, not
for upholding the kingdom of God newly born in
heaven, but for maintaining its own political domination and its commercial supremacy. (Revelation
11:15-18) God's law since A.D. 1914 was that the
good news of the setting up of the promised,
prayed-for kingdom should be preached in all the
inhabited earth for a witness to all the nations
by his dedicated witnesses. (Matthew 24:14) The
Anglo-American dual world power outstandingly
opposed the carrying out of that law by the holy
people of Jehovah God. In doing so it fulfilled the
angelic prophecy: "He . . . shall wear out the
saints of the Most High, . . . and they shall be
given into his hand for a time, two times, and half
a time."—Daniel 7:25, *RS*.

[25] A time, two times and half a time amount to
three times and a half, or, all together, to half of
seven times. The "seven times" that literally
passed over King Nebuchadnezzar during his madness at Babylon amounted to seven literal years.
Measured by this, a half of "seven times," or three
times and half a time, amounts to three years and
a half.† During this time the "saints" or holy ones
of the Most High God were given into the hand
of the Anglo-American dual world power, and
"this horn made war with the saints, and prevailed over them." (Daniel 7:21, *RS*) This occurred during World War I, beginning in 1914, the

* See chapter 4, pages 94 (paragraph 28) to 103.
† See chapter 4, page 101, paragraph 40.

25. How much time did the time, times and half a time amount
to, and what kind of war did the symbolic horn make against
God's "saints"?

year when the seven "appointed times of the nations" came to their end. The British part of the dual world power entered World War I on August 4, 1914, the American part on April 6, 1917. But they waged a spiritual warfare against Jehovah's "holy nation" of spiritual Israelites, especially during the foretold three times and half a time.

[26] This period of three years six months corresponds with the forty-two months or a thousand two hundred and sixty days during which Jehovah's "two witnesses" were to prophesy dressed in spiritual sackcloth or mourning. (Revelation 11:1-3) This period began in the first half of November, 1914, and ended on May 7, 1918. On this latter day the president, the secretary-treasurer and the publication writers of the Watch Tower Bible & Tract Society were arrested on false charges. They were railroaded off to Federal penitentiary for nine months until bail, improperly denied them, could be furnished and they could be released.* As a consequence of this action the Bible educational work of the witnesses of the Most High God was affected throughout the entire earth.

[27] Meantime, on February 12, 1918, the British Dominion of Canada led off in this final attack. That day the Canadian Secretary of State banned the Society's seventh volume of *Studies in the Scriptures,* entitled "The Finished Mystery," and also its series of tracts entitled "The Bible Students Monthly." To possess any prohibited books laid the possessor open to a fine of not more than $5,000 and five years in prison. In America, the very next month, or on March 14, 1918, the De-

---

* See *The Watch Tower* as of March 1, 1918, pages 77, 78, under the title "Religious Intolerance."

---

26. When did those three times and a half a time begin and end, and how?
27. How was this warfare against God's saints brought to a climax?

partment of Justice at Washington, D.C., pronounced the distribution of the seventh volume of *Studies in the Scriptures* to be a violation of the Espionage Act. Confiscation of literature, searching of homes of Jehovah's people and seizure of books, and arrests of worshipers of the Most High God followed the above acts of the Canadian and American governments. The arrest, mistrial and imprisonment of outstanding representatives of the Watch Tower Bible & Tract Society followed in the ensuing months.

[28] True, the governmental release of the banned literature after World War I and the judicial exoneration of the Society's imprisoned officers and writers came as an obligation of justice. Nonetheless, this did not wipe out the record of fighting against the God of heaven, whose will was being done on earth by his servants. Furthermore, this shameful record stamps the prophecy as true, and gives us the assurance that the rest of Daniel's vision will come true.

DIVINE JUDGMENT CONCERNING WORLD DOMINATION

[29] As the eyes of the prophet Daniel turned from the dreadful fourth beast out of the sea, he was given a vision of a heavenly scene. "As I looked, thrones were placed and one that was ancient of days took his seat; his raiment was white as snow, and the hair of his head like pure wool; his throne was fiery flames, its wheels were burning fire. A stream of fire issued and came forth from before him; a thousand thousands served him, and ten thousand times ten thousand stood before him; the court sat in judgment, and the books were opened." (Daniel 7:9, 10, *RS*) The One that was ancient of days is Jehovah, the One who from time

---

28. Despite the postwar righting of matters, what record remains, and how does this stamp the prophecy?
29. What heavenly vision does Daniel then see, and who is the one ancient of days, what is the issue to be judged, and what do the opened books disclose?

indefinite to time indefinite is God. (Psalm 90:2) "For God is the judge. This one he abases, and that one he exalts." (Psalm 75:7) The matter upon which the Most High God must judge is the domination of the earth. For 2,520 years the worldly nations of earth have ruled it without interference from earth's Creator. But now the autumn of 1914 (A.D.) has come and the "appointed times of the nations" have run out. The books, the records made by the nations during the "seven times," are opened. A beastly record stares the great Judge in the face. The nations deserve no further lease of sovereignty over the earth.

[30] See there! A certain one is summoned to the divine Court. Says Daniel: "I looked then because of the sound of the great words which the horn was speaking. And as I looked, the beast was slain, and its body destroyed and given over to be burned with fire. As for the rest of the beasts, their dominion was taken away, but their lives were prolonged for a season and a time. I saw in the night visions, and behold, with the clouds of heaven there came one like a son of man, and he came to the Ancient of Days and was presented before him. And to him was given dominion and glory and kingdom, that all peoples, nations, and languages should serve him; his dominion is an everlasting dominion, which shall not pass away, and his kingdom one that shall not be destroyed." —Daniel 7:9-14, RS.

[31] When on earth Jesus Christ repeatedly spoke of himself as the Son of man. (Matthew 16:13; 25:31) When the Sánhedrin or Supreme Court of Jerusalem put Jesus under oath to say who he was, Jesus said: "Yet I say to you men, From henceforth you will see the Son of man sitting

---

30. What does Daniel see done to the fourth beast and the others, and who is brought before the Judge, and what is given to him?
31. Who is that one like a son of man, and when is it that he appears in the Court, and for what does he ask the Judge?

at the right hand of power and coming on the
clouds of heaven." (Matthew 26:59-64) So in
Daniel's heavenly vision the one that came with
the clouds of heaven and was presented before
the Ancient of Days is the resurrected, glorified
Jesus Christ. He is the one with whom Jehovah,
the Ancient of Days, has made a covenant for a
kingdom, as pictured by the covenant for the
kingdom made with King David, David being a
prophetic picture of Jesus Christ. Through the
inspired King David, Jehovah had prophetically
invited his Son Jesus Christ to ask of Him at the
right time for the nations as his inheritance and
the ends of the earth as his own possession.
(Psalm 2:7, 8; Acts 4:24-26) The time is the close
of the "appointed times of the nations" in 1914.
Now, at the time for which Jesus Christ had
waited in heaven, he appears in the court of the
Ancient of Days. He asks the Judge for the things
that are due to him according to the covenant
for the kingdom over all the earth. All the evidence visible and spiritual proves that he was
given the dominion over all earth's inhabitants,
to fulfill Daniel's vision.

[32] Between the Son of man enthroned in the
heavens as New World king in 1914 and the symbolic beasts of Daniel's vision there can be no
enduring peaceful coexistence. According to the
vision, the symbolic fourth beast, namely, the
Anglo-American dual world power and the other
ten "horns" or "kings" that sprang from the
Roman Empire and that are still claiming sovereignty and maintaining themselves on earth, must
be destroyed. They must disappear as if hurled
into a fiery lake that burns with sulphur. (Revelation 19:19, 20) Particularly concerning the symbolic horn with eyes and mouth the angel said:

---

32. What must happen to the horns of the fourth beast, and
particularly the one with eyes and mouth, and where will this
happen?

"But the court shall sit in judgment, and his dominion shall be taken away, to be consumed and destroyed to the end." (Daniel 7:26, *RS*) This utter destruction will be carried out by decree of the great Judge, the Ancient of Days, at the battlefield of Armageddon, in the "war of the great day of God the Almighty."—Revelation 16:14, 16.

[33] As regards the other three symbolic beasts, Babylonia, the Medo-Persian Empire and the Macedonian (Grecian) Empire, when they were anciently overthrown, their national foundations were not completely destroyed. For instance, in 483 B.C. Babylon rose in arms against the Persian ruling power, and Xerxes I had to capture it by months of siege, after which he plundered it. Alexander the Great died at Babylon in 323 B.C. Turning Babylonish, he had wanted to make Babylon the capital of his empire, but God's decree was against Babylon. Persia, too, has had a continuous history since Alexander's death, down to the kingdom of Iran today. Alexander's successor, General Seleucus Nicator, who died in 280 B.C., transferred his capital from Babylon to Seleucia in Syria, a new city that he had built. Greece has kept its existence till today, and the kingdom of Iraq occupies the territory of ancient Babylon.

[34] The remnants of those ancient beastly world powers, together with the symbolic horns of the dreadful fourth beast, are found united today with other nations around the globe in that international organization, the United Nations, which is the eighth world power of Biblical history. (Revelation 17:11) The vision to Daniel foretold correctly: The dominion of the Babylonian, Medo-Persian and Grecian world powers was taken away, but they had their lives "prolonged for a season

---

33. In the vision, what happened to the other three beasts, and how has this been fulfilled?
34. How are the remnants of those three ancient world powers and the horns of the fourth beast united today, but when will their prolonged lives be ended?

and a time." At Armageddon God's kingdom, like the stone that struck Nebuchadnezzar's dream image on the feet and then ground it to powder, will destroy all remaining traces of those ancient symbolic beasts, the fourth beast also.

[35] The One like a son of man will not be alone in his everlasting dominion and indestructible kingdom. The "saints" or holy ones of God will be with the glorified, enthroned Son of man in his heavenly kingdom. In support of this, Daniel said: "As I looked, this horn made war with the saints, and prevailed over them, until the Ancient of Days came, and judgment was given for the saints of the Most High, and the time came when the saints received the kingdom." In interpretation of this, the angel told Daniel: "But the court shall sit in judgment, and his dominion shall be taken away, to be consumed and destroyed to the end. And the kingdom and the dominion and the greatness of the kingdoms under the whole heaven shall be given to the people of the saints of the Most High; their kingdom shall be an everlasting kingdom, and all dominions shall serve and obey them." (Daniel 7:21, 22, 26, 27, *RS*) The chief one of the "saints of the Most High" is Jesus Christ.—Acts 3:14; 4:27, 30.

[36] However, those whom Jesus Christ takes into the Kingdom covenant with him form a "holy nation," a nation of his spiritual "brothers," all "called to be holy ones." (1 Peter 2:9; Hebrews 2:11; Romans 1:7) According to the covenant for the Kingdom they experience a resurrection from their death in faithfulness and are joined with Jesus Christ in his reign on the heavenly Mount Zion.—Revelation 2:10; Hebrews 12:22-28.

---

35. Will the One like the son of man be alone in his dominion and kingdom, and how does Daniel's vision give us the answer?
36. What do those taken into the Kingdom covenant form, and how do they get into their reigning positions, and where?

[37] In the vision to him, the apostle John, who was one of those saints or holy ones, said: "I saw, and look! the Lamb standing upon the mount Zion, and with him a hundred and forty-four thousand having his name and the name of his Father written on their foreheads." Also: "Happy and holy is anyone having part in the first resurrection; over these the second death has no authority, but they will be priests of God and of the Christ, and will rule as kings with him for the thousand years." (Revelation 14:1; 20:6) These 144,000 followers of the sacrificed Lamb have endured suffering with him during vicious world control by the symbolic fourth beast with its horns. For this they are promised that they will "also rule together as kings." (2 Timothy 2:11, 12) They will reign that the heavenly Father's will may be done on earth as well as in heaven.

---

37. Those who share in the resurrection to that position on Mount Zion are pronounced what, and for having endured what do they reign with the Son of man?

CHAPTER 9

Restoring The Sanctuary To Its Rightful State

*D*URING the sixty-nine years that Babylon dominated as the third world power of Bible history the sanctuary of Jehovah God at Jerusalem lay desolate. With heartfelt interest in the worship of the Most High God at the place that he had chosen in ancient times, the prophet Daniel in exile prayed: "For thy own sake, O Lord, cause thy face to shine upon thy sanctuary, which is desolate." (Daniel 9:17, *RS*) His concern for Jehovah's sanctuary was heightened by the vision that the Lord God sent him during the reign of the last king of the Babylonian world power, that is, "in the third year of the reign of King Belshazzar."

[2] It is not certain whether Daniel was still in the city of Babylon and merely saw himself in another location in the vision or was actually in the other location named. Changing from Aramaic back to Hebrew, Daniel writes: "And I saw in the vision; now it was so, that when I saw, I was in Shushan the castle, which is in the province of Elam; and I saw in the vision, and I was by the stream Ulai. And I lifted up mine eyes, and saw, and, behold, there stood before the stream a ram which had two horns; and the two horns were high, but one was higher than the other, and the higher came up last. I saw the ram pushing westward, and northward, and southward; and no beasts could stand before him, neither was there any that could deliver out of his hand; but he did according to his will, and magnified himself." —Daniel 8:1-4, *JPS*.

[3] We today, who are living in the last half of this twentieth century, can take up examination of this exciting prophecy with an assurance that it has to do with our own critical time, "the time of the end," for no one else but a prominent angel of Jehovah God has said so. In his ancient day

1. During Babylon's world domination, what was the state of Jehovah's earthly sanctuary, and what heightened Daniel's concern about it?
2. What did Daniel first see in this vision during Belshazzar's third year of rule?
3. Who was instructed to make Daniel understand the vision, and why do we know it has to do with our own critical time?

Daniel could not understand the vision, but he writes: "And I heard the voice of a man between the banks of Ulai, who called, and said: 'Gabriel, make this man to understand the vision.' So he came near where I stood; and when he came, I was terrified, and fell upon my face; but he said to me: 'Understand, O son of man; for the vision belongeth to the time of the end.' Now as he was speaking with me, I fell into a deep sleep with my face toward the ground; but he touched me, and set me upright. And he said: 'Behold, I will make thee know what shall be in the latter time of the indignation; for it belongeth to the appointed time of the end.' " So we today ought to be interested.

⁴ Beginning the interpretation, the angel Gabriel said: "The ram which thou sawest having the two horns, they are the kings of Media and Persia." (Daniel 8:15-20, *JPS*) This symbolic ram stands for the fourth world power, Medo-Persia. The two high horns picture kings. The Median horn was first to come up as direct successor to the Chaldean kings of Babylon, but it practically ended with Darius the Mede. His nephew Cyrus the Great had joined him in conquering Babylon. Cyrus the Persian succeeded his uncle Darius as king over all Babylonia. The Persian kings continued in the controlling position. During the later reign of the Persian King Darius I, there was a rebellion among the Medes, but the Persians put this down. So the Persian horn became the higher of the two. As a sign of this, Daniel 5:28; 6:8, 12, 15; 8:20 speak of the Medes ahead of the Persians, but the later book of Esther speaks of the Persians ahead of the Medes. (Esther 1:3, 14, 18, 19; 10:2) Through the prophet Isaiah, Jehovah spoke of stirring up the Medes rather than the

---

4. What did the ram of the vision symbolize, and how did the horn coming up last become higher?

Persians to overthrow Babylon.—Isaiah 13:17; 21:2.

[5] In the previous vision to Daniel, Babylon had been pictured by the wild beast that arose out of the sea and that was like a lion having eagles' wings. This symbolic beast proved to be unable to stand before the symbolic ram of this new vision. With Babylon's capture in 539 B.C. it fell, and for almost fifty years afterward none of the other beasts of political government were able to stand up against the Medo-Persian world power. The prophecies speak of Jehovah as raising up a conqueror "from the sunrise" and calling him like a "bird of prey" from the sunrising. (Isaiah 41:2; 46:11) "Kings from the rising of the sun" is the way Darius the Mede and his nephew Cyrus the Great are alluded to in Revelation 16:12. In harmony with this, Daniel saw the symbolic ram "pushing westward," or from the east, as well as pushing northward and southward.

[6] Until the Medo-Persian Empire had expanded far beyond the size of the Babylonian Empire, there was no political power that could resist seizure by the hand of this fourth world power, particularly on the Asiatic continent. It did as it pleased and enlarged its realm. King Cambyses, who succeeded Cyrus the Great, conquered Egypt. His successor, the Persian King Darius I, moved westward across the Straits of Bosporus in 513 B.C. and invaded the European territory of Thrace, the capital of which was Byzantium (now Istanbul). By the year 508 he had subdued Thrace, and by 496 he had conquered Macedonia. Thus in the days of Darius I the empire became the greatest that the world had seen up to that time. Darius I is noted also for having redug the Suez Canal, and

---

5. What world power proved unable to stand before this symbolic ram, and how is the ram pictured as pushing from the east?
6. Until what expansion was there no standing up against the Persian Empire or delivering out of its hand, and for what is the king of its greatest dominion noteworthy?

for permitting the restored Jews in Palestine to complete their rebuilding of Jehovah's sanctuary in Jerusalem, despite wicked enemy opposition. —Ezra 4:1-5, 24; 5:1 to 6:15.

[7] Testifying to the greatness of the empire, Darius' successor, Xerxes I, is spoken of in sacred Scripture as "Ahasuerus who was ruling as king from India to Ethiopia, over a hundred and twenty-seven jurisdictional districts."—Esther 1:1.

[8] In vindication of Jehovah's prophecies, a successful challenger of the domination of the earth by the Persian world power arose in due time. As a hint of this long in advance, even King Darius I met with defeat at the hands of the Greeks at Marathon, Greece, in 490 B.C. Foreseeing not a mere defeat but total overthrow, Daniel tells more of his vision: "And as I was considering, behold, a he-goat came from the west over the face of the whole earth, and touched not the ground; and the goat had a conspicuous horn between his eyes. And he came to the ram that had the two horns, which I saw standing before the stream, and ran at him in the fury of his power. And I saw him come close unto the ram, and he was moved with choler [bitterness] against him, and smote the ram, and broke his two horns; and there was no power in the ram to stand before him; but he cast him down to the ground, and trampled upon him; and there was none that could deliver the ram out of his hand. And the he-goat magnified himself exceedingly; and when he was strong, the great horn was broken; and instead of it there came up the appearance of four horns toward the four winds of heaven."—Daniel 8:5-8, *JPS*.

[9] For the inspired interpretation of this prophetic vision, we must again listen to what the

---

7. How is the successor of Darius I the Persian spoken of in the book of Esther?
8. In Daniel's vision, what animal charged against the ram, and what happened to its conspicuous horn?
9. How did the angel Gabriel explain the goat and its conspicuous horn?

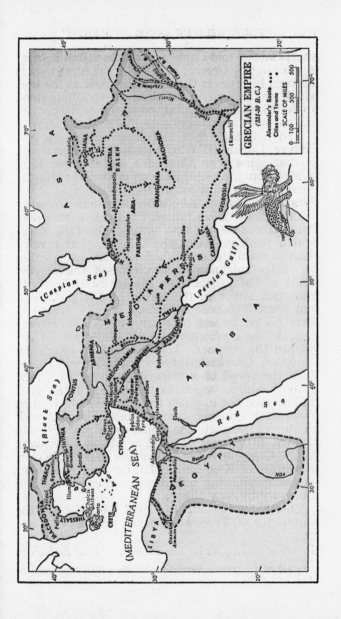

angel Gabriel told Daniel: "And the rough he-goat is the king of Greece; and the great horn that is between his eyes is the first king. And as for that which was broken, in the place whereof four stood up, four kingdoms shall stand up out of the nation, but not with his power."—Daniel 8:21, 22, *JPS*.

[10] In 336 B.C. that last king of the Persian Empire, Darius III (Codomannus), was crowned. In that same year Alexander was crowned king in Macedonia, which had been delivered from the Persians away back in 479 B.C. by a defeat of the Persians at Plataea. Alexander determined to carry out the plans of his father, Philip II of Macedon. Philip II was the one who had organized the Macedonian phalanx, with which he coupled cavalry charges upon the enemy's flank. His son Alexander, after subduing Greece, crossed the narrow strait of the Dardanelles (anciently Hellespont) into Asia Minor in the spring of 334 B.C. With him went 30,000 foot soldiers heavily armed to form his phalanxes, together with 5,000 cavalrymen, soldiers of many Greek dialects who developed the common (*koiné*) Greek in which the Christian Greek Scriptures were later written. With the speed of a leopard equipped with four birdlike wings, yes, with the speed of the goat that seemed not to touch the ground as he dashed toward the symbolic ram, Alexander moved with his forces through the domains of the Persian Empire, fifty times as large as his own kingdom. At the Granicus River he won his first battle over the forces of King Darius III. Onward Alexander moved, conquering and to conquer, capturing city after city in Asia Minor.

[11] On his way south to Egypt he destroyed the island city of Tyre, after seven months of siege.

---

10. When did Alexander invade Asia Minor, and with what forces, and where did he gain his first victory over King Darius III's forces?

11. What other exploits did Alexander do until he reached the Punjab of India?

Then he entered Jerusalem. Before him Egypt fell, and there in 332 B.C. he founded the city which bears his name, Alexandria, which became the largest ancient city in the Hellenic realm. At Gaugamela, not far from the ruins of ancient Nineveh on the Tigris River, Alexander totally defeated the Persian army and put Darius III to flight. The city of Babylon fell before him (331 B.C.). When he reached Balkh, in what is now Afghanistan, in 328 B.C., he had completely annexed the Persian Empire. Desirous of going on to the Pacific Ocean, he moved on into the Punjab of India, but did not get as far as the Sutlej River (327-326 B.C.). Because of his weary, homesick troops he chose now to turn back to the west.

[12] Truly in Alexander the Great the symbolic he-goat "magnified himself exceedingly." From India's threshold Alexander made his way back to Babylon, with the thought of making it the supreme capital of his empire. In this regard the Bible prophecy was at odds with him. In Babylon he was stricken with malaria, but continued feasting to drunkenness, and suddenly died, in his thirty-third year of life, in 323 B.C. Thus the symbolic "great horn" of the he-goat, which was the "first king," was broken. In place of the broken horn (Alexander) there arose four symbolic horns, but not in Alexander's natural successors. By the year 301 B.C. four of Alexander's generals had established themselves in power, General Ptolemy Lagus in Egypt and Palestine; General Seleucus Nicator in Mesopotamia and Syria; General Cassander in Macedonia and Greece; and General Lysimachus in Thrace and Asia Minor. The four symbolic horns wielded power "toward the four winds of heaven," south, north, west and east. The prophetic "king of the north" and "king of the south" now came on the international scene.

12. How was the "great horn" of the symbolic goat broken, and how did four horns come up in place of it to the four winds?

[13] What Daniel next saw in the vision astonished or appalled him. He saw more than the arising of the four horns, for he adds: "And out of one of them came forth a little horn, which waxed exceeding great, toward the south, and toward the east, and toward the beauteous land. And it waxed great, even to the host of heaven; and some of the host and of the stars [some of the host of the stars, *RS*] it cast down to the ground, and trampled upon them. Yea, it magnified itself, even to the prince of the host; and from him the continual burnt-offering was taken away, and the place of his sanctuary was cast down. And the host was given over to it together with the continual burnt-offering through transgression; and it cast down truth to the ground, and it wrought, and prospered." (Daniel 8:9-12, *JPS*) Who is this "little horn" that defied Jehovah God?

[14] The angel Gabriel, after explaining the "four horns," says: "And in the latter time of their kingdom, when the transgressors have completed their transgression, there shall stand up a king of fierce countenance, and understanding stratagems. And his power shall be mighty, but not by his own power; and he shall destroy wonderfully, and shall prosper and do; and he shall destroy them that are mighty and the people of the saints [holy ones]. And through his cunning he shall cause craft to prosper in his hand; and he shall magnify himself in his heart, and in time of security shall he destroy many; he shall also stand up against the prince of princes; but he shall be broken without hand."—Daniel 8:23-25, *JPS*.

[15] The arising of the symbolic "little horn" occurs in the latter time of the rulerships of Alexander's successors, when the transgressors against

13. In the vision, what did Daniel next see that appalled him?
14. How did the angel Gabriel then explain the rise and the course of action of the "little horn"?
15. Where does the prophecy locate the arising of the symbolic "little horn," and what in the foretold time corresponds with it?

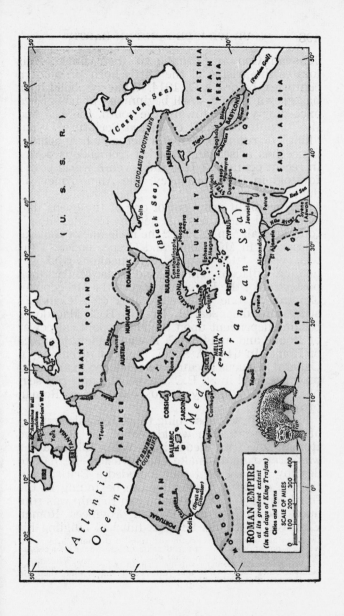

ROMAN EMPIRE
at its greatest extent
(in the days of King Trajan)
• Cities and Towns

SCALE OF MILES
0 100 200 300 400

Jehovah God are coming to their finish. This locates the arising of the "little horn" in modern centuries, before A.D. 1914. What symbolic horn has grown from a small beginning but has grown exceedingly great toward the south, the east and the "beauteous land" of sacred Scripture? What "king" or ruling power of a fierce or bold countenance has arisen and wielded tremendous power in recent centuries? It is the seventh world power foretold in Bible prophecy, the Anglo-American dual world power.

[16] How did it grow out of one of the horns that symbolized the kingships set up by Alexander's four generals? In 298 B.C. the male line of General Cassander in Macedonia and Greece ended. Thirteen years later General Lysimachus, who was holding adjacent Thrace and Asia Minor, took possession of the European part of the Macedonian Empire. So one of the empires of Alexander's successors disappeared. In 168 B.C. Macedonia became dependent upon the rising political power of Rome, and in 146 B.C. it was made a province of Rome. In 64 B.C. Syria, the seat of empire of General Seleucus Nicator, was reduced to a Roman province; and in 30 B.C. Egypt, the imperial seat of General Ptolemy Lagus, became a Roman province.

[17] While it was absorbing those Hellenic empires of the Grecian fifth world power, the aggressive Roman power invaded Britain. When Julius Caesar was preparing to make the invasion, he had to destroy a great fleet that included a British contingent of ships. It was by the beginning of the third century A.D. that southern Britain was subdued and divided into Roman provinces. Roman Emperor Septimius Severus finished building his

16. Tending toward the arising of the "little horn," by what western power were the imperial seats of Alexander's successors reduced to provinces, and in what order?
17. When did the Romans subdue Britain, who made it an independent state for a while and fathered its navy, and when did the Romans quit Britain?

wall there and died at York in Britain A.D. 211. Toward the end of that century General Carausius, a lieutenant of Roman Emperor Maximianus, crossed over into Britain and usurped the throne of Britain, and declared himself Augustus (emperor). After Carausius had defeated the Roman fleet that was sent to chastise him, Rome had to acknowledge his imperial position. "He ruled the country well for seven years when he was murdered in 293 A.D. He made Britain an independent state and incidentally became the 'father of the British Navy.' "* Three years later Emperor Constantius recovered Britain, and in 306 (A.D.) he too died in York in Britain. The figure of Britannia on money coins was first struck by the Romans. In the fifth century the Romans began gradually withdrawing from Britain, and by A.D. 436 they had quit Britannia.

¹⁸ It was in the seventeenth century, during the days of Queen Elizabeth I, that Britain set out on its imperial course, and the British navy was the convenient means for its colonialism and imperial expansion. By the year 1815 the rival navies of The Netherlands, Spain and France had practically ceased to exist; and down till World War I in 1914 the British navy was virtually the "water police of the world; . . . that navy has been the principal instrument in building and holding together the greatest empire the world has yet seen."† At the close of World War II Britain's war ally, the United States of America, which had been built up from the original thirteen British colonies, emerged with the greatest navy in the world. From the foregoing it is seen how the seventh

---

* *The Encyclopedia Americana,* Volume 13, page 322b.
† *Ibidem,* Volume 13, page 325b.

18. How, now, did the "little horn" come forth out of one of the four horns and wax great toward the south, the east and the "beauteous land"?

world power, or the Anglo-American dual world power, came forth like the "little horn" from one of those four horns into which the symbolic "great horn," Alexander the Great, was broken. History well bears witness to how this dual world power of Britain and America, as close allies with strong ties, waxed exceedingly great toward the south and east and toward the "beauteous land."

[19] The "beauteous land" is the Bible expression that means the prophet Daniel's land. (Daniel 11:16, 41, *JPS*) Jehovah himself speaks of it as the "land that I had sought out for them, flowing with milk and honey, which is the beauty of all lands." (Ezekiel 20:6, 15, *JPS*) It is true that during World War I the British expeditionary forces carried on a military campaign in Palestine against Turkey, and on December 9, 1917, Jerusalem was captured by the British General Allenby. After the war the newly begun League of Nations assigned to Britain the mandate over Palestine, to continue till May 14, 1948. But since this is prophecy and contains many symbols, the "beauteous land" symbolizes rather the earthly condition of Jehovah's people in his new covenant, his faithful witnesses on earth, during the existence of the seventh world power. These are Jehovah's "saints" or holy ones on earth; and the apostle Paul says to them: "He raised us up together and seated us together in the heavenly places in union with Christ Jesus."—Ephesians 2:6.

[20] From this standpoint we can understand how the Anglo-American "little horn" waxed great "even to the host of heaven; and some of the host and of the stars it cast down to the ground, and trampled upon them." The angel Gabriel also explains: "And he shall destroy them that are mighty and the people of the saints." (Daniel 8:10,

19. What is meant here in the prophecy by the "beauteous land"?
20. In view of that fact, how could the Anglo-American "little horn" reach some of the host and of the stars to cast them down?

24, *JPS*) The seventh world power could reach the "host of heaven" and "stars" only because these are Jehovah's saints or holy ones who are on earth but who have a heavenly calling and a heavenly resurrection in view, in order to reign with Jehovah's anointed King on his heavenly throne. Over the congregation of Jehovah's dedicated people who follow in the footsteps of Jesus Christ there are overseers, who are likened to "stars" that the glorified Jesus holds in his right hand. (Revelation 1:16, 20) This symbolic "host of heaven" and their "stars" beam with the heavenly light of the good news of God's kingdom, for which the prayer is offered: "Let your kingdom come. Let your will come to pass, as in heaven, also upon earth." —Matthew 6:10.

[21] These "people of the saints" the seventh world power did try to destroy, but only with part success, when it cast them to the ground and trampled upon them during World War I in America and in British possessions "for a time, two times, and half a time." (Daniel 7:25, *RS*) * The heavenly light on earth then burned low.

CASTING DOWN THE PLACE OF JEHOVAH'S SANCTUARY

[22] To those who long ago rebuilt Jehovah's sanctuary in Jerusalem after the land of Judah had lain desolate seventy years, the prophet Zechariah said: "For thus saith Jehovah of hosts: . . . he that toucheth you toucheth the apple of his eye." (Zechariah 2:8, *AS*) So in assaulting his dedicated "host," his sanctuary class on the earth, the seventh world power really assaulted Jehovah of armies. The symbolic "little horn" was really mag-

---

* See chapter 8, pages 180, 181, paragraphs 25-27.

---

21. When did the seventh world power cast them to the ground and trample upon them, and how far to their destruction?
22. How was the symbolic "little horn" able to magnify itself "even to the prince of the host"?

nifying itself "even to the prince of the host; and
from him the continual burnt-offering was taken
away, and the place of his sanctuary was cast
down." (Daniel 8:11, *JPS*) Jehovah God is the
"prince" or theocratic Chief of his host of saintly
ones, and they make up "his sanctuary" in which
he dwells by his holy spirit. (Ephesians 2:21, 22)
The symbolic "little horn" or seventh world power
magnified itself as greater than the kingdom of
God. It refused to surrender its world-wide sovereignty in the earth, giving it to God's kingdom
that had been established in the heavens at the
close of the "appointed times of the nations" in
the year 1914. It treated with contempt the good
news of God's kingdom that his sanctuary class,
his dedicated saints or holy ones, were trying to
preach throughout the domain of the seventh
world power, the British Empire and America.

[23] Daily that Kingdom message was ascending
to Jehovah God in praise of him, like a sacrifice
that was daily, continually, constantly being rendered up to the "prince of the host," by the earth-
wide efforts of his saintly people to preach the
message. These were conscientiously striving to
obey the command to Jesus' followers: "Through
him let us always offer to God a sacrifice of praise,
that is, the fruit of lips which make public declaration to his name. Moreover, do not forget the
doing of good and the sharing of things with
others, for with such sacrifices God is well
pleased." (Hebrews 13:15, 16) The sacrificers of
praise were harmonizing their purpose in life
with the apostle Peter's words: "You yourselves
also as living stones are being built up a spiritual
house for the purpose of a holy priesthood, to
offer up spiritual sacrifices acceptable to God
through Jesus Christ." (1 Peter 2:5) The symbolic "little horn," the "king of fierce countenance,

---

23. How and when did the symbolic "little horn" take away from
him the "continual burnt-offering"?

and understanding stratagems," did not want to
be overshadowed by God's kingdom or to have
sheeplike people turn to it for salvation. So it felt
grieved at this "sacrifice of praise," these "spiritual sacrifices acceptable to God" that were daily
and continually being made to ascend to God.
Under patriotic pretexts, and urged on by the religious clergy of Christendom, the seventh world
power took away "from him the continual burnt-
offering" during the "times, two times, and half
a time."

²⁴ Thus the sacrificial place or very basis upon
which "his sanctuary" rested as a spiritual house
for sacrifices of praise and worship to him "was
taken away." The casting down of the base or
"place" did not mean that the symbolic "sanctuary" itself was destroyed; but this could have
led to the destruction of the remnant of the sanctuary class. Isaiah 12:1 prophetically tells of how
God was incensed at his dedicated people, his nation of spiritual Israel, for yielding to fear of the
seventh world power and practically stopping the
offering of the sacrifice of praise and of public
declaration to his name. In mercy he cut short
the tribulation that he had begun to bring upon
Satan the Devil's organization. Why? That the
chosen sanctuary class, who were being trampled
upon, might not be destroyed with the seventh
world power, but that they might be saved while
still in the flesh.—Matthew 24:21, 22.

²⁵ Their failure for a time to obey God and render up the "continual burnt-offering" in a spiritual
way was a transgression upon the part of the sanctuary class. For this they came under the power
of the oppressive symbolic "little horn," by Jeho-

---

24. Thus how was the "place of his sanctuary" cast down, but
why was the sanctuary class then not destroyed?
25. What was the "transgression" on the part of the sanctuary
class because of which they were surrendered, and hence why
was it not "by his own power" that the "little horn" captured
them?

vah's permission and in expression of his anger
with them. Hence, although the military and commercial power of the "little horn" was mighty, yet
it was "not by his own power" that this "king of
fierce countenance" brought the host of Jehovah's
holy people under foot. "And the host was given
over to it together with the continual burnt-
offering through transgression; and it [the little
horn] cast down truth to the ground, and it
wrought, and prospered." (Daniel 8:12, 24,* *JPS*)
During this time of failure spiritually the sanctuary class became captive to the worldly powers,
just as in Daniel's day he and the rest of Jehovah's
people went into captivity to Babylon and their
homeland and sanctuary lay desolate for seventy
years.

²⁶ The seventh world power, the Anglo-American
dual world power, cared nothing for the truth of
God's Kingdom message, nor for the faithfulness
and integrity of God's people. It cast truth and
faithfulness to the ground. For this action Jehovah
did not at once execute judgment against the
seventh world power. Why not? In order that he
might not at the same time execute destructive
judgment on his own dedicated "people of the
saints." So the seventh world power acted and
prospered and came forth victorious from World
War I, rendering great destruction upon its mighty
foe, Imperial Germany.

²⁷ During the truce of peace that followed from

---

* In Daniel 8:24 the words "but not by his own power" are not found in the papyrus fragments from Egypt
that contain the original text of the Greek *Septuagint
Version,* in the Chester Beatty collection of papyri. They
contain Daniel 3:27 to 6:18 and 7:1 to 8:27. Neither are
the words found in Theodotion's second-century Greek
version. But the Hebrew text has the words.

---

26. How did the "little horn" cast truth and faithfulness to the
ground and yet operate prosperously?
27. During the peace that followed November 11, 1918, how did
the "little horn" magnify itself still more against the "prince
of the host" by setting up an idol?

November 11, 1918, it magnified itself still more
against Jehovah, "the prince of the host." In re-
jecting the message that the sanctuary class had
tried to proclaim to all nations, the Anglo-
American dual world power promoted the establishment of a modern world idol, the League of
Nations. The British war premier, Lloyd George,
had had thoughts of such an international alliance
of nations;* and the American war president, T.
Woodrow Wilson, included it in his Fourteen
Points which he submitted for a peace settlement.
Although acting president, he emboldened himself
to attend the Paris Peace Conference in order to
push through his Points, including the international pact, the League of Nations.

²⁸ The Anglo-American dual world power thus
fulfilled the prophecy concerning the "beast" that
"had two horns like a lamb" but that "began
speaking as a dragon" in telling earth's inhabitants to make an "image to the wild beast." The
Anglo-American dual world power gave "breath
to the image" so that it would speak with some
authority and cause itself to be worshiped by
those who were against God's established kingdom

------
* Said Lloyd George in a speech near the beginning
of 1931: He "proposed the first resolution in the gathering of the principal Allied statesmen in Paris in 1919
upon which the Covenant of the League of Nations was
afterwards based. The cabinet of which I was the head
was the only government in the world that had, before
the [Peace] conference met, and even before the Armi-
stice was signed, prepared carefully thought-out plans
for putting the principle of that resolution into operation. Even during the most anxious moments of the
war, there were committees of that cabinet sitting to
frame a scheme for setting up an association of nations
for ensuring peace on earth."—See *The Watch Tower* as
of January 15, 1931, page 31, column 1, under "A Large
Portion," paragraph 5.

------
28. What prophecy of Revelation did the Anglo-American dual
world power thus fulfill, and what was this political idol as
respects God?

and who were in favor of the "wild beast," Satan's visible world system of government. (Revelation 13:11-15) The symbolic "image to the wild beast," this League of Nations, was an abomination, a disgusting thing, to Jehovah God, just as much so as the golden image sixty cubits high and six cubits broad that Nebuchadnezzar, king of Babylon, set up for all the provinces of his empire to worship, including Daniel's companions Shadrach, Meshach and Abednego. (Daniel 3:1-15) Jehovah's witnesses saw that the League of Nations was disgusting to him just as an idol is.

"THE ABOMINATION THAT MAKES DESOLATE"

[29] The peace conference opened in Paris, France, on January 18, 1919, attended by the American President Wilson. The resulting peace treaty, including the covenant of the League of Nations, was signed in Versailles, France, on June 28, 1919. On October 13 that year it had been ratified by three big allied powers and it went into effect with its League of Nations covenant. The United States Senate refused to go along with President Wilson and ratify this treaty. The Senate considered that America's national sovereignty was not safeguarded enough in the League of Nations covenant. America concluded a separate peace with Germany later. The League of Nations, the symbolic "image of the wild beast," really began to function on January 10, 1920, at Geneva, Switzerland. But before this event religious Christendom led off in idolizing the symbolic "image."

[30] The Federal Council of the Churches of Christ in America offered itself at once as a priest to minister before the "image." Ahead of the peace conference, and while President Wilson was mere-

29. When was the League of Nations covenant made effective, when did the League begin to function, but what did Christendom lead off in doing?
30. What did the Federal Council of the Churches of Christ in America offer to do, and how did it give the proposed League a Messianic role?

ly advocating the League of Nations, the Federal
Council of the Churches of Christ in America
spoke forth in favor of it and gave to it the role
of Christ the Messiah. The executive committee
of this Federal Council met in Atlantic City, New
Jersey, and on December 12, 1918, it passed an
endorsement of President Wilson's plan for a
League of Nations. It adopted the following Declaration (quoted in part):

The war crisis of the world has passed, but a
world crisis is upon us.

. . . "Are we to lapse back," asked Lloyd George,
"into the old national rivalries, animosities and
competitive armaments, or are we to imitate the
reign on earth of the Prince of Peace?"

The time has come to organize the world for
truth and right, justice and humanity. To this end,
as Christians we urge the establishment of a
League of Free Nations at the coming Peace Conference. Such a League is not a mere political ex-
pedient; it is rather the political expression of the
Kingdom of God on earth.

. . . The heroic dead will have died in vain unless out of victory shall come a new earth where-
in dwelleth righteousness.

The Church has much to give and much to gain.
It can give a powerful sanction by imparting to
the new international order something of the prophetic glory of the Kingdom of God. What is the
Kingdom of God, if it be not the triumph of God's
will in the affairs of men, "righteousness and
peace and joy in the Holy Spirit"? And what is
this vision of a world-federation of humanity organized on a basis of justice and fair-dealing, for
the effective and impartial maintenance of peace,
if it be not of the Kingdom of God?

The Church can give a spirit of good-will, without which no League of Nations can endure. . . .

The League of Nations is rooted in the Gospel.
Like the Gospel, its objective is "peace on earth,
good-will toward men." Like the Gospel, its appeal
is universal.

Let us implore our Heavenly Father, God Almighty, that the Peace Delegates of the Nations
may be guided by the Divine Spirit and enlightened by the Divine Wisdom to the end that they
may embody in the new fabric of the world's life
His righteous, loving and holy will. . . .

[31] The executive committee of the Federal Council of the Churches also passed supporting Resolutions. One of these was for the appointing of a "suitable Special Commission representing, so far as practicable the Protestant Churches of America, to present the above documents to the Peace Conference of the Allied and Associated Nations." Following the adoption of the Declaration and Resolutions, a recommendation was acted upon and a cablegram was sent to President Wilson at Paris by the executive committee, advising him of its action. Later, a letter dated December 18, 1918, was addressed to President Wilson, enclosing a copy of the cablegram, the Declaration and the supporting resolution. It also told of the appointing of the Special Commission to present officially the Declaration to the Peace Conference soon to convene.*

[32] Did this Special Commission present the Declaration to the Paris Peace Conference after it opened on January 18, 1919? In the annual report of the Federal Council of the Churches of Christ in America for the calendar year of 1919 there appeared on page 11 this sentence:

> At the Peace Conference in Paris a representative committee of the Federal Council was received by officials of the government and presented the actions of the executive committee which they were instructed to convey to the Peace Conference.

[33] More action than the above was taken. The Peace Treaty was signed on June 28, 1919. The Federal Council Bulletin as of June, 1919, on page 94, said the following in an article entitled "Reso-

---

* See Federal Council Bulletin, Volume II, No. 1, as of January, 1919, pages 12-14.

---

31. What did the Council's executive committee do for having the above documents presented, and what did it send to President Wilson?
32. What record do we have that the Special Commission presented the Declaration to the Paris Peace Conference?
33. What further action was taken by the Federal Council of the Churches toward idolizing the League of Nations?

lutions Adopted by the Federal Council of the Churches of Christ in Special Session at Cleveland, Ohio, May 6-8, 1919":

I. Social Justice

. . .

II. National and International Affairs

RESOLVED: That we express our gratitude for the establishment of the League of Nations as agreed upon by the Paris Peace Conference and pledge our support in securing its ratification by the Senate of the United States and our devotion to make it a success.

[34] Vain were their efforts. The U.S. Senate never did adopt the Paris Peace Treaty, with its League of Nations charter. The devotion of the Federal Council of the Churches never did make the League of Nations a success. Neither did the devotion of the religious organizations in the British realm of the seventh world power. The League of Nations failed to prevent World War II and the introduction of the atomic bomb. It was formally dissolved on January 10, 1946.

[35] Even apart from the prophetic Word of God, the telltale facts of history disclose that the League of Nations was not an earthly image of the Kingdom of God rooted in the Gospel but was a blasphemous man-made counterfeit for the Kingdom of God. It was an idolatrous "image of the wild beast," to which political beast the great dragon Satan the Devil had given "its power and its throne and great authority." (Revelation 12: 3, 4, 7-9, 13-17; 13:1, 2) The Declaration that the Church Council's executive committee adopted in Atlantic City and presented by its Special Commission to the Paris Peace Conference in the last part of January, 1919, was a foul blasphemy against the true Kingdom of God. It was a false prophecy that deceived the world and was a disgusting act

---

34. How did the Council's efforts prove vain?
35. As respects God's Kingdom, what was that Declaration as presented to the Paris Peace Conference? and what action did the churches of Christendom thus take toward the nominal temple of God?

of idolatry to a beastly "image." By this action in January, 1919, the religious leaders of Christendom and the politicians of the seventh world power and its allies set an abomination before Jehovah God, a thing disgusting to him. Since the churches of Christendom claimed to be the temple of God, they in effect brought an abominable idol into the religious temple.

³⁶ By setting up this "abomination that makes desolate" the religious clergy of Christendom imitated those who rejected Jesus Christ in 33 (A.D.) and who cried out to the Roman governor Pontius Pilate: "We have no king but Caesar." (John 19:15) Here the seventh world power became the instrument of the "god of this system of things" in setting up the "abomination that makes desolate," "the disgusting thing that causes desolation." (Matthew 24:15) This marks an important point in the count of prophetic time.

"THE TRANSGRESSION THAT MAKES DESOLATE"

³⁷ However, there is a "transgression" that is connected with the "abomination that makes desolate." Daniel says that an angel asked a question about it: "Then I heard a holy one speaking; and another holy one said unto that certain one who spoke: 'How long shall be the vision concerning the continual burnt-offering, and the transgression that causeth appalment [the transgression that makes desolate, *RS*], to give both the sanctuary and the host to be trampled under foot?' And he said unto me: 'Unto two thousand and three hundred evenings and mornings; then shall the sanctuary be victorious [be restored to its rightful state, *RS*].'"—Daniel 8:13, 14, *JPS*.

³⁸ The "continual burnt-offering" was taken

---

36. Whom did Christendom's churches thus imitate, and what was the seventh world power the instrument in setting up?
37. What is there connected with this desolating abomination, and what did Daniel learn about it from the angel?
38. What questions arise concerning the "transgression that makes desolate," and why are the answers needed?

away at the culmination of the "time, two times, and half a time" on May 7, 1918.* It was toward the end of January, 1919, that the "abomination that makes desolate" was set up for adoration. But at that time the "transgression that makes desolate" had not been committed, so as to begin counting the two thousand three hundred evenings and mornings. What, then, was this "transgression"? When was it committed, and by whom? Jehovah's witnesses present these facts:

³⁹ On March 26, 1919, the officers and writers of the Watch Tower Bible & Tract Society were released on bail from their detention in the Federal Penitentiary in Atlanta, Georgia.† The following day the Society's officials began to formulate plans for organizing and carrying on the postwar witness work by the sanctuary class of Jehovah God. This resulted in a great reviving of Jehovah's sanctified people. He poured his energizing spirit out upon them that they might discern his work for them and brace up their minds for performing it. On September 1-8 of that year they held a general convention at Cedar Point, Ohio. There the erstwhile imprisoned president of the Society laid out the fearless witness work to be performed from then on until the universal battle of Armageddon. Prophecy became clearer, and on page 12 of its issue of January 1, 1921, the Society's official magazine *The Watch Tower* pointed out that the League of Nations was the "abomination that makes desolate" as foretold by Jehovah's prophet Daniel. (Matthew 24:15) The following year a still larger international convention was held, again at Cedar Point, Ohio. By a Resolution adopt-

------

* See pages 180, 181, paragraphs 25-27.
† See page 180, paragraph 26; also the publication *Light,* Volume I, page 249.

39. How did the postwar witness work open up following World War I, and what revelation and action concerning the League of Nations occurred?

ed there on Sunday, September 10, 1922, the nations of the earth that adhered to the abominable League of Nations were challenged and notified of the League's failure decreed by God.*

[40] This second Cedar Point convention began a series of yearly conventions of world-wide importance. The fifth one was held in London, England, the capital of the globe-girdling British Empire. In attendance were delegates from Britain's partner in the Anglo-American dual world power and from other foreign lands.

[41] The convention opened on Tuesday, May 25, 1926, and continued through the following Monday, May 31. Friday afternoon, at the close of his address on Isaiah, chapter 49, the Society's president submitted to the convention a Resolution entitled "A Testimony to the Rulers of the World." It called attention to the responsibility that was placed upon all rulers because all the evidences of the times bore testimony to the establishment of God's kingdom in the heavens in 1914. The fifth clause of the Resolution then said that, despite this conclusive proof, "contrary to the Word of God the commercial, political and ecclesiastical rulers attempted to stabilize the world and keep the peoples under control by adopting that makeshift which is called the League of Nations and which was wrongfully and blasphemously hailed as the political expression of God's kingdom on earth; that the real author and father of the League of Nations compact is Satan the Devil, the god of this evil world, [it] was put forward by him as his last desperate effort to deceive the peoples, turn them away from the true God, and hold them under his wicked control; that now

* See *The Watch Tower* as of November 1, 1922, pages 324, 325.

40. What did the second Cedar Point convention begin, leading up to what in London, England?
41. What was adopted by that convention on Friday afternoon, and what did the fifth clause have to say to the world rulers?

after seven years of laborious effort on the part of the proponents of that compact to establish peace and prosperity, it is practically conceded that the League of Nations is a complete failure and that its utter collapse is a matter of only a brief space of time; . . . "

[42] Not only was this Resolution enthusiastically adopted by the convention of Jehovah's saintly people that Friday, but the following Sunday night it was submitted to a public audience that packed out the Royal Albert Hall. Then the Society's president gave a masterly address in support of and in enlargement upon the Resolution. The League of Nations was exposed to all, not alone as the "abomination that makes desolate," but also as the "eighth" king of Revelation 17:11, the British Empire being the seventh "king" and being the main support of the League of Nations. "Let Britain withdraw from it tomorrow, and it will go down immediately," declared Joseph F. Rutherford, to a round of applause. After the close of the address, which described the blessings of mankind under God's kingdom, the vast audience rose solidly in expressing itself in favor of God's government just described.

[43] Next day, except for the full page devoted by the *Daily News* to reporting the Resolution and the public address, the London newspapers hushed up the biggest, most important news of the times.* Still reprints of the full page of the *Daily News* of May 31, 1926, were widely circulated, and the Resolution was published around the earth. The Testimony was served upon the nations of the earth, the League of Nations was exposed for

---

* See *The Watch Tower* as of July 15, 1926, pages 211-217; also *The Golden Age* as of September 8, 1926, pages 780-791.

42. How was this Resolution submitted to a public audience, and with what reception?
43. Upon whom was this Testimony then served, and how was the "transgression that makes desolate" thus committed?

what it was, and the responsibility fell where it belonged. But the seventh world power and the other political powers of the earth did not heed the Testimony. They did not turn from the "abomination that makes desolate" to the support of God's proclaimed kingdom. Their continued worship of this "image of the wild beast" was dramatized on September 8, 1926, by the readmission of Germany into the family of nations in good standing and this by the admission of Germany into the League of Nations. What did such spurning of Jehovah's message concerning the League of Nations as the Devil-schemed, man-made makeshift for God's kingdom under Christ constitute? A "transgression" against God, a "transgression that makes desolate," that appals and astonishes all who long and pray for God's promised kingdom of his Christ. What disgusting conduct on the part of the worldly nations!

⁴⁴ If we accept this as fulfilling the prophecy of the "transgression that causeth appalment" or "that makes desolate," when is it that the sanctuary should be "victorious" (*JPS*), "vindicated" (*Ro*), "justified" (*Le*), "cleansed" (*AS, AV, LXX*), or "be restored to its rightful state" (*RS*)? It should be "two thousand and three hundred evenings and mornings" after that transgression so appalling and so certain to result in a desolation. If the Bible rule for counting prophetic time is applied as already set out,* a prophetic year of 360 days being taken as the basic unit, 2,300 evenings and mornings would amount to six years four months and twenty days, each day being composed of an evening and a morning. (Genesis 1:5, 8, 13,

---

* See page 101, paragraph 40. Remember that a thirteenth Jewish month is regularly added seven times every nineteen years in order to equalize lunar time with solar time with its leap years.

---

44. From when, therefore, may we count the 2,300 evenings and mornings, and when do they end?

19, 23, 31) Count now from the beginning of this
International Convention of London on May 25,
1926, and we shall find that the 2,300 days of
evenings and mornings bring us to October 15,
1932.

[45] How was Jehovah's "sanctuary" cleansed, vindicated or restored to its rightful state by that
date? Examine the official journal of Jehovah's
witnesses, *The Watchtower*, as of that date. Note
page 319. That page sets out the Resolution adopted by the New York company of Jehovah's witnesses on October 5, 1932. It called for a cleansing
of the congregational organization, a restoring of
it to the rightful state of Jehovah's sanctuary
class. How? By the ridding of the organization of
"elective elders," or elders that had been elected
to the office of eldership by the stretching out of
the hands of the members of the congregation in
a popular or democratic election, after the political style of the ancient Greek states and the democratic Anglo-American dual world power.

[46] For decades the congregations of Jehovah's
sanctuary class had been locally electing men to
eldership by local congregational hand-voting.
This, of course, was due to misunderstanding the
apostolic procedure of the first century as described in the Christian Greek Scriptures.* Now
at God's chosen time the article entitled "Jehovah's Organization" appeared in *The Watchtower*,
Part 1 in the issue of August 15, 1932, and Part 2

---

* See the book *The New Creation*, by C. T. Russell,
copyrighted 1904, pages 276-282; *Zion's Watch Tower*
as of March 15, 1906, on page 91, paragraph 7. See also
chapter 7 of this book, pages 161 (paragraph 29) to 165,
paragraph 38.

45. As of that date, what did the Watch Tower Society's official
journal point out?
46, 47. (a) How had the congregations been proceeding in the
matter of putting elders into office, and in what had this resulted?
(b) What Resolution did the *Watchtower* magazine submit for
adoption?

in the following issue of September 1. This exposed the system of "elective elders" as conforming to the democratic part of this world and hence as being unclean and not theocratic, not submissive to the great Theocrat who rules his sanctuary from the top down. This democratic electing of elders had resulted in many being appointed to this office who were not really mature or spiritually grown up, who felt independent of superior control, who felt self-important in their local congregation as having the assignment to run the local congregation, being responsible primarily to the congregation to which they had looked for votes. This had resulted in much obstruction by such type of "elders" to the world-wide witness work that the Watch Tower Bible & Tract Society was encouraging by its service representative in each congregation. The article on "Jehovah's Organization" closed, submitting for adoption by all congregations a Resolution, which said, in part:

[47] "Therefore be it resolved that there is no Scriptural authority for the existence of the elective office of elders in the church and that henceforth we will not elect any person to the office of elder; that all of the anointed of God are elders, as that term is defined by the Scriptures, and all are servants of the Most High. . . . A service director who shall be nominated by us and confirmed by the Society's executive or manager, and which service director shall be a member of the service committee of this company."

[48] This Resolution was adopted by congregations of Jehovah's witnesses throughout the earth. The announcement in the *Watchtower* magazine of October 15, 1932, at the end of 2,300 evenings and mornings was the official notification made by

---

48. What, therefore, did the announcement in the October 15, 1932, issue of *The Watchtower* constitute, and how did this harmonize with the meaning of the "twenty-four elders" and the "seven stars"?

Jehovah through his visible channel of communication that his sanctuary of anointed "living stones" had been cleansed, vindicated and justified. It had been restored to its rightful state as regards the elimination of democratically elected "elders" and as regards the theocratic appointing of the congregational overseer. Certainly the twenty-four elderly persons whom the apostle John saw in his heavenly vision crowned and seated on thrones around the throne of the Most High God were not "elders" democratically elected by the congregations on earth below. They were "elders" chosen by the Sovereign of the universe because of their full Christian growth and proved integrity. Certainly, too, the "seven stars" whom John saw upon the right hand of the glorified Jesus Christ and who pictured the "angels" or overseers of the congregations of Jehovah's anointed sanctuary class were full-grown "elders" chosen and controlled, not by the congregations after the democratic procedure of the seventh world power, but by the Supreme Head of the theocratic organization through Jesus Christ. (Revelation 1:16, 20; 2:1; 4:4, 10, 11) Rightly the remnant of the sanctuary class on earth was brought into accord with this theocratic rule in Jehovah's due time.

[49] That was only a right beginning, for the sanctuary had to be made theocratic in all respects. Six years later *The Watchtower* published the article "Organization," Part 1 in its issue of June 1, 1938, and Part 2 in its next issue of June 15. This article opened, saying: "Jehovah's organization is in no wise democratic. Jehovah is supreme, and his government or organization is strictly theocratic." This article also proposed a resolution for each congregation to adopt, the resolution recognizing that "God's government is a pure theocracy" and requesting "The Society" as his visible

---

49. What thereafter did the *Watchtower* issues of June, 1938, declare, and what resolution did it propose for adoption?

representative to organize the congregation for God's service and to appoint theocratically from the visible top the various servants of the congregation.—Part 2, ¶ 15.

⁵⁰ This theocratic resolution was adopted and acted upon by the congregations of Jehovah's witnesses wherever found; and the visible governing body at the Society's headquarters in Brooklyn, New York, proceeded with theocratically organizing all willing congregations. All new congregations established since then have been organized theocratically in this manner from their very start. This has resulted in a better, more peaceful and more productive organization of Jehovah's dedicated people, in fulfillment of Isaiah 60:17. This theocratic organization went through World War II, terrifically persecuted indeed by the seventh world power and its allies and its enemies. But in no way did the theocratic organization bow fearfully in slavish bondage to dictatorial or regimented governments and in no way did it cease to render to Jehovah God the daily, continual or constant burnt offering of praise to him and his kingdom.

⁵¹ Cleansed, vindicated and in its rightful theocratic state, the sanctuary continues rendering divine service till now, regardless of what the symbolic "little horn," the "king of fierce countenance," may yet do. The sanctuary class look to the complete fulfillment of the angel Gabriel's explanation to Daniel concerning this cunning political "king": "By his cunning he shall make deceit prosper under his hand, and in his own mind he shall magnify himself. Without warning he shall destroy many; and he shall even rise up against the Prince of princes; but, by no human hand, he shall be broken. The vision of the eve-

---

50. What action followed on this resolution, what reorganization then took place, and in what did this result?
51. What has the sanctuary in its rightful state continued to do, and to what fulfillment of prophecy does it look?

nings and the mornings which has been told is true; but seal up the vision, for it pertains to many days hence."—Daniel 8:25, 26, *RS*.

[52] The Anglo-American dual world power still holds its position as the active seventh world power of Biblical prophecy. It has not yielded place to the threatening Communist bloc, which has openly boasted that it will establish itself at last in the world domination. The most flagrant mistake that the seventh world power has made is in high-mindedly standing up against the Prince of princes, Jehovah God, who took to himself his power in 1914 (A.D.) and who is the Most High over all the earth and its princes, including the "king of fierce countenance." (Psalm 83:18, *AV*) For especially this reason the seventh world power will shortly be broken, not by the hand of world communism, but by superhuman hand or power.

[53] God's kingdom, against which the seventh world power has committed the abominable "transgression," will strike it during the progress of the "war of the great day of God the Almighty," just as the stone cut out of the mountain in Nebuchadnezzar's dream struck the symbolic image of successive world powers on its feet and ground it to a powder for winds to blow away. The vision of the evenings and the mornings is no more shut up. After the "many days" of thousands of years it has been opened up. The greater part of the vision has already been fulfilled. The symbolic "king of fierce countenance" is yet to be broken by divine hand. Then Jehovah God, who dwells by his spirit in his sanctuary, will be vindicated as Universal Sovereign. His will must be done on earth.

---

52. What has been the seventh world power's most flagrant mistake, and hence what must happen to it?
53. What is now the state of the "vision of the evenings and the mornings" after these "many days," and what is yet to be expected?

CHAPTER 10

The North Against The South

SINCE World War II the tension and "cold war" between the two great blocs of nations have been said to be between the East and the West. The final prophetic vision that was given to Daniel presents it as a climactic conflict between the North and the South. The vision is so accurate in prophetic detail that unbelievers have denied that Daniel received and wrote down the description of the vision. Porphyry, a Greek philosopher of the third century (about 233-304 A.D.), who produced a work called *Against the Christians* in fifteen volumes, was one of these.

[2] Porphyry recognized Jesus Christ merely as an outstanding philosopher but did not agree with him that Daniel was the author of the Bible book bearing his name. Because Daniel's last vision seemed to describe so closely the Syrian King Antiochus IV Epíphanes, Porphyry could not accept it as history written in advance by inspiration, but looked on it as a history written after it happened. Hence Porphyry viewed the author of the book of Daniel as a fraud, putting on the appearance of being a prophet to whom Jehovah God sent angels and revealed visions. However, the foolishness of Porphyry and of skeptics like him is stripped naked. How so? Because the vision is found to have foretold events really happening in this twentieth century and Daniel has not been here to write them down after they have happened. Truthfully the angel had told Daniel: "I . . . came to make you understand what is to befall your people in the latter days. For the vision is for days yet to come."—Daniel 10:13, 14, *RS*.

[3] From no one else but an angel of Jehovah God the seventh world power, the Anglo-American dual world power, should learn that world powers prior to it have had demon princes in unseen charge of them. The angel of God that came in answer to

---

1, 2. (a) How does Daniel's final vision present the conflict now on between the two great blocs of nations? (b) How did Porphyry view the book of Daniel, but how is his foolishness stripped naked?

3. Who were in unseen charge of past world powers, and how did the angel disclose this fact to Daniel?

Daniel's prayer was held up three weeks by one
such demon prince. He explained his delay, telling
Daniel: "The prince of the kingdom of Persia
withstood me twenty-one days; but Michael, one
of the chief princes, came to help me, so I left
him there with the prince of the kingdom of Persia
. . . Do you know why I have come to you? But
now I will return to fight against the prince of
Persia; and when I am through with him, lo, the
prince of Greece will come. But I will tell you what
is inscribed in the book of truth: there is none who
contends by my side against these except Michael,
your prince." This angelic appearance to Daniel
was on the twenty-fourth day of Nisan in the
third year of Cyrus king of Persia.—Daniel 10:
1-4, 10-14, 20, 21, *RS*.

⁴ Darius the Mede, the uncle of Cyrus and the
first ruler of the Medo-Persian world power, had
now passed off the scene. But the angel refers
back to him in starting off his wonderful prophecy
concerning Daniel's people in days yet to come,
down to the "latter days." He said: "And as for
me, in the first year of Darius the Mede [539-
538 B.C.], I stood up to be a supporter and a
stronghold unto him." (Daniel 11:1, *JPS*) This
pagan ruler Darius the Mede was not the one
whom Jehovah's angel had stood up to confirm
and strengthen, but it was Michael. The angel had
just spoken of Michael as contending by his side.
In view of Jehovah's purposes that had to be
carried forward concerning Daniel's people, over
whom the heavenly chief prince Michael was the
prince, this angel stood up to offer his strength
and aid to Michael as against the demon prince
of the Medo-Persian world power. Darius had to
be maneuvered in harmony with Jehovah's purposes, as, for instance, when Jehovah sent his

4. To be a supporter and stronghold, to whom did this angel
stand up in the first year of Darius the Mede, and what is there
to show an effect of this?

angel to "shut the lions' mouths" from devouring Daniel. So King Darius was glad to take Daniel out of the lions' den into which the envious enemies had forced King Darius to lower him. As a result of this deliverance of Daniel, one of the three presidents of Darius' kingdom, Darius the Mede of his own accord made a decree for all his subjects to "tremble and fear before the God of Daniel, for he is the living God, enduring for ever; his kingdom shall never be destroyed, and his dominion shall be to the end." Thus it was that "this Daniel prospered during the reign of Darius and the reign of Cyrus the Persian."—Daniel 6: 21-28, *RS*.

⁵ What now follows in the prophecy to Daniel is important, all of it. It is God's own message through an angel associate of Michael the prince. It is in answer to Daniel's prayer for three weeks. It is no mere heavily detailed prophecy of political intrigues and fighting between ancient rival kings, that is not worthy of our time-consuming study and examination today. Since God's own angel took time and fought for the opportunity to bring the prophetic message to Daniel because God had sent him with this message; also since God inspired Daniel to write the vision down just as given by the angel, then we should be slighting God and his angel and Daniel were we to pass over any part of the prophecy as unessential or unimportant to us in these critical days. Why so? Because our study of the events that match the prophecy shows the accuracy of Jehovah God's foresight and vindicates him as the great Prophet. Hence our study and proving of the first part of the prophetic vision strengthens our faith and confidence in the certainty of fulfillment of the last part of the prophecy. Yes, it fortifies our

---

5. Whom would Bible students be slighting by passing over any part of this final vision as unimportant now, and what is the value of understanding the first part of it?

faith in *all* the prophecies of God's Word as being true and reliable.

⁶ Having referred to Darius the Mede, the first Medo-Persian world ruler, Jehovah's angel went on to say: "And now will I declare unto thee the truth. Behold, there shall stand up yet three kings in Persia; and the fourth shall be far richer than they all; and when he is waxed strong through his riches, he shall stir up all against the realm of Greece." (Daniel 11:2, *JPS*) The three kings of Persia that were to "stand up" or assume world rulership were (1) Cyrus the Great, (2) Cambyses (530-522 B.C.), the conqueror of Egypt, and (3) Darius Hystaspes (521-485 B.C.), the son-in-law of Cyrus. In listing these three, no count is made of the usurper, the Magian named Gaumata, who pretended to be Smerdis Bardija the brother of Cambyses. He reigned less than eight months and was discovered to be false and was put to death by the Persian Darius I (Hystaspes). Under orders of this Darius an invasion of Greece began in 499 B.C. During a second invasion the Persians were routed at Marathon, September 28-29, 490 B.C., and their army was obliged to retreat to Asia Minor. Five years later Darius I died and was succeeded by the "fourth" king, Xerxes I.

⁷ The Persian defeat at Marathon called for revenge. So Xerxes, having become strong through his riches, made empire-wide preparations for humbling the Greeks. He is understood to be the Ahasuerus who took Esther the Jewess as wife and who ruled over 127 provinces from India to Ethiopia. (Esther 1:1) Collected from all these provinces, his host of troops included East Indians and Ethiopians. The Phoenicians furnished 1,200 warships with crews, besides which there were 3,000 ships for transport of his grand mixture of

6. Who were the three kings of Persia that were yet to stand up, and who was the fourth one foretold?
7. Why and how did this fourth rich king stir up all against the realm of Greece?

troops. The historian Herodotus says there were
1,700,000 footmen, 100,000 horsemen and 510,000
sailors and marines, a total of 2,310,000 men. In
the spring of 480 B.C. this huge war machine
moved against Greece.

⁸ A heroic Greek delaying action at Thermopylae,
Greece, was overcome at great cost to the Per-
sians. They ravaged Athens, but at Salamis these
Persians met with terrible defeat, for here the
Greeks had determined to make their last stand.
Another victory for the Greeks at Plataea the
following year proved decisive. Greece was no
place for the Persians, and back to Asia Minor
King Xerxes fled. Even Byzantium, the capital of
Thrace, was wrested from the Persians by the
courageous Spartans from southern Greece.

⁹ Despite this ouster from Greece, the Persian
Empire continued as the fourth world power for
about 150 years longer. Consequently seven more
Persian kings followed Xerxes, namely, Artaxerxes I, Xerxes II, Darius II (Ochus), Artaxerxes II,
Artaxerxes III, Arses and Darius III. For this
reason "higher critics" say that the angel erred
in telling Daniel: "Now I will show you the truth."
But not so, for the angel did not say that the
"fourth" Persian king would be the last or that
Xerxes I would be the fourth and last world ruler,
counting from Cyrus the Great. He merely stops
with this "fourth" Persian king who was to make
such an all-out, vengeful campaign against Greece,
only to meet with bitter defeat and loss of prestige.
He was the last Persian emperor to carry war into
Greece. So the angel condensed history by passing
over the succeeding reigns of the seven remaining
Persian kings and by taking a prophetic preview
of the European king who reversed matters and

8. How were the invading Persians obliged to leave Greece?
9. Why do higher critics say that the angel erred regarding the
kings of Persia, but why did the angel mention only four kings
and proceed to the next world power?

carried the war into Persia. The angel was therefore historically right as he now said:

¹⁰ "And a mighty king shall stand up, that shall rule with great dominion, and do according to his will." (Daniel 11:3, *JPS*) This was in 336 B.C., in the same year that the eleventh and last Persian world ruler counting from Cyrus the Great was crowned. In that year the Macedonian Alexander 'stood up,' being crowned king of Macedonia as successor to his father, Philip II, after whom the Biblically famous city of Philippi was named. This twenty-year-old ruler did prove to be a "mighty king" and came to be called Alexander the Great.

¹¹ Fired with the scheme originated by his father, he launched out on the conquest of Asia and met with speedy success. He seized the Persian provinces in the Middle East and in Egypt, where he founded the city that exists to this day, Alexandria. Turning northward, he crossed the Euphrates and Tigris Rivers to meet Darius III on the field of battle at Gaugamela near where Nineveh the ancient capital of Assyria lay moldering in ruins. Alexander's phalanxes and cavalry, 47,000 strong, dashed against Darius' host of 1,000,000 warriors and scattered them. Darius III fled, only to be murdered, thus bringing to an end the rule of the Achaemenian dynasty that had begun with Darius I. With the Persian Empire now under his sway, Alexander the Great did "rule with great dominion" and did do "according to his will." He married Roxana, the daughter of the conquered Bactrian king, and also Statira, a daughter of the Persian King Darius III. By Roxana he had a son who was named Alexander (Allou). By a certain Barsine he had an illegitimate son named Heracles (Hercules).

---

10. Who was the "mighty king" that then stood up, and where?
11. How did Alexander come to "rule with great dominion," and do "according to his will"?

[12] Alexander's enjoyment of world rulership was short-lived. Jehovah's angel foretold this: "And when he shall stand up, his kingdom shall be broken, and shall be divided toward the four winds of heaven; but not to his posterity, nor according to his dominion wherewith he ruled; for his kingdom shall be plucked up, even for others beside these." (Daniel 11:4, *JPS*) At the height of his career, when but in his thirty-third year, the carousing Alexander was struck down by malarial fever at Babylon in 323 B.C., and his plans to make this Scripturally doomed city his world capital collapsed. His vast empire in Europe, Asia Minor, Asia, the Middle East and Egypt broke up to the four winds of the heavens. His body was transported into Egypt and buried in Alexandria by his General Ptolemy, the satrap of Egypt.

[13] The empire did not pass to Alexander's posterity. He had left behind in Macedonia an incapable brother, Philip Aridaeus. He reigned for less than seven years, and then was murdered by his own mother in 317 B.C. Alexander's legitimate son by Roxana, Alexander Allou, followed and ruled but about six years. In 311 B.C. he too met violent death at the hand of one of his father's generals, Cassander, who now usurped the throne of Macedonia and Greece. Alexander's illegitimate son, Heracles, undertook to rule in his father's name, but was murdered in 309 B.C. With him the line of Alexander the great blood-spiller died out, in blood. The dominion had departed from his house. The angelic prophecy proved true.

[14] The Alexandrian Empire was plucked up for men other than Alexander's posterity to rule. His generals quarreled among themselves and grabbed for territory; and the broken kingdom was for a

12. How long did Alexander enjoy world rulership, and when was his kingdom broken?
13. How did the prophecy prove true that the kingdom should not be divided to Alexander's posterity?
14. How was Alexander's kingdom divided for a time "toward the four winds of heaven," and how was this reduced later on to three?

time divided four ways, "toward the four winds of heaven." One-eyed General Antigonus tried to set himself up as lord of all Asia and finally took the title of king, claiming to be the heir of Alexander the Great. He had to meet the confederacy of the three other generals against him, Cassander, Seleucus and Lysimachus. He fell in battle against them at Ipsus in Phrygia, Asia Minor, in 301 B.C. The four Hellenic empires that resulted were (1) that of General Cassander in Macedonia and Greece; (2) that of General Lysimachus in Asia Minor and European Thrace, including Byzantium; (3) that of General Seleucus Nicator (the Conqueror), who secured Babylon, Media, Syria, Persia and the provinces eastward to the Indus River; and (4) that of General Ptolemy Lagus, who secured Egypt, Libya, Arabia and Palestine and Coele-Syria. In a few years the male line of General Cassander died out, and in 285 B.C. General Lysimachus took possession of the European part of the Macedonian Empire. However, in 277 B.C. Antigonus Gonatas, the grandson of one-eyed General Antigonus, gained possession of the throne of Macedonia. This reduced the Hellenistic empires to three, till Macedonia became dependent upon Rome in 168 B.C. and ended up as a Roman province in 146 B.C.

[15] In 281 B.C. General Lysimachus fell in battle before General Seleucus Nicator and thus left Seleucus practically the master of the Asian territories. Seleucus became the founder of the Seleucidae or house of Seleucid kings in Syria. Shortly after the decisive battle of Ipsus he founded the city of Antioch in Syria, naming it after his father Antiochus. As a seaport for it he founded a coastal city, which he named after himself, Seleucia. Centuries later the Christian apostle

---

15. How did General Seleucus the Conqueror become master of the Asian territories, and what cities of apostolic interest did he establish?

Paul used the seaport of Seleucia and taught Christian truth in Antioch of Syria, where the followers of Jesus first came to be called Christians.—Acts 11:25-27; 13:1-4.

¹⁶ Seleucus transferred his seat of government from Babylon to his new Syrian capital, Antioch. He was assassinated in 280 B.C. The Seleucid dynasty of kings that he left to succeed him continued in power until 64 B.C., when the Roman General Pompey made Syria a Roman province. Long before he died Seleucus gave to his son Antiochus I the sovereignty over all the lands beyond the Euphrates River as well as the title of king. With King Seleucus Nicator the long warfare between the Biblical "king of the north" and the "king of the south" began. Foresightedly Jehovah's angel left the names of the "king of the north" and the "king of the south" unmentioned, because the nationality and the political identity of these "two kings" change with the course of centuries and even become matters of vital concern to us in this twentieth century A.D.

RIVALRY OF THE TWO KINGS*

¹⁷ Jehovah's angel now begins narrating many details of the long-drawn-out warfare: "And the king of the south will become strong, yea, he who is one of his princes; but another will become strong against him, and will rule; a great dominion will his dominion be." (Daniel 11:5, Le) This "king of the south" is south of what, and the "king of the north" is north of what? They are north and south of Daniel's people, who, by the time of this vision to Daniel, had been freed from Babylon and restored to the land of Judah.

* See the map of the Hellenic kingdom of the north and that of the south on page 372.

16. To where did Seleucus transfer his capital, and with him what long warfare began, as described in this final vision?
17. With respect to whom were the two kings to the north and to the south?

[18] Who personally is this "king of the south" of Daniel 11:5? He is one of the "princes" or military chiefs of Alexander the Great, namely, Ptolemy I, the son of Lagus. He was, in fact, one of Alexander's eight bodyguards. He was made the satrap of Egypt but assumed the title of king in 306 B.C., in imitation of one-eyed General Antigonus. He was the first of thirteen or fourteen Macedonian kings or Pharaohs of Egypt. According to his name, he established the Ptolemaic line of rulers over Egypt. About 312 B.C. he captured Jerusalem on a sabbath day. He persuaded Jews to come south to Egypt as colonists, and a colony of them was established in Alexandria. With his son and successor he shared in founding the famous library and museum in Alexandria. The Jewish province of Judea stayed under control of Ptolemaic Egypt or the "king of the south" till 198 B.C., when the "king of the north" took over. Ptolemy I invaded the Syrian territory of King Seleucus a number of times.

[19] Who, now, is the other prince or military chief of Alexander who the angel said would "become strong against him" and whose dominion would be a "great dominion"? This is General Seleucus Nicator, who now assumes the role of "the king of the north." At his death he was succeeded by his son Antiochus I (Soter or Savior). This king is not taken note of in the angel's prophecy, as he died fighting, not the "king of the south," but the Galatians in Asia Minor. He was succeeded by his son Antiochus II, who came to be called *The.os'* or "God." He married a woman named Laodice, and his oldest son by her he named after his grandfather Seleucus.

[20] But what of this? The angel tells: "And at

18. Who personally was this "king of the south" in Daniel 11:5, and what line of rulers did he establish?
19. Who personally was the prince that became "strong against him," and what role did he and his successors play?
20. Who was the daughter of this "king of the south," and what translation did her father cause to be begun?

the end of years they shall join themselves together; and the daughter of the king of the south shall come to the king of the north to make an agreement; but she shall not retain the strength of her arm; neither shall he stand, nor his arm; but she shall be given up, and they that brought her, and he that begot her, and he that obtained her in those times." (Daniel 11:6, *JPS*) Who is this "daughter of the king of the south"? It is Berenice, the daughter of Ptolemy II (Philadelphus) of Egypt. According to tradition, this Egyptian king showed kindness to his Jewish subjects and arranged for beginning the translation of the inspired Hebrew Scriptures into Greek. This resulted at length in the famous Greek *Septuagint Version*, which the Greek-speaking Christians used in the first century A.D.

[21] King Ptolemy II waged two wars with the Syrian "king of the north," Antiochus II (Theos). In the year 250 B.C. the two kings entered into a peace arrangement. As the price of this alliance or "agreement" the Syrian king of the north, Antiochus II, must marry Berenice the daughter of King Ptolemy II. But Antiochus II was already married to Laodice. So this obliged him to divorce her in order to marry the Egyptian Berenice. By Berenice, Antiochus II of Syria had a son, who became heir to the throne of the "king of the north," to the exclusion of the sons of his first wife Laodice.

[22] The "arm" or supporting power of Berenice was her father, King Ptolemy II. Hence when he died in 246-7 B.C., Berenice did not "retain the strength of her arm" with her husband, King Antiochus II of Syria. He rejected her, and took back his first wife, Laodice, and named her oldest son, Seleucus Callinicus, to be his successor to the

21. According to the agreement, what was done with this daughter of the king of the south, and what resulted from this?
22. How did Berenice's "arm" not stand, and how were she and those who brought her and he who got her "given up"?

Syrian throne. Calamity befell all connections of
Berenice, as prophecy had foretold. Not only did
her father, "her arm," not endure, but also "his
offspring," her own self. She was given up with
her infant son to be murdered, Laodice planning
it. Those who brought her, evidently her attend-
ants who brought her from Egypt to Syria, also
suffered. This did not pacify Laodice. Doubtless
by her, as the saying went, Antiochus II (Theos),
who had taken her back, was poisoned to death.
What an end for a "god"! This was evidently to
prevent her from being divorced a second time.
So Berenice's father that had begotten her and
her Syrian husband that had obtained her for a
while both died. This left Laodice's oldest son,
Seleucus II, as rightful successor to his father on
the Syrian throne. Certainly the cause of peace
was not strengthened by this.

[23] To this there would be a reaction, the angel
foretold, saying: "But one of the shoots of her
roots shall stand up in his place, and shall come
unto the army, and shall enter into the stronghold
of the king of the north, and shall deal with them,
and shall prevail." (Daniel 11:7, *JPS*) The "roots"
of Berenice were, of course, her parents, Ptolemy II
(Philadelphus) and his sister-wife Arsinoë.

[24] The particular 'shoot of her roots' that stood
up in place of her father was her brother, who
now became "king of the south" as Ptolemy III,
surnamed Evergetes ("Benefactor"). He began to
"stand up" at his father's death by assuming authority as king. At once he set out to avenge the
murder of his sister Berenice at the Syrian capital
of Antioch. With an army he marched against
Syria's king, Seleucus II Callinicus, whom Laodice
his mother had used in murdering Berenice and
her infant son. Ptolemy III came into the strong-

23. Who were the "roots" of Berenice?
24. How did "one of the shoots of her roots" stand up, enter the
stronghold of the king of the north and prevail in dealing with
those up there?

hold of the king of the north and dealt out death to the queen mother Laodice. Moreover, he overran Syria, captured the fortified part of the capital city Antioch and also its seaport, Seleucia. Then he moved eastward through the "great dominion" of the king of the north and plundered Babylonia and Susa and continued his march as far east as the shores of India. In this manner the murderous Seleucus II was forced from his Syrian throne.

²⁵ That the king of the south would wipe out a religious indignity also, Jehovah's angel foretold: "And also their gods, with their molten images, and with their precious vessels of silver and of gold, shall he bring into captivity into Egypt; and he shall desist some years from the king of the north." (Daniel 11:8, *JPS*) More than two hundred years previously, during the days of Pharaoh Psammetichus III, the Persian King Cambyses of the fourth world power had conquered Egypt and had carried home in triumph the conquered Egyptian gods, "their molten images." Now, when plundering Susa, the former royal capital of Persia, and Babylonia, the victorious king of the south, Ptolemy III, recovered the deported gods of ancient Egypt and took these captive from the temple robbers. He brought them back to their homeland. By this he won for himself the name Evergetes or Benefactor from the grateful Egyptians.

²⁶ It was internal troubles down south in Egypt that called the conquering Ptolemy III back to the land of the Nile. Being obliged to quell revolt at home, he was prevented from taking advantage of his successes over the king of the north. So he desisted from inflicting further injuries upon the northern king. Besides the gods stolen from Egypt,

<hr/>
25. How did he wipe out a religious indignity, and for this what name did he win for himself?
26. Why did he "desist some years from the king of the north," and what did he bring home with him?

Ptolemy III brought back as spoils of war no fewer than 2,500 "precious vessels of silver and of gold." How he died in 221 B.C., whether naturally or by being murdered, is not known. History is divided on that question. But he outlived the Syrian King Seleucus II upon whom he had taken vengeance.

27 Taking advantage of the situation, what did the king of the north do? The angel foretold this: "And he shall come into the kingdom of the king of the south, but he shall return into his own land." (Daniel 11:9, *JPS*) The humiliated Seleucus II struck back in revenge. He came south into the realm of the king of the south but met defeat. In disgraceful flight, with but a small remnant of his army, he retreated to his Syrian capital, Antioch, in 242 B.C. His surname Callinicus, "the Gloriously Triumphant," proved to be a misnomer. He died before his humiliator, Ptolemy III of Egypt, did and was succeeded by his son Seleucus III, surnamed Ceraunus ("Thunderbolt"). Assassination put a sudden end to this son's reign of less than three years. His brother succeeded him in the Syrian throne as Antiochus III and became called "the Great."

28 Concerning these two sons of the Syrian King Seleucus II Callinicus, the angel prophesied: "And his sons shall stir themselves up, and shall assemble a multitude of great forces, and he shall come on, and overflow, as he passeth through; and he shall return and stir himself up, even to his stronghold."—Daniel 11:10, *JPS*.

29 The one son, Seleucus III (Ceraunus), died under an assassin's weapon while on a campaign toward the west in Asia Minor. His brother, the other son, Antiochus III the Great, assembled great forces for an assault on the kingdom of the

27. Why did the king of the north return after coming into the kingdom of the southern king?
28, 29. (a) What happened to the older son of that king of the north? (b) How did the younger son come on, overflow, return and stir himself up?

king of the south, who was now Ptolemy IV, surnamed Philopator. The new king of the north,
Antiochus III, finally came into conflict with the
rising power of Rome. But first he led his military
forces to wipe out Egyptian gains and he won back
the seaport of Seleucia, also the province of Coele-
Syria (Hollow Syria), and the seacoast cities of
Tyre and Ptolemais and nearby towns. The first
Egyptian army that Ptolemy IV sent against him
he routed. He also took many cities of the province
of Judea in Palestine. During the winter victorious
Antiochus III went into winter quarters with his
60,000 warriors at Ptolemais, about twenty-five
miles south of Tyre. The following spring (217
B.C.) he did "return and stir himself up, even to
his stronghold."

³⁰ Jehovah's angel showed that the tide of battle
would turn, saying: "And the king of the south
shall be moved with choler, and shall come forth
and fight with him, even with the king of the
north; and he shall set forth a great multitude,
but the multitude shall be given into his hand."
(Daniel 11:11, *JPS*) Embittered, the king of the
south, Ptolemy IV Philopator (or Tryphon), moved
north with 70,000 troops against the advancing
enemy. At the coastal city of Raphia, about twenty miles southwest of Gaza and not far north of
Egypt's border, they met. Syrian King Antiochus III had raised a "great multitude" 60,000
strong, but it was given into the hand of the king
of the south.

³¹ "And the multitude shall be carried away, and
his heart shall be lifted up; and he shall cast down
tens of thousands, but he shall not prevail." (Daniel 11:12, *JPS*) The king of the south, Ptolemy IV,
carried 10,000 enemy Syrian troops and 300 horse-

---

30. Where did the king of the south meet him for a fight, and
what was given into his hand?
31. How was a multitude carried away at that battle, what were
the terms of the peace treaty signed, but why did the king of the
south not prevail but have his heart lifted up?

men to their death and took 5,000 more as prisoners, a big loss for the king of the north. The
two kings now signed a peace treaty, and Antíochus III was obliged to give up Phoenicia, including
Tyre and Ptolemais, and Coele-Syria, that he had
conquered. But he still held on to his Syrian seaport of Seleucia. This peace was to his advantage,
for the king of the south did not follow up his
victory, to "prevail." He turned to a life of dissipa-
tion in Egypt and left no successor to take up an
aggressive lead against Syria, only his five-year-
old son, Ptolemy V, as successor to Egypt's throne.
This was many years before his Syrian opponent,
Antíochus III, himself died. Jehovah's angel had
foretold: "He shall not prevail." Over this victory
his heart did get "lifted up," but specially against
Jehovah God. Judah and Jerusalem still continued
under his domination, but he worked himself up
to an attitude against Jehovah's people.

[32] The king of the north, Antíochus III, after
being defeated at Raphia, retired to his Syrian
capital at Antioch. Unlike his victorious opponent,
he went on to earthly greatness, gaining his title
Mégas, the Great. He directed his military genius
eastward and defeated the Parthians in 209 B.C.
The following year he carried his expedition still
further eastward, against the Bactrians deep in
Asia. These successful expeditions earned for him
the title "the Great." Turning now westward, he
captured Ephesus in Asia Minor and made it his
capital. He crossed the Hellespont (the narrow
strait of the Dardanelles) into Europe. There he
rebuilt the city of Lysimachia that had been
founded by Alexander's general Lysimachus. At
this point Rome asked him to quit interfering in
Europe. In 191 B.C. the Romans formally declared
war upon him. He was finally defeated at Magnesia
in Asia Minor, not far from his capital, Ephesus.

32. How did this defeated king of the north go on to greatness,
and how did he run into conflict with Rome, disastrously?

When settling for peace with Rome, he yielded up everything on the Roman side of the Taurus Mountains of Asia Minor and also paid a fine. He became the father of Cleopatra, whom he engaged in marriage to the king of the south, Ptolemy V. From then on Cleopatra became the regular name of Egypt's queens in the Ptolemaic line.

³³ With regard to the northern King Antiochus III the Great, Jehovah's angel further prophesied: "And the king of the north shall again set forth a multitude, greater than the former; and he shall come on at the end of the times, even of years, with a great army and with much substance." (Daniel 11:13, *JPS*) The "times" or years here foretold turned out to be twelve or more years after the battle of Raphia, where he had suffered defeat at the hand of Ptolemy IV. After that lapse of years, the victor of the battle of Raphia died and his five-year-old son became the king of the south, bearing the name Ptolemy V. Taking advantage of this tender age of the king of the south, Antiochus III set out to reconquer all the territories he had lost. To this end he leagued himself with Philip V, king of Macedonia, against young Ptolemy V. He then invaded Phoenicia and Syria and captured the coastal city of Gaza near Egypt. He had a great army with substantial supplies.

³⁴ The times had to become hard for the king of the south according to the further prophecy of Jehovah's angel to Daniel: "And in those times there shall many stand up against the king of the south; also the children of the violent among thy people shall lift themselves up to establish the vision; but they shall stumble." (Daniel 11:14, *JPS*) Besides Syrian King Antiochus III and his Macedonian ally, King Philip V, the young king of the south had other troublemakers to contend

---

33. How did this king of the north come at the end of years with a well-supplied army and take territory from Egypt?
34. What troubles did the young king of the south have?

with right at home in Egypt. As his guardian, Agathocles ruled in the king's name, but he dealt arrogantly with the Egyptians. On this account many Egyptians revolted.

[35] According to the prophecy, even some of Daniel's people became disturbers. They were "children of the violent," or were men of violence, revolutionists in some sort of way. The "vision" that they may have had from Jehovah's Word they tried to establish before the time in harmony with their selfish understanding of the matter. Their effort or movement had nothing to do with the building of a temple in Egypt, the one called the temple of Onion after the Jewish priest Onias and built by this son of the high priest, Onias III, to force a material fulfillment of Isaiah 19:19. These Jewish men of violence were mistaken if they were thinking of putting an end to the "appointed times of the nations" that had begun in 607 B.C., when Jerusalem was desolated and the Jews came under the "seven times" of Gentile domination. In trying to run ahead of the Most High God in this or in any other matter that is not disclosed in Daniel 11:14, they were doomed to "stumble," fail.

[36] Jehovah's angel now looked north of those violent men among Daniel's people and said: "And the king of the north shall come, and cast up a mound, and take a well-fortified city; and the arms of the south shall not withstand; and as for his chosen people, there shall be no strength in them to withstand. But he that cometh against him shall do according to his own will, and none shall stand before him; and he shall stand in the beauteous land, and in his hand shall be extermination." (Daniel 11:15, 16, *JPS*) The military forces or "arms of the south" that King Ptolemy

---

35. How did some of Daniel's people become disturbers but stumble in failure to establish the vision?
36. How did the king of the north now come and the arms of the south not withstand him?

V Epíphanes sent under General Scopas proved unable to "withstand" the pressure from the north. Egypt's general met Antíochus III the Great far to the north of Jerusalem, at Paneas (later called Caesarea Philippi). This was at the headwaters of the Jordan River, near Mount Hermon, and so near the place where Jesus Christ was later transfigured. (Matthew 16:13; 17:1-9) Here the battle was joined.

[37] Antíochus III proved victorious. He drove Egypt's General Scopas and his 100,000 picked troops or "chosen people" back into the Phoenician seaport of Sidon, a "well-fortified city." Here he "cast up a mound" or siegeworks. He took Sidon, in 198 B.C., for the bottled-up General Scopas was forced to surrender because of famine. Antíochus III pressed forward "according to his own will," as the forces of the king of the south were unable to stand before him. He captured more cities and proceeded against the capital of the "beauteous land," Jerusalem, with its rebuilt sanctuary.

[38] The military garrison that the king of the south had stationed in Jerusalem failed to hold the holy city. Finally Antíochus III entered Jerusalem and was given a welcome by its inhabitants who seem to have been alienated from the king of the south. Thus, in 198 B.C., Jerusalem and Judea passed from under the domination of Egypt to under that of the Syrian king of the north. In Antíochus III the Great, the king of the north began to "stand in the beauteous land," but how long would he remain standing there?

[39] "And in his hand there shall be extermination." Indeed, extermination for opposing Jews or Egyptians was within his power. But the He-

---

37, 38. (a) Where did he cast up a mound, and what well-fortified city did he take? (b) How did he come to "stand in the beauteous land"?
39. How was there "extermination" in his hand, and what questions arise here?

brew word in Daniel 11:16 for "extermination" may also be read "all of it" or "wholly." He did take over the "beauteous land," all of it, to the exclusion of the king of the south. How long, though, will the Jews keep submissive to the Syrian king of the north? Furthermore, will this king yield to the demand of Rome and surrender his captured territories? What does the prophecy foretell?

ROME MAKES ITSELF FELT

⁴⁰ "He will also direct his face to enter with the strength of his whole kingdom, having professions of peace with him; and thus will he do it: and he will give him the daughter of his wife [the daughter of women, *JPS*] to destroy it; but it will not stand, and it will not remain his." (Daniel 11:17, *Le*) Antiochus III aimed to have Syria dominate Egypt. He directed his face to enter into dominance over Egypt with the strength of his whole kingdom, now that he had taken away Judea. But why did he have professions of peace and enter an agreement with the king of the south, Ptolemy V Epiphanes? It was to get around the demands of jealous Rome. Ptolemy V was but five years old when becoming king. And when Antiochus III and King Philip V of Macedonia leagued against the boy king to take over his territories and split them between themselves, the guardians of Ptolemy V made a tragic mistake. They turned to Rome and placed him under the protection of that aggressive power. Rome gladly took advantage of extending its sphere of influence; and to protect Ptolemy V it felt it had the right to block Syrian Antiochus III, to keep him from becoming too great.

---

40. (a) Though the king of the north entered with the strength of his kingdom, yet why was it with the "professions of peace"? (b) How did he here run counter to Rome?

[41] Under compulsion of Rome, Antiochus III brought terms of peace to the king of the south. For a selfish reason he decided to make the young king his son-in-law. Instead of making an outright surrender of his conquered territories in obedience to Rome, he would make a nominal transfer of territory to King Ptolemy V by means of the "daughter of women," Cleopatra, the "daughter of his wife." In consideration of this political marriage she was to receive as dowry from her father the conquered provinces of Coele-Syria, Palestine (including the "beauteous land") and Phoenicia.*

[42] However, Antiochus III did not actually let these provinces pass over to his southern son-in-law by way of his daughter Cleopatra. In 196 B.C. Ptolemy V was declared of legal age and was crowned king of the south. In 193 B.C. his marriage to Cleopatra was performed. The intent of this political marriage was to "destroy it," or to bring Egypt to ruin, making it subject to Syria. But this scheme did not stand, and the advantage did not remain with Syrian King Antiochus III. In the difficulties that followed, Cleopatra took the side of her young husband rather than that of her Syrian father. In this way she frustrated the selfish designs of her father Antiochus III. When at last war broke out between her father and Rome, Egypt took the side of its protector, Rome.

[43] After marrying off his daughter Cleopatra for political advantage, Antiochus III met with reverses. Jehovah's angel had said in advance:

---

* See Josephus' *Antiquities of the Jews,* Book 12, Chapter 4, paragraph 1; and Polybius' Book 28, Chapter 17.

---

41. What were the terms of peace that he made with the king of the south, involving the "daughter of women"?
42. What was the purpose of this political marriage, but why did it not stand in his favor and the advantage not remain in his favor?
43. To what coastlands did he turn his face, and why?

"Then will he turn his face to the Coastlands and will capture many,—but a commander will bring to an end his reproach against himself, that his reproach return not unto him. Therefore will he turn his face towards the fortresses of his land,—but he shall stagger and fall and shall not be found." (Daniel 11:18, 19, *Ro*) The coastlands were those of Asia Minor and Greece and Macedonia. It happened that war broke out in Greece in 192 B.C. and King Antiochus III was induced to come to Greece. He landed there that year. He captured Chalcis, gained a foothold in Boeotia and tried to take over Thessaly but retreated before the Macedonian army.

[44] The following year Rome formally declared war on Antiochus III, who was then at Acarnania. He returned to Chalcis. At Thermopylae he met the Romans and suffered defeat. So he sailed back to Asia Minor to his capital at Ephesus. But now the Romans purposed to oust this king of the north from Asia. Battles at sea were fought. First the admiral of Antiochus III defeated the Roman fleet, but soon afterward his own admiral sustained a heavy defeat from the Roman fleet. Following this, Antiochus III abandoned Lysimachia on the Chersonese peninsula. By giving up Lysimachia he left the way open for the Romans to cross the Hellespont into Asia Minor.

[45] In 190 B.C. a decisive battle took place at Magnesia, near Ephesus, and Antiochus III with 80,000 men lost to the Roman "commander," Lucius Scipio Asiaticus. The king of the north was now willing to make peace with Rome. Commander Scipio instructed him to send envoys to Rome. In 189 B.C. the final peace arrangement was made. Antiochus III was required to disown everything in Asia Minor, everything west of the Taurus

---

44, 45. How did a "commander" bring his reproach by the king of the north to an end, and how was a domination established over the king of the north?

Mountains, as well as everything in Greece. He must pay 15,000 talents to Rome and 500 talents to her ally, Eumenes, king of Pergamum, who had helped in whipping Antiochus III at Magnesia. As a further reward King Eumenes received European territory and all the possessions of Antiochus III in Asia Minor as far as the Taurus Mountains. Rome thus established a domination over the Syrian king of the north. One of his sons, who became King Antiochus IV, lived as a boy at Rome as a hostage.

[46] After being driven from Greece and losing Asia Minor and practically all his fleet, Antiochus III turned his face back toward the strongholds of his own land. The Romans had turned back his reproach against themselves upon his own self. He was pressed to pay the big fine to Rome. In 187 B.C., while trying to rob the temple of Belus at Elymais in Persia, he was killed. He staggered and fell in death. He left two sons, Seleucus and Antiochus, to succeed him.

[47] Here the king of the north became Seleucus IV, surnamed Philopator ("Fond of His Father"). Despite the great losses that resulted from his father's defeat in the battle of Magnesia, at which he himself was present, Seleucus IV continued to be called "King of Asia." His son Demetrius felt the domination of Rome by serving as a hostage at Rome. Ptolemy V, the Egyptian brother-in-law to Seleucus IV by marriage to Cleopatra, tried to regain the lost provinces that should have come to him as Cleopatra's dowry. Poison stopped his preparations. He was succeeded by Ptolemy VI Philometor ("Fond of His Mother").

[48] The king of the north, Seleucus IV, needed money to pay on the heavy fine owed to Rome as

46. Toward what did he now turn his face, and how did he stagger and fall so as not to be found?
47. Who became the new king of the north, and what did he still continue to be called?
48. How did this king of the north come to fall and not be found, and who succeeded him?

one of the penalties from his father's defeat at
Magnesia. Wealth was said to be stored up in Jerusalem's rebuilt temple or sanctuary. Onias III
was the Jewish high priest at the time. To get
his hands on money, Seleucus IV sent his treas-
urer Heliodorus to plunder Jehovah's temple.
Heliodorus himself wanted to ascend the Syrian
throne as king of the north. So he murdered Seleucus IV. But Eumenes and Attalus, the kings of
Pergamum, blocked the murderous Heliodorus and
had the brother of the murdered king placed upon
the throne to become Antíochus IV.

⁴⁹ For fourteen years the new king had lived at
Rome as a hostage. He reigned for about twelve
years (175-163 B.C.) and was surnamed Epíphanes. This is a shortening of the title that Antíochus IV gave himself on coins that he had struck,
namely, *Theós Epiphanés.* This name means "God
Manifest," that is, the god that appears or reveals
himself. The Egyptians translated this inscription
as "God who comes forth," that is, coming forth
like the blazing sun, Horus, on the eastern horizon.
The Egyptians thus identified King Antíochus IV
Epíphanes with the triumphal, appearing god.

⁵⁰ He tried to show himself mightier than Jehovah God. He tried to Grecize or Hellenize Judea
and Jerusalem. He put High Priest Onias III out
of office. For a bribe he put the high priest's
brother Jesus into that high office, in order to
further the Hellenizing of the Jews. He went to
the extreme of trying to eradicate the Jewish religion, the worship of Jehovah God. In defiance
of their God he rededicated the temple that had
been built by Governor Zerubbabel and assigned
it to the Olympian Zeus or Jupiter. The rededicated temple's high priest was Jesus, who Grecized
his name to Jason. On Chislev 15 of the year 145

49. What surname did the king of the north now assume, and
what was this interpreted to mean?
50. How did Antíochus IV Epíphanes try to show himself mightier
than Jehovah God?

of the Seleucid era, or in December, 168 B.C., a
pagan altar was erected on top of the great altar
of Jehovah in the temple courtyard where Jehovah's daily burnt offering used to be offered. Ten
days later, or Chislev 25, a sacrifice was offered
on the pagan altar for the first time. (1 Maccabees 1:54-59) It was offered to Zeus of Mount
Olympus in Greece.*

* See also Josephus' *Antiquities of the Jews*, Book 12,
Chapter 5, paragraph 4; also 2 Maccabees 6:2.

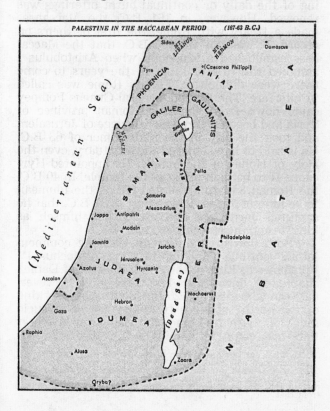

PALESTINE IN THE MACCABEAN PERIOD   (167-63 B.C.)

⁵¹ This desecration of the sanctuary of Jehovah led to the Jewish uprising under the leadership of the Maccabees in 167 B.C. For three years Antiochus IV Epiphanes waged a bitter war against them and proved himself no god in comparison with Jehovah. In 165 B.C., on the exact anniversary of the desecration of the sanctuary, Judas Maccabeus, the leader, rededicated the temple to Jehovah and the festival of dedication (Hanukkah) was established. (John 10:22) The sacrificing of the daily or continual burnt offerings was renewed. However, in 161 B.C. the Maccabees made a treaty with Rome, the first of theirs on record. It was not till 104 B.C. that the Maccabees established a kingdom, when Aristobulus I assumed the title of king. In the years to come there were difficulties. Finally Rome was called to interfere. The Roman General Gnaeus Pompey came down from the now Roman province of Syria and began a three-month siege of Jerusalem and took the city in the midsummer of 63 B.C. He is said to have entered the sanctuary, even the Holy of Holies of the temple. He appointed Hyrcanus II to be high priest at the temple. In 40 B.C. the Roman Senate appointed Herod the Idumean to be king of Judea. It was first in 37 B.C. that he captured Jerusalem and established himself as king, to end the Maccabean rule.

⁵² Both Jewish and Roman Catholic commentators continue applying to King Antiochus IV Epiphanes as king of the north the rest of Daniel, chapter 11, down to its last verse (45). However, between verses 19 and 20 the identity of the "king of the north" changes from the line of Seleucid kings of Syria to Rome, the rising world power that had come to dominate the affairs of the

51. To what did this desecration of the temple lead, and how did the Maccabean rule finally come to an end?
52. How do Jewish and Catholic commentators apply the rest of Daniel, chapter 11, but who, and by what prophecy, makes it certain that the identity of the king of the north must change from that?

Middle East. It is evident that the identity of the king of the north does not stay the same down to Daniel 11:45, for Jesus Christ referred to Daniel, chapter 11, to show that the identity must change and become very modern, even as modern as our twentieth century. Jesus gave a marvelous prophecy on the "time of the end" of this world and quoted from Daniel 11:31. This prophecy was given in the spring of 33 (A.D.), or 195 years after Antiochus IV died in 163 B.C.

[53] Jesus said to his questioning apostles: "Therefore, when you catch sight of the disgusting thing that causes desolation, as spoken of through Daniel the prophet, standing in a holy place, (let the reader use discernment,) then let those in Judea begin fleeing to the mountains. . . . for then there will be great tribulation such as has not occurred since the world's beginning until now, no, nor will occur again." (Matthew 24:15-21) Jesus was looking beyond his own day for Daniel 11:31 to be fulfilled, not back to the days of the Syrian Antiochus IV Epiphanes. At the historical fulfillment of Daniel 11:31 the king of the north is not Syrian or Seleucid. Hence after Daniel 11:19 a change in person and nationality of the king of the north must occur. Historical facts establish that the change began in the next verse, Daniel 11:20. The king now becomes Roman.

[54] Already before Antiochus IV Epiphanes, Rome was taking a dominant role in the affairs of the Middle East and dictating to Syria. Even this so-called "God Manifest" bowed to dictation from Rome. In his war with Egypt, Antiochus IV won. He had himself crowned as king of Egypt. Then the Roman fleet brought its ambassador Caius Popilius Laenas with the orders of the Roman

53. In his prophecy, which way did Jesus look for the fulfillment of Daniel 11:31, and so of what nationality did the king of the north now become?
54. How did Antiochus IV Epiphanes bow to dictation from Rome, and how did Syria finally become a Roman province, to mark definitely what change in the king of the north?

Senate that Antiochus IV renounce his kingship of Egypt and quit the country. The Syrian king did so, but kept his hold on Coele-Syria, Palestine and Phoenicia. In 163 B.C. he died as a temple looter in Persia. After him there were many more independent kings of the Seleucid dynasty in Syria. But in 65 B.C. the Roman General Pompey the Great dethroned the last one, Antiochus XIII Asiaticus; and in 64 B.C. Syria became a Roman province. There definitely Rome took up the role of the king of the north. Before this king of the north Jerusalem fell in 63 B.C. The Egyptian king of the south was powerless to prevent it.

[55] The Ptolemaic dynasty down in Egypt held the position of king of the south somewhat longer. In 31 B.C. the decisive battle of Actium was fought, in which Egypt's Queen Cleopatra deserted the fleet of her Roman lover, Antony, to his defeat. The victor, Octavius, the grandnephew of Julius Caesar, then proceeded to the conquest of Egypt. In 30 B.C. Cleopatra committed suicide, and Egypt became a Roman province, subject to the new king of the north.

THE "PRINCE OF THE COVENANT" BROKEN

[56] In the battle for power Octavius finally came forth as the sole ruler of Rome and became the first Roman emperor. He turned down the titles of *rex* ("king") and *dictator*. Finally, in 27 B.C., by decree of the Roman Senate, he was styled Augustus. The Greeks translated this title as *Sebastós*, which means "Reverend One." (Acts 25: 21, 25) To his acting as king of the north in place of the Seleucid dynasty of Syrian kings, Jehovah's angel refers in continuing the long-range prophecy on the contest between the north and the south: "Then shall stand up in his place one that shall

---

55. How long did the Ptolemaic dynasty last, and what did Egypt become?
56. Who became the first Roman emperor, and what does Daniel 11:20 say regarding him?

cause an exactor to pass through the glory of the kingdom; but within few days he shall be destroyed, neither in anger, nor in battle." (Daniel 11:20, *JPS*) The "glory of the kingdom" of Augustus Caesar included the "beauteous land" of Daniel's people.—Daniel 11:16, *JPS*.

[57] The sending of the "exactor" took place in the year 2 B.C. The Christian historian Luke made record of this particular event in these words: "Now in those days a decree went forth from Caesar Augustus for all the inhabited earth to be registered; (this first registration took place when Quirinius was governor of Syria;) and all people went traveling to be registered, each one to his own city. Of course, Joseph also went up from Galilee, out of the city of Nazareth, into Judea, to David's city which is called Bethlehem, because of his being a member of the house and family of David, to get registered with Mary, who had been given him in marriage as promised, at present heavy with child. While they were there, the days came to the full for her to give birth. And she gave birth to her son, the firstborn, and she bound him with cloth bands and laid him in a manger, because there was no place for them in the lodging-room."—Luke 2:1-7.

[58] P. Sulpicius Quirinius, Roman senator, was the Roman governor of Syria twice, the first time about the death of King Herod the Great, who had reconstructed the temple at Jerusalem. This period of governorship was from 750 to 753 from the founding of Rome, or from 4 to 1 B.C.* The

* See Zumpt's *Commentat. epigraph.*, II, 86-104; *De Syria romana provincia*, 97, 98; and Mommsen's *Res gestae divi Augusti*. Also *Dictionary of the New Testament* in the French Bible translation by Canon A. Crampon, 1939 edition, page 358. Compare also Werner

57. When was this "exactor" made to pass "through the glory of the kingdom," and what record does Luke make of this?
58. When was this Quirinius governor of Syria, and why was this registration one of the most important events of Augustus' reign, deserving of mention in Daniel's prophecy?

census or registration was not for merely learning
the number of the population but for the purpose
of taxation and conscription of men for military
service. This particular census was one of the
most important events that occurred during the
rule of Caesar Augustus as king of the north. It
served to maneuver the carpenter of Nazareth
and his wife Mary into going to Bethlehem, that
Jesus might be born there in fulfillment of Micah
5:2. (Matthew 2:1-11) With good reason, then,
Jehovah's angel included the important mention
of this in the vision to Daniel, so as to aid us also
in determining when the prophetic "king of the
north" changed from Syrian kings of the fifth
world power to Roman rulers of the sixth world
power.

[59] Caesar Augustus set up the emperor's bodyguard known as the Praetorian Guards, which was
later enlarged by his successor. He died in the
forty-fifth year of his reign, on August 19, A.D.
14. This was comparatively a "few days" after
his having the important registration taken during which Jesus the Son of God was born at the
city of King David as his royal heir. Like an actor
in a theater, Augustus had ruled well; and he was
numbered among the Roman gods, and temples
and altars were erected in his honor.

[60] The angelic prophecy showed that Augustus'
successor also would have a close connection with

Keller's *The Bible as History*, 1956 edition, pages 326,
327, which tells that, according to a fragment of a
Roman inscription discovered in Antioch, Syria, Quirinius had been Emperor Augustus' legate in Syria in the
days of Saturninus the proconsul before the Christian
era, and how Quirinius had set up his seat of government and his military headquarters in Syria at that
time.

---

59. How was he, as king of the north, "destroyed, neither in
anger, nor in battle"? And within a "few days"?
60, 61. (a) Who was the "contemptible person" that then stood up,
and how did he become related to Caesar Augustus? (b) How had
the "majesty of the kingdom" not been conferred upon him?

the earthly life of God's only-begotten Son: "And in his place shall stand up a contemptible person, upon whom had not been conferred the majesty of the kingdom; but he shall come in time of security, and shall obtain the kingdom by blandishments [flatteries, *RS*]. And the arms of the flood shall be swept away from before him, and shall be broken; yea, also the prince of the covenant." (Daniel 11:21, 22, *JPS*) The mysterious "contemptible person" here was Tiberius Caesar, the son of Livia. She became the third wife of Emperor Augustus; so naturally Tiberius became the stepson of the emperor. Caesar Augustus did not want Tiberius to be his successor, for he hated this stepson because of his bad qualities. It was not willingly that the "majesty of the kingdom" was at last bestowed upon Tiberius. Augustus was forced to accept Tiberius as his successor to the emperorship only after every other hope had failed. How was that?

[61] Emperor Augustus had no sons. His sister had a son Marcellus, but this nephew died. His daughter had two sons, Gaius and Lucius, and these Augustus appointed to be his successors. These also Augustus lost by death. He loved his dear stepson, Drusus, the younger brother of Tiberius, but this loved one died early, on September 14, 9 B.C. This left Tiberius, who was a capable general, in the position of the top-ranking soldier of the Roman Empire. It was in the year 12 B.C. that Agrippa, the great general of Emperor Augustus, died at the age of fifty-one years. In view of this Livia, the mother of Tiberius, induced the emperor, with great difficulty, however, to replace the dead Agrippa by her son Tiberius. To replace Agrippa, though, it required Tiberius to become the son-in-law of the emperor. So to his great grief, Tiberius was compelled to exchange Agrippina, the daughter of General Agrippa, for the emperor's daughter Julia. In the year 4 (A.D.)

Emperor Augustus adopted Tiberius and Agrippa Postumus. Nine years later, by a special law, Tiberius was raised to the coregency with Emperor Augustus. The next year, on August 19, A.D. 14, Augustus died, and Tiberius was made emperor. This is how this "contemptible person" came to "stand up" or assume power in the place of unwilling Caesar Augustus.

[62] As to the part that blandishments or flatteries played with the new king of the north, Tiberius, *The Encyclopœdia Britannica*, Volume 26, page 916 (eleventh edition), says: "Historians of Rome in ancient times remembered Tiberius chiefly as the sovereign under whose rule prosecutions for treason on slight pretexts first became rife, and the hateful race of informers was first allowed to fatten on the gains of judicial murder. . . . But the history of the state trials of Tiberius' reign shows conclusively that the straining of the law proceeded in the first instance from the eager flattery of the senate, . . . and was by him acquiesced in at the end of his reign, with a sort of contemptuous indifference, till he developed, under the influence of his fears, a readiness to shed blood."*

[63] At the time that Tiberius became king of the north his nephew Germanicus Caesar was commander of the Roman troops on the Rhine River. Soon after Tiberius' enthronement a dangerous mutiny broke out among these troops, but Germanicus kept the discontented legions from marching upon Rome. In 15 (A.D.) Germanicus led his troops against the German hero Arminius (Hermann) and put him on the run, even capturing

---

* See also *The Eighteen Christian Centuries*, by James White (1884), pages 18, 19; and *Thy Kingdom Come*, by C. T. Russell (1891), page 30, paragraphs 1, 2.

62. How did Tiberius Caesar "obtain the kingdom by blandishments"?
63. How were the "arms of the flood" then "swept away from before him"?

his wife Thusnelda, and defeating him the following year. Finally the foreign policy, or the policy with regard to the Roman frontier, became one of peace and met with fair success. "With few exceptions the duties of the Roman forces on the borders were confined to watching the peoples on the other side while they destroyed each other."* In this way the "arms of the flood" were held in check or were "swept away from before him" and were "broken."

[64] Even the "prince of the covenant" was broken in death. This was not any Jewish high priest, whom the Roman political representatives had put into office. It was the Leader of the covenant that Jehovah God had made with Abraham for blessing all the families and nations of the earth. It was the Seed of Abraham promised in this covenant. It was Jesus Christ. On Passover day, Nisan 14, of the year 33 (A.D.) Jesus stood in the governor's palace (the Praetorium) in Jerusalem, before Pontius Pilate, who represented Tiberius Caesar and before whom the Jewish priests charged Jesus with treason against the emperor. Jesus said to the Roman governor: "My kingdom is no part of this world. . . . my kingdom is not from this source." In order that the Roman governor might not release the faultless Jesus, the Jews shouted to Pilate: "If you release this man, you are not a friend of Caesar. Every man making himself a king speaks against Caesar. . . . We have no king but Caesar." Then, according to the recent law of *laesa majestas* ("injured majesty"), the Roman governor handed Jesus over to be "broken," impaled on a torture stake.—John 18: 36; 19:12-16; Mark 15:14-18.

* *The Encyclopædia Britannica,* Volume 26, page 915, paragraphs 2, 3.

64. How was also the "prince of the covenant" then "broken" before him?

[65] Yes, because of being very suspicious, Emperor Tiberius had extended the law of *laesa majestas* to include offenses against his own person and he also encouraged the informer system (delation). The land became like a police state and the latter part of his imperial rule became one of terror. The Roman author Pliny the Elder called Tiberius the "gloomiest of men." Because he was so reserved, uncommunicative and retiring, the people could not understand him, and this made him unpopular.

[66] Still speaking in advance about Tiberius, the angel said to Daniel: "And after the league made with him he shall work deceitfully; and he shall come up and become strong, with a little nation." (Daniel 11:23, *JPS*) Tiberius was constitutionally in league with the Roman Senate; he depended upon them formally, according to the constitution. Actually, though, he depended upon the "little nation." Which "nation"? The Praetorian Guards, which had been formed by Caesar Augustus in 13 B.C. as Imperial Lifeguards, like the bodyguard around the person of the commander in chief of a Roman army. Up till now this imperial guard had been seen only near Rome in small detachments. Tiberius changed this. On the advice of his favorite, Sejanus, the commander of the Praetorian Guards, Tiberius had these Guards encamp permanently in full force close to the city walls. By this arrangement he held in check any unruliness of the people. This attached great importance to the commander of the Guards. The Guards came to enjoy special privileges and in time became so powerful that they were able to put emperors in office or to dethrone them, according to their will. By means of the Guards, just about 10,000 strong, Emperor Tiberius kept strong. With-

---

65. Why was the law of *laesa majestas* established, and what made Tiberius Caesar unpopular?
66. With whom was Tiberius Caesar in league, and to what extent, and how did he become strong "with a little nation"?

out much trouble, any risings within the Roman domain against his authority were put down. He almost completely abolished the popular assemblies known as the *comitia*.

[67] "In quiet and into the fattest portion of the province will he enter; and he will do what his fathers have not done, nor his fathers' fathers: the prey, and spoil, and riches will he divide freely to them, and against the strong-holds will he devise his plans, but only till a certain time." (Daniel 11:24, *Le*) This is what Tiberius did by the way he expressed his suspicions, largely under the influence of Sejanus, commander of the Praetorian Guards, till finally Sejanus himself fell under suspicion and was killed.

[68] Ceaselessly Emperor Tiberius expended great care on the Roman provinces. At his death he left all the peoples subject to the empire in a condition of prosperity that they had not known under Augustus or previously and did not know again. Because of strict government economies, taxes were light and Tiberius was able to show generosity when times were exceptionally bad anywhere. If representatives of the empire, whether soldiers, governors or other officials, oppressed anyone below them and promoted any sort of irregularity in handling matters, they could be sure of imperial vengeance. A firm grip on power kept up the public security and quiet both in Italy and in foreign lands. The improvement in the communications system helped along commerce. With what were considered the sterner Roman virtues, the emperor saw to it that affairs were administered fairly and steadily both inside and outside Rome. In many respects the laws were improved, and social and moral relations were safeguarded by holding on to and furthering the reforms insti-

---

67, 68. How did he enter into the fattest portion of the province, doing what his fathers and fathers' fathers had not done, yet how did he die?

tuted by Caesar Augustus. However, the Roman
historian Tacitus describes the personality of Tiberius as "one of studied dissimulation and hypocrisy from the beginning." He was considered
a tyrant, and after his death, in the latter half
of March, A.D. 37, he was not honored with any
deification. A "contemptible person"!

[69] Tiberius was succeeded by Gaius Caesar, commonly called Caligula, who, in turn, was succeeded
by his uncle, Claudius, in 41 (A.D.). Besides what
Tiberius, as king of the north, had done for the
improvement of the Roman Empire, Claudius saw
to the further development of the empire along
the lines that Augustus had in mind. Says one
authority: "Client-states were absorbed, southern
Britain was conquered, the Romanization of the
West received powerful impulse, public works were
executed in Rome and Italy, and the organization
of the imperial bureaucracy made rapid strides."[*]
Says a history: "An important extension of the
state was made under Claudius, who sent a successful expedition into Britain in A.D. 43 and
added the southern portion of the island as the
province of Britannia. Later the British frontier
was pushed farther northward and secured by a
line of defenses. Trajan (A.D. 98-117) . . . ambitious to build a great oriental empire, entered
upon a war of aggression in which he defeated
the Parthians in Persia and added Armenia, Mesopotamia and Assyria to the empire as provinces.
This represents the expansion of Rome to its
greatest extent, but these conquests by Trajan in
the East were abandoned by his successor."[†]

---

[*] *The Encyclopædia Britannica*, Volume 23, page 651b.
[†] *On the Road to Civilization,* by Heckel and Sigman
(1937), page 198, paragraph 1.

---

69. How did the king of the north, in Claudius, develop the empire still further, and under which emperor did it attain its
greatest expansion?

[70] Continuing his preview of the activities of the prophetic king of the north, Jehovah's angel told Daniel: "And he will then stir up his power and his courage [heart] against the king of the south with a great army: and the king of the south will prepare himself for the war with an exceedingly great and mighty army; but he will not stand; for they will devise evil plans against him. Yea, they that eat of his food will bring his downfall, and the army of the other will overflow; and many will fall down slain." (Daniel 11:25, 26, *Le*) With this verse the king of the north has become Emperor Aurelian (A.D. 270-275). One of his great problems was Queen Septimia Zenobia, of Palmyra in the Syrian desert. An ancient city, Palmyra was favored in its growth by the wars between the Romans and the Parthians in Persia. When Emperor Hadrian visited the town about A.D. 130 he named it Adrianopolis. It became a Roman colony and an important military post. The wars with Persia brought Palmyra to political importance for a time and it became for a few years the mistress of the Roman East. It became a danger to Rome, because of the ambitions of Queen Zenobia. Her native name was Bath Zabbai. Her husband, King Odaenathus, was the supreme commander of the East. After he died (A.D. 266-267), Zenobia planned to lift her position higher than his by making Palmyra the dominant city of the Roman Empire in the East. Already skilled at government administration, she took over the reins of government entirely.

[71] Her general-in-chief was Zabdā, a kinsman of her husband, and under him the Palmyrene army occupied Egypt A.D. 270 under the pretext of making it secure to Rome, for there were pre-

---

70. With Daniel 11:25, who does the king of the north become, and during his reign whose ambitions became a danger to the empire?
71. How did she, with her son, come to occupy the position of king of the south toward the Roman Empire?

tenders that disputed the Roman emperor's authority along the Nile River. Zenobia directed this conquest, and her son governed Egypt with the title of king, whereas his mother was titled queen. Garrisons of Palmyrene troops were established in Asia Minor as far west as Ancyra (now Turkish Ankara) and even opposite European Byzantium. Zenobia came to be called Augusta or empress. When Aurelian became the Roman emperor in 270 (A.D.) he became king of the north. He soon appreciated that the ambitious policy of Queen Zenobia was putting the unity of the Roman Empire in danger. In his second year the breach between him and Queen Zenobia occurred. Zenobia was now faced with an invasion by the king of the north, to whom she held the position of king of the south. She had gained worldly greatness by uniting the desert Arabs with the Egyptians. Besides Mesopotamia and part of Asia Minor, she held Egypt as well as Syria. She could rely on the Arabs and the Armenians, but not too strongly on the loyalty of the Syrians.

[72] It required Emperor Aurelian to stir up his power and his heart to proceed against this warlike queen of Egypt and Syria. For her part, she had to prepare herself for war with the king of the north by an exceedingly great and mighty army under her two generals Zabdā and Zabbai. Aurelian first recovered Egypt for himself by Probus. Then he got ready for a big expedition into Asia Minor and Syria. Zenobia with her two generals was defeated at Emesa (now Homs) and retreated to Palmyra. Although this city was bulwarked by the desert, Aurelian finally formed and kept up a siege of the strongly fortified and well-provisioned city. Under the siege the courage of Zenobia cracked. She and her son got out of the

---

72. What did the king of the north have to stir up, and how did the king of the south have to prepare himself, and how did the contest result?

city and fled toward Persia for help. The Romans captured them on the bank of the Euphrates River. The besieged Palmyrenes lost heart and surrendered their city, A.D. 272. Aurelian spared the life of Zenobia and took her to Rome to be his prize feature in his great triumphal march through the imperial capital A.D. 274.* After that she was permitted to spend the rest of her life as a Roman matron.

[73] Not only had Queen Zenobia in the role of king of the south not stood before the armed might of Rome, but even her conqueror, Emperor Aurelian, did not stand against conspirators. The Roman Senate rightly conferred upon him the title Restorer of the Roman Empire. He was the first Roman emperor to wear the diadem, and on medals he was entitled Lord and God. Toward the end of his triumphal year he set out on an expedition against the Persians. While waiting in Thrace for the opportunity to cross the straits into Asia Minor, those who ate his food carried out their evil plans against him and broke him. He was going to call his secretary Eros to account for certain irregularities. Eros incited certain officers to conspire against the emperor by forging a list of men who were marked out for death and including these officers. The sight of this list moved them to devise his assassination.

[74] The career of the king of the north did not end with Emperor Aurelian. Other emperors followed him, and for a time there were an emperor of the west and an emperor of the east, within the one empire. Under these the army of the king of the north was swept away and many fell down

* See *Thy Kingdom Come*, by C. T. Russell (1891), pages 33, 34.

73. How was it that the king of the north did not stand, those who ate of his food bringing about his downfall?
74. As regards the further representation of the king of the north, how did the "army of the other" overflow, so that many fell down slain?

slain, as prophesied, due to the invasions of barbarians from the north. These invasions were thrown back until the fourth century, when the barbarians successfully broke through. The Goths or Germans found out that the armed legions of Rome were invincible no more. Now that they had broken the Roman frontiers, invasion followed invasion. By the beginning of the sixth century they had shattered the Roman Empire in the West, and German kings bore rule in Italy, Britain, Gaul, Spain and North Africa. In the eastern part of the empire, Constantinople (Byzantium) had failed to fall before the threatening Attila the Hun, who then went west.

[75] Emperor Constantine (324-337) gave state recognition to the popular form of Christianity and even presided over the Council of Nice in Nicomedia, Asia Minor, less than a hundred miles from Byzantium, A.D. 325. Later he moved the imperial residence from Rome to Byzantium. There, on May 11, A.D. 330, he founded the new imperial capital and dedicated it as New Rome or Constantinople. But there was still one Roman Empire. On the death of the later emperor, Theodosius, January 17, 395, the empire was finally divided between his sons, Honorius receiving the western section and Arcadius the eastern, with his capital at Constantinople. Egypt fell to the lot of Constantinople and became a province of the eastern division of the Roman Empire. In 641 (A.D.), when Heraclius was the emperor of the East, the Egyptian capital, Alexandria, fell to the Mohammedan Saracens and Egypt became a province of the caliphs or successors of Mohammed. Long afterward, in 1516-1517, Egypt became a Turkish province, governed by a pasha. When World War I broke out in 1914, Egypt belonged to Turkey and

---

75. How did the Roman Empire finally become divided into two parts, with two emperors, and how did Egypt eventually come under British domination?

was ruled by a *khediv* or viceroy. Because of siding with the Germans, the Khedive Abbas Pasha was deposed on December 18 that year, and Egypt was declared a British Protectorate, particularly with a view to protect the Suez Canal.

[76] Constantine P. XII was the last emperor of the East, ascending the throne in 1448. The Mohammedans had repeatedly tried to capture Constantinople. After centuries of attempts they at last succeeded. It was besieged fifty-three days by Turkish Sultan Mahomet (Mohammed) II and was taken on May 29, 1453. With its capture the Eastern Roman Empire definitely ended.

[77] In the western part of the Roman Empire a new religious political figure arose in the Catholic bishop of Rome, particularly with Pope Leo I, the Great, who is noted as the real founder of the papacy in the fifth century. In course of time the pope took it upon himself to crown the emperor of the Western Roman Empire. This occurred when Pope Leo III crowned Frankish King Charles (Charlemagne) on Christmas Day, A.D. 800, at Rome, as emperor of the Western Roman Empire. Pope Leo III said: "To Charles the Augustus, crowned by God, great and pacific emperor, life and victory." So from then on the political ruler was supposed to rule "by the grace of God." However, says one recent history: "The coronation of Charlemagne was a usurpation, for the government at Constantinople was still the legal governing authority in the Empire."* This was true even though at the time a woman usurper, Empress Irene (780-802), sat on the throne at Constantinople. From this point forward it is proper to speak of the Eastern Empire and the Western

---

* *On the Road to Civilization,* by Heckel and Sigman, page 275, paragraph 3.

76. When and how was the Eastern Roman Empire ended?
77. In what line of bishops did a new political religious figure arise, and when did it become proper to speak of an Eastern Empire and a Western Empire?

Empire, both claiming to be Christian. Charlemagne added a second head to the eagle in his insignia, to denote that the Empires of Rome and of Germany were united.

[78] In 911 (A.D.) the emperorship of the West became elective. Five centuries later it was obtained by the members of the house of Hapsburg of Austria, and was held by them till 1806, when the Holy Roman Empire was dissolved. The German Empire received this title during the reign of Otho (Otto) the Great. In 961 he was crowned as king of Italy; and on February 2, 962, Pope John XII crowned him at Rome as Otho I, emperor of the Holy Roman Empire. It came to be known as the Holy Roman Empire of the German Nation. It had its capital in Germany, and the emperors and most of their subjects were Germans. So under Otho I Germany and Italy were brought into close relationship, but with Germany on top, for Italy was treated finally as a conquered province. Napoleon Bonaparte was the one that brought the Holy Roman Empire to its end in 1806. When he, as emperor of the French, refused to recognize the Holy Roman Empire as existing, Emperor Francis II released the Germanic states from their allegiance to the Holy Roman Empire. He resigned from the Roman Imperial dignity and withdrew to his national government as emperor of Austria. Thus after 1,006 years the Holy Roman Empire, which had been founded by the Roman Catholic pope and by Frankish Charlemagne, came to an inglorious end. It had proved to be no millennial kingdom of God.

[79] In 1870 Italy was established as a kingdom independent of the Roman popes of the Vatican.

---

78. When emperorship of the West became elective, to whom did it finally come, to remain till the end, and how was the Holy Roman Empire of the German Nation established and brought to an end?

79. When was the new German Empire established, and what triple alliance was formed?

In the next year the new Germanic Empire was begun, with William I being declared Caesar or Kaiser. The modern king of the north was becoming identifiable. In time Germany and Austria-Hungary and Italy entered into an alliance, in which the outbreak of World War I found them.

[80] Great Britain took on imperial power in the beginning of the seventeenth century and rose to the position of the seventh world power of Bible history, it being joined in this position by the United States of America to form the Anglo-American dual world power. During Britain's war with Napoleon Bonaparte the British army drove the French out of Egypt, the whole of which the French had conquered in 1798. Although Egypt came again under the overlordship of Turkey, the British government virtually controlled Egypt since 1882. Egypt was in fact a British dependency, although under its native khedive, for the British army stayed in Egypt and the British will was really the law. Then in 1914, because the Egyptian khedive sided with Turkey, which had joined Germany in the first world war, the British took over in Egypt, deposed the khedive and declared Egypt a British Protectorate. Thus democratic Britain and America became opponents of the prophetic king of the north, and together they came into the position of the king of the south.

[81] From this standpoint, the rest of the historical preview that Jehovah's angel brought to Daniel in the third year of Cyrus the Great of Persia takes on a gripping meaning for us in this "appointed time of the end" of this old world.—Daniel 8:19, *JPS; RS.*

---

80. How did the seventh world power come into existence, and when particularly did it come into the position of king of the south?
81. From this standpoint, what does the rest of Daniel's prophecy take on for us?

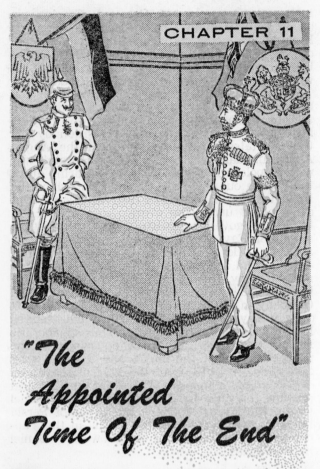

CHAPTER 11

"The Appointed Time Of The End"

IN THE "appointed time of the end" the warfare cold and hot between the king of the north and the king of the south has threatened modern man-made civilization with ruin. The two kings have carried on their deceptive diplomacy and their warfare not only without regard for the best interests of mankind but also without respect for the kingdom of God, the rightful government of all the earth. Bringing the long-range prophecy down to our times, God's angel said to the prophet Daniel: "And as for both these kings, their heart is bent on mischief, and at one table will they speak lies; but it shall not prosper; for the end is yet for the time appointed."—Daniel 11:27, *Le; JPS.*

[2] Shortly after the re-establishment of the German Empire on January 1, 1871, the interests of this king of the north began to clash with those of the modern king of the south, the Anglo-American dual world power. The Germanic king of the north was the most lively and mighty champion of the former sixth world power of Rome. When the German parliament opened in October of 1871, Emperor William I voiced the conviction that "the new German Empire will be a reliable shield of peace." Did this prove to be the truth or a lie?

[3] The king of the north and the king of the south were seated "at one table," having mutual contacts and expressing friendliness. But their hearts were bent on mischief, if not toward each other, then certainly toward the promised, prayed-for kingdom of God. The two kings claimed to rule "by the grace of God" and to rule by divine right as the "higher powers" that were "ordained by God." (Romans 13:1, *AV; Luther*) The king of the south already held world empire, the greatest that the world had known till then. It resented

1. In this "appointed time of the end," what has the warfare between the king of the north and the king of the south threatened, and why?

2. From 1871 onward, what interests began to clash, and yet what conviction concerning peace was voiced?

3. In what way were the hearts of these two kings "bent on mischief"?

the rising power of the new German Reich or Empire.

⁴ In 1888 the grandson of William I came to the German imperial throne as William II, commonly called Kaiser Wilhelm. Says one authority: "He was a firm believer in the divine right of kings and of kaisers in particular. On numerous occasions he spoke of himself as 'the instrument of the Lord,' and took such excessive interest in the army, . . . But his selfish ambition had no bounds. It is now generally conceded that almost from the first day of his reign he began to plan for world domination; that he . . . resolved that he, William, would show the world that one man could raise himself to the topmost pinnacle and not only rule Germany, but through Germany might rule the civilized earth."* "He declared that he owed his 'awful responsibility toward the Creator alone, wherefrom no man, no minister, no parliament, no people can relieve the sovereign.' . . . "† He built up a powerful, well-trained army in which he had great confidence: he also developed a mighty navy, including many *untersee* boats or submarines; he launched out on great commercial and colonial expansion of the German Reich. He extended the Reich's influence to Turkey and Asia Minor, seeking a direct railroad route to the Persian Gulf. He built up German interests in the Far East, Africa and South America. Mischief afoot!

⁵ Both kings became members of the Hague Court of International Arbitration. So presumably they were for peace between themselves and other nations, but hardly for "peace with God" or peace with his coming kingdom. What else could be

---

* *The Encyclopedia Americana,* Volume 29, page 333b.
† *Ibidem,* Volume 12, page 520b.

4. Evidently for what did Kaiser Wilhelm II plan, and what moves did he make to that end?
5. At what "one table" were the two kings seated, and what did they speak there?

expected but that they should "speak lies" diplomatically "at one table"? Not at the "table of Jehovah," which is a table of truth, but at the "table of demons," which is the table of "teachings of demons." (1 Corinthians 10:20, 21; 1 Timothy 4:1, 2, *NW; RS;* Malachi 1:7, 12, *AS*) However, this lying course of speech and conduct toward each other and toward Jehovah God and his Christ did not prosper into a peaceful world or toward any willing submission to the oncoming kingdom of God and of his Christ. It did not prosper for their perpetually holding on to political, commercial and military power, because the end of both "kings" is "yet for the time appointed" by Jehovah God.

⁶ Having the king of the north in mind, Jehovah's angel said to Daniel: "Then will he return into his land with great riches, and his heart will be against the holy covenant: and he will do it, and return to his own land." (Daniel 11:28, *Le*) Kaiser Wilhelm returned to the land or earthly condition of the ancient king of the north by building up an absolutist imperial form of rule, for increasing the German Reich and extending its influence to all quarters. By this course "great riches" in many ways resulted to imperial Germany. He made Germany the chief part in a Triple Alliance or *Dreibund* made up of Austria-Hungary, Italy and Germany, with the favor of the pope of the Vatican. To quote an authority:

⁷ "Notably in maintaining the Triple Alliance, the emperor followed the policy of [Chancellor] Bismarck. . . . Bismarck's [anti-Catholic] *kulturkampf* legacy William sagaciously disposed of through concessions which he turned to profit by making an implicit alliance of the Vatican and

---

6, 7. (a) How did the king of the north now "return into his land with great riches"? (b) The favor of what religious potentate did he win?

the German schools in his anti-revolutionary policies and by remodeling the schools themselves."*

[8] Since not only Italy but also Austria-Hungary was Roman Catholic and intimate with the Vatican pope, it was only to be expected that the pope would favor the Triple Alliance (*Dreibund*) against the king of the south and his Triple Entente of Protestant Britain, republican France and Russian Orthodox Czarist Russia.

[9] In the early days of the revived German Empire, in fact, from 1877 onward, Jehovah's dedicated people of his "sanctuary" class were openly declaring in their publications that the Gentile times or "appointed times of the nations" would end in 1914. In that year the kingdom of God was to be fully established in the heavens to see that His will should be done on earth. This was in harmony with Jehovah's covenant with King David for an everlasting Kingdom in the hands of his permanent Heir, Jesus Christ. (2 Samuel 7:12-16; Psalm 89:28-37; Luke 22:28, 29) Kaiser Wilhelm as well as the other worldly rulers treated the message of Jehovah's sanctuary class concerning the end of the Gentile times in 1914 with contempt. Yet the Watch Tower Bible & Tract Society had had a vigorous branch office in Barmen-Elberfeld, Germany, since 1903. Undeniably the heart of the Germanic king of the north was against the holy Kingdom covenant of Jehovah God. The Kaiser's plans were not for handing over the imperial sovereignty to Jesus Christ at his heavenly enthronement in 1914, the Kaiser thus to acknowledge him as the rightful Heir of the kingdom over all the earth. So he "did it" or acted with effect and returned to his own schemes of an earth dominated by the German Kaiser. By

---

* *The Encyclopedia Americana*, Volume 29, page 333a.

8. Which did the pope favor, the Triple Alliance or the Triple Entente, and why?
9. How was this king of the north at heart "against the holy covenant"?

commercial rivalry and military build-up he sowed the seeds for hot war, World War I.

[10] The question of world domination was becoming a sizzling one. During the four decades from 1870, when the Franco-Prussian war began and the German Reich again sprouted, down to 1910 there was more headway made in the "European domination of the world" than during the four preceding centuries.* It was due to materialism! Already in 1895 Kaiser Wilhelm declared† that "the German Empire has become a world empire." He mixed himself in with the Middle East, for, four years later, a group of German bankers got from the Turkish sultan a concession for building a railroad across Asiatic Turkey from the Straits of Bosporus, opposite Constantinople, southeastward to Baghdad in Mesopotamia (now Iraq). Looking to further imperial communications, he said: "Germany's future lies upon the water." The total tonnage of his navy became second only to that of Britain. The king of the south looked on nervously.

[11] With so much inflammable material piled up, it needed only a spark to touch off a world conflagration. It was struck—on June 28, 1914, by the assassination of Austrian Archduke Ferdinand and his wife in Bosnia, which Austria-Hungary, Germany's ally, had annexed in 1908. The king of the north seized upon this to realize his scheme of world domination at the expense of the king of the south. Jehovah's angel had said: "At the time appointed will he return, and enter into the south; but not as in the former will it be in the latter time." (Daniel 11:29, Le) The "time appointed"

---

* Contemporary Europe Since 1870, by Carlton J. H. Hayes (1953), page 264.
† Ibidem, pages 149, 150.

10. From 1870 onward, how did the question of world domination become a sizzling one?
11. How was a world conflagration finally sparked, and how was it "at the time appointed"?

was the year 1914, which God's time schedule had marked for the 2,520 years of the "appointed times of the nations" to end in the fall of the year. At that time their allowance from Jehovah God to enjoy terrestrial rule without interference from God's kingdom ended. That was "seven times" from 607 B.C., from the Gentile overturning of Jehovah's typical kingdom in Jerusalem, the destruction of his typical sanctuary in that city, and the desolating of the kingdom realm of Judah.—2 Chronicles 36:17-21; Luke 21:24.

[12] In the fall of 1914, therefore, was Jehovah's appointed time for his kingdom to be restored, not on earth at Jerusalem, but up in heaven at his right hand where his Son, Jesus Christ, had sat waiting for his enemies to be made his footstool. —Psalm 110:1; Hebrews 10:12, 13.

[13] In 1914, were the nations of "Christendom" glad that the time was at hand for the kingdom of God to be fully set up, as proclaimed by Jehovah's people of the "sanctuary" class? The symbolic twenty-four elders seated before God upon their thrones were glad and said: "We thank you, Jehovah God, the Almighty, the one who is and who was, because you have taken your great power and begun ruling as king." But prophecy said that the worldly nations would not be glad: "But the nations became wrathful, and your own wrath came, and the appointed time . . . to bring to ruin those ruining the earth." (Revelation 11:16-18) Even before the "seven times" expired in the fall of 1914 the nations put themselves in no condition to hail and accept the then-to-be-restored kingdom of God.

[14] Austria-Hungary, having had her heir to the royal throne murdered, declared war on Serbia

---

12. For what to be restored was it the time in the fall of 1914?
13. At the kingdom's establishment in 1914, did the nations of Christendom share the gladness of the "twenty-four elders"?
14. How did the king of the north "return, and enter into the south" in 1914?

on July 28. Her partner in the *Dreibund,* Germany, backed her up and declared war upon Russia on August 1, then upon France on August 3. The next day the king of the south, through Britain, declared war upon Germany. Italy, a member of the *Dreibund,* declared neutrality, but joined the king of the south in war the following year. Turkey and Bulgaria joined Germany. After that Britain took over Egypt as her protectorate, to block the troops of the Kaiser and of Turkey in Palestine from cutting off the Suez Canal and invading Egypt, the ancient land of the king of the south. Britain being now in control of Egypt, the king of the south now represented the system of liberal democracy or constitutional rule, together with free, capitalistic enterprise.

¹⁵ Thus for the autocratic king of the north in this "latter time," in 1914, it was not "as in the former" time when he was the Roman imperial world power, the sixth world power of Bible history. In this "latter time" the second-rate king of the north had to face the king of the south, who was holding the role of the seventh world power, the greatest of the seven world powers. Not only that, but from about October 1, 1914, the king of the north had to face also the restored kingdom of Jehovah God ruling in the heavens for universal domination.

¹⁶ Commenting on this lack of sameness with former times, the angel said to Daniel: "For there will come against him the ships of Kittim; and he will become fainthearted, and return, and will rage against the holy covenant; and he will do it: and he will return, and have an understanding with those that forsake the holy covenant." (Daniel 11:30, *Le*) Although armed with the second-largest navy and many destructive U-boats, the

---

15. For the king of the north, how was it "in the latter time" not as "in the former"?
16. At first what mainly was the "ships of Kittim" that came against the king of the north?

king of the north proved no match for the "ships of Kittim" that came against him. These were not literally ships of Cyprus, the ancient Kittim, although on November 5, 1914, Great Britain annexed the island of Cyprus, to keep pro-German Turkey out. According to the Jewish historian Josephus, the term Kittim was applied not only to Cyprus but also to the coasts of Italy. Interestingly, Italy joined the warring Britain in 1915, according to the Treaty of London, and thus put her own Roman navy alongside that of the king of the south. But the "ships of Kittim" were at first mainly the great British navy.

[17] More "ships of Kittim" came from the west later, after the German submarine, U-20, sank the British Cunard Liner Lusitania off Ireland on May 7, 1915, and 124 American lives were lost. A diplomatic controversy arose between America and Germany. Matters worsened, and on April 6, 1917, American President Wilson declared a state of war existed with Germany. Then from the west came the American warships in the fight against the king of the north, and American troops were poured onto the European continent. The king of the south, the Anglo-American dual world power, was now fully at war with the rival king. In September, 1916, however, the British had introduced a strange kind of armor-clad land battleship against the king of the north, in the form of the tractored "tanks."

[18] Significantly, in 1917, after Russia's czar abdicated, Kaiser Wilhelm sent Nikolai Lenin from Switzerland across Germany and Sweden to Russia to spread Bolshevism or communism, for the purpose of weakening and destroying the Russian armies. (So says General Ludendorff, the ally of Adolf Hitler, in his memoirs.) By this war strat-

---

17. How did more ships of Kittim come later when the seventh world power fully got into the war with the king of the north?
18. In 1917, how did the king of the north help world communism?

egy the king of the north helped the cause of world communism.

[19] However, in November, 1918, the king of the north grew "fainthearted" and returned, withdrawing from the war, whipped. Kaiser Wilhelm, who had ruled since his father, Frederick III, died in 1888, gave up the throne and fled into exile, and Germany became a republic. So World War I ended. But it, together with the food shortages, pestilences and the persecution of Jehovah's sanctuary class, stamped A.D. 1914 as the year when the "seven times," "the appointed times of the nations," ended and when God's kingdom was born in the heavens and this Devil-ruled old world entered in upon its "appointed time of the end." —Matthew 24:7-9; Luke 21:10-17.

[20] In Kaiser Wilhelm's case, his heart had been against the holy covenant. (Daniel 11:28, *JPS*) With him in exile till his death on June 4, 1941, how did the king of the north now "rage against the holy covenant" and "do it"? This was by the rise to power of Adolf Hitler, the Austrian, aided by German Catholic politicians, for example, Franz von Papen. In January, 1933, President von Hindenburg put out Schleicher and put in Hitler as German chancellor, with Von Papen as vice-chancellor. Then President von Hindenburg declared: "And now, gentlemen, forward with God!"* It was really 'FORWARD AGAINST GOD!' By then Jehovah's witnesses numbered more than 19,200 in Germany and were very prominent. One of the first things that the Nazi Fuehrer Hitler did was to ban Jehovah's witnesses, seize their witnessing equipment and consign them

---

* See *Contemporary Europe Since 1870,* by C. J. H. Hayes, pages 583ff.

19. When did the king of the north "become fainthearted, and return," and how, and by what world events had 1914 now become stamped as significant?
20. With Kaiser Wilhelm now in exile, how did the king of the north "rage against the holy covenant"?

to prisons and concentration camps.* On April 1, 1933, Hitler became dictator, for the German Reichstag delegated its lawmaking powers to Hitler's government for a term of four years. By this stroke the German republic ceased and was followed by the "Third German Empire." The First had been the Germanic Holy Roman Empire from 962 to 1806; and the Second, the Hohenzollern Empire from 1871 to 1918. The Third was the Hitler dictatorship.

21 Still, how did he "do it"? On September 8, 1926, Germany had been admitted to the League of Nations, but Nazi dictator Hitler marched Germany out of the League on October 14, 1933. Boldly he went from one worldly success to another, annexing Austria and then Sudetenland in Czechoslovakia and forming the Axis Powers, including faraway Japan. Much of his success was due to his having an "understanding with those that forsake the holy covenant." Those who claimed to be in favor of God's covenant for the Kingdom were the clergy of Christendom, particularly those of the Roman Catholic Hierarchy. These had not waited upon the rightful Heir, Jesus Christ, to come into his kingdom in 1914, but established a religious-political government of their own and set up the Holy Roman Empire. Early in July of 1933 Vice-Chancellor von Papen negotiated in Hitler's behalf a concordat with Pope Pius XI; and through this the pope agreed to dissolve the Catholic Center party in Germany in return for Hitler's pledge that the Catholic Church should keep on having full religious freedom in Germany. This paved the way for Hitler to decree that there should be a single political party in the land, the National Socialist party.

---

* See 1934 *Yearbook of Jehovah's Witnesses,* pages 127-146.

---

21. How did the king of the north now "do it" by having an "understanding with those that forsake the holy covenant"?

[22] During World War II the New York *Times* as of February 17, 1940, stated in a dispatch dated "Washington, Feb. 16," the following Roman Catholic information: "The German war aims were outlined tonight as a re-establishment of the Holy Roman Empire by [the Roman Catholic priest] Dr. Edmund A. Walsh, regent of the Foreign Service School of [Catholic] Georgetown University, . . . Dr. Walsh said that he had heard Adolf Hitler say that the Holy Roman Empire, which was a Germanic empire, must be re-established." It is well known that the Axis Powers partner of baptized Catholic Hitler was the Italian Duce Mussolini, who signed a concordat with Pope Pius XI in 1929 by which Vatican City was set up as an independent state. Years later, under the blessing of Catholic priests, Mussolini's troops invaded non-Catholic Ethiopia, and on July 9, 1936, Mussolini proclaimed the restoration of the Roman Empire of the Caesars and proclaimed King Victor Emmanuel to be Emperor of Ethiopia. In December of 1937 Duce Mussolini withdrew Fascist Italy from the League of Nations.

THE "SANCTUARY" AND THE "ABOMINATION"

[23] However, what about those who refuse to come to any understanding with the king of the north and who hold fast to the holy covenant for the kingdom of Jehovah's reigning Son? The angel answers the question. Rather than discuss the many details of World War II he confines his words mainly to these of the loyal sanctuary class. In doing this the angel points to a remarkable transformation in the personality and nationality of the king of the north, saying: "And arms shall stand up on his part, and they shall profane the

---

22. According to Roman Catholic information, what were the war aims of the king of the north, and how were the imperial ambitions of his Italian partner disclosed?
23. At this point, how does Jehovah's angel make reference to the sanctuary class in connection with the king of the north?

sanctuary, even the stronghold, and shall take away the continual burnt-offering, and they shall set up the detestable thing that causeth appalment [the desolating abomination, *Le*]."—Daniel 11:31, *JPS*.

[24] The mention of "arms" that "stand up on his part" denotes supporters of the king of the north, military forces with which he engages the democratic king of the south in a second world war. But before, during and after this second war for world domination, surprising developments took place. The king of the north had already aided world communism in 1917, when the revolutionary Lenin went back to Russia from exile in Switzerland under safe conduct from Kaiser Wilhelm's government. Since then the Communists had seized the Russian government and set up the Union of Soviet Socialist Republics with its totalitarian government and dictatorship. This U.S.S.R. was admitted to the League of Nations September 17, 1934. It carried on negotiations with the western democracies.

[25] In August of 1939 Britain and France were negotiating with the Communist government when suddenly came what was called the "betrayal of the western democracies." The Nazi king of the north was about ready to launch World War II and needed to protect his eastern flank. To this end he entered into co-operative pacts with Russia. So on August 19 the Russian capital announced that it had concluded a seven-year trade agreement with Nazi Germany. Stranger still, on August 24, Moscow again caused surprise and consternation in the West by signing a ten-year nonaggression pact with Germany. Was there a deal between them? Time told. On September 1

---

24. Aided by Kaiser Wilhelm in 1917, what did the Communists do in Russia, and to what League was the new Russia admitted? 25. How did the "betrayal of the western democracies" come by the Communist Soviet government, and why was it read out of the League?

the Nazi "arms" or military forces invaded Poland, to light the fires of World War II.* In lightning warfare or *Blitzkrieg* they moved forward. Then on September 17 the Communist government ordered its own troops into Poland from the other side. Five days later Nazi Germany and the Communist Soviet Union announced an agreed-upon dividing line across Poland between the territories grabbed. Two months later Soviet Russia attacked Finland, and Russia became the first member to be read out of the League of Nations.

[26] For almost two years Communist Russia continued as an ally of the Nazi king of the north. It was dictatorial; it was aiming at world domination, like its ally. Only Hitler's crafty action in attacking Russia on June 22, 1941, forced Russia onto the side of the democratic king of the south. But Russia's fighting on the side of the western democracies would help it to defeat Nazi Germany and take over the position of the totalitarian, dictatorial king of the north. In 1945 Communist

---

* "Principal Events in 1939.— . . . on 1 September, at the outbreak of the war, Egypt proclaimed emergency measures. The following day German nationals were asked to leave the country and to return to Germany." (*The Encyclopedia Americana*, 1940 Annual, page 259b, paragraph 2) Egypt, though not declaring war on Germany and Italy, played a vital role as the base from which Britain and its allies could launch a campaign against the Italian and German forces. Throughout July and August of 1940, British planes bombed the Fascist Italian base at Tobruk, Libya; and Italian planes bombed the British bases at Mersa Matruh and Alexandria, Egypt. On July 9, 1940, the French naval authorities at Alexandria, Egypt, demilitarized the French warships in that port rather than risk a battle with the British Mediterranean Fleet.—*Ibidem*, 1941 Annual, page 233.

By July 1, 1942, German General Erwin Rommel had driven through with his Nazi forces to El Alamein, Egypt, only 70 miles west of Alexandria.—*Ibidem*, 1943 Annual, page 819b.

---

26. How did the Third German Empire lose the position of king of the north?

Russia shared in the Allied victory over the Nazi-Fascist foe. The dividing up of conquered Germany between the Big Four, namely, France, Britain, America and Russia, followed. According to the Yalta agreement, Russia took over eastern Germany. The Germanic king of the north as a rival of the seventh world power, the Anglo-American world power, no longer existed. A new politically strong power must step into his shoes, that the rivalry between the two kings for world domination might go on to a final decision or a draw, a standstill.

[27] Who could do so? Who did? Events quickly revealed—the Soviet Union, the Communist power that, since it seized power in Russia in 1917, has held world domination as its aim to this day. It felt its strength. It did not reduce its military forces below a war footing. It began to act according to its position of strength, against its chief rival. The United States of America had stepped forth from World War II as the most powerful nation on earth. So a propaganda and economic warfare was begun against the American democracy, a cold war. In effect, Communist Russia declared it early in 1947. The Communist land blockade of western Berlin, beginning June 26, 1948, was a tense feature of the cold war, but was overcome by the American airlift. Communist Russia long blocked the reuniting of all Germany under one government. It held on to eastern Germany as a satellite, making sure that a Communist form of rule was set up there before it recognized Eastern Germany as a political state inside the Communist sphere. There is no mistaking the identity of the king of the north since World War II.

[28] Before and during World War II the angelic prophecy was fulfilled: "They shall profane the

sanctuary, even the stronghold." This sanctuary is the remnant or remaining ones of Jehovah's "spiritual house" made up of "living stones." In this house he dwells by his spirit. Jesus Christ, the reigning King, is the Chief Cornerstone of this sanctuary or spiritual house. It is Jehovah's house and is dedicated exclusively to his worship. Associated with it now is a "great crowd" of dedicated persons of good will who worship and serve Jehovah God in company with the sanctuary class of holy ones or "saints." The sanctuary is a stronghold, because it is filled with unconquerable spiritual strength. It is filled with strength from Almighty God. Its strength is a tested one, proved by the fact that it has survived World War II and the collapse of Nazism, Fascism and Stalinism clear down to this day.

²⁹ Daniel 8:11, 13 foretold the casting down of the place or base of this sanctuary and the trampling of it under foot. That occurred during World War I. It took place at the hands of the symbolic "little horn," the "king of fierce countenance," that is, the seventh world power, the Anglo-American dual world power.* But the later profaning of the "sanctuary, even the stronghold," was the terrible persecution of the sanctuary class before, during and since World War II at the hands of the king of the north in the lands of the Axis Powers and of the Soviet Union. All the loyal "great crowd" of good will who worshiped Jehovah with his sanctuary class suffered along with these holy ones or "saints" of Jehovah's "holy nation" of spiritual Israel. This persecution by means of concentration camps, prisons, slave labor camps, firing squads, beheading, banning of meetings and of Bible literature, and by other means, was a prof-

* See chapter 9, pages 201ff.

29. How did the profaning of this sanctuary proceed, and by whom was it done?

anation of Jehovah's sanctuary, an abuse of it. The king of the north was not alone in this outrage to God. The king of the south showed the same spirit as during World War I and committed his own wicked profanations. But was the sanctuary and were those who worshiped at it destroyed by this rabid persecution? Not at all. But why not? Jehovah's angel explains later.

³⁰ Along with the profaning of Jehovah's sanctuary went the taking away of its "continual burnt-offering." In the English translation the word "burnt-offering" is supplied. In the Hebrew text the word "continual" is applied to a number of sacred things having to do with Jehovah's temple and its priesthood. So here the word "continual" could apply to numbers of things besides a "burnt-offering." "Continual" could embrace the entire worship at the sanctuary that was to be performed daily, constantly, regularly. During the Nazi-Fascist heyday of power the king of the north did take away the means of spiritual sacrifice from the sanctuary remnant and from their fellow worshipers of good will. By banning and by seizing Bibles and Bible literature and by penning up Jehovah's witnesses or by driving them underground, the king of the north and his allies caused the open, public offering of the "sacrifice of praise" always to God to cease. To observers it was seemingly taken away; but underground and wherever Jehovah's witnesses were held prisoner it went on fearlessly.

"THE DESOLATING ABOMINATION"

³¹ How is it, though, that at this stage of progress of the angelic prophecy it is said: "And they shall set up the detestable thing that causeth appalment," "the desolating abomination"? Does

---

30. How, too, was the "continual burnt-offering" taken away in fulfillment of Daniel 11:31?
31. What was the "desolating abomination," and how did Revelation 17:7-11 state there must be a reappearing of it?

this disagree with the setting up of the League of Nations, which has been styled the "abomination that makes desolate" and which was set up at the instance of the king of the south in 1919?* No, indeed! Let it be remembered that that abominable counterfeit for God's established kingdom, the League of Nations, was the "image of the wild beast." This image of that wild beast with seven heads and ten horns was proposed by the symbolic two-horned beast, the dual world power of Britain and America, and this was done toward the close of World War I in 1918. (Revelation 13: 11-15) That "image," being a League, was made up of the seventh world power and of remnants of the preceding six world powers. As a result, it was an expression of all seven world powers and was itself the "eighth king," the eighth world power. Revelation 17:7-11 shows that the career of this symbolic seven-headed wild beast included a disappearance: "The wild beast that you saw was, but is not, and yet is destined to ascend out of the abyss." Hence the wild beast must reappear!

[32] Although the League of Nations was formally dissolved on January 10, 1946, when the first General Assembly of the United Nations opened in London, England, it had really ceased as a world-peace organization in September, 1939. At that time World War II burst forth at the rash conduct of the Nazi king of the north. There the League of Nations showed itself a disastrous failure, and it went down into the "abyss" dead, with only some corpselike structure remaining but without any peace-preserving energy.

[33] However, would it stay down in the abyss? In September, 1942, Jehovah's sanctuary class held

---

* See chapter 9, pages 204 (paragraph 27) to 210.

---

32. When and how did that "wild beast" disappear into the "abyss"?
33. By what stages did this world-peace "beast" reappear from the "abyss"?

an assembly, with fifty-three conventions in as many American cities holding simultaneous sessions September 18-20. The assembly grew to earth-wide proportions when over eighty conventions on four continents besides islands joined in having the same program. Sunday, September 20, at the key city of Cleveland, Ohio, the president of the Watch Tower Bible & Tract Society spoke to the visible and invisible conventions in the public address "Peace—Can It Last?" In it he dealt with Revelation 17:7-11. He showed from this that World War II would end and, during the peace that would not last, the international world-peace beast would ascend out of the abyss but finally go off into destruction.* The following year the foreign ministers of Communist Russia, Great Britain, America and China held a meeting in Moscow and expressed the need for a new world organization to include all "peace-loving states," as the League of Nations was considered dead. The Dumbarton Oaks Conference took place in early autumn of the following year, and there a proposed charter for a permanent United Nations Organization was outlined by representatives of the same four nations. This Charter had a thorough discussion and was finally adopted by a conference of fifty-one nations at San Francisco, California. On October 24, 1945, Communist Russia deposited its instrument of ratification of the United Nations and the Charter of this international organization went into force that day, which was shortly after Japan surrendered and World War II ended on September 2.

[34] The seven-headed scarlet-colored beast was again out of the abyss, and on January 10, 1946, its first General Assembly opened in London,

---

* See the booklet *Peace—Can It Last?* pages 18-22. Copyright 1942.

---

34. How was it the same beast, and thus how is Daniel 11:31 in full agreement with Daniel 8:11-14?

England. It was the same beast, for the United Nations had a striking resemblance to the League of Nations, which now closed up and later turned over its physical properties to the U.N. So Daniel 11:31 does not disprove that the "abomination that makes desolate" was first given life in 1919 by the seventh world power, the king of the south. Rather, Daniel 11:31 implies that this abominable "image of the wild beast" was to be plunged into the abyss of helplessness by the Nazi king of the north through bringing on another world war; and that the abominable "image" for international worship was to be brought out with the aid of the Communist king of the north. Seen in this light, Daniel 11:31 and Daniel 8:11-14 are in full harmony with each other. Together, they are in agreement with Revelation 13:11-15 and Revelation 17:7-11. Jehovah's angel showed the truth.

EDUCATIONAL WORK UNDER DIFFICULTY

[35] If the king of the north cannot destroy by persecution, he seduces by slippery, smooth talk. Jehovah's angel warned of this, saying: "And such as act wickedly against the covenant will he corrupt by flatteries; but the people that do know their God will be strong, and deal valiantly. And the intelligent among the people will impart understanding to many: yet they will stumble through the sword, and through flame, through captivity, and through being plundered for some time." (Daniel 11:32, 33, *Le*) The king of the north, whether Nazi or Communist, tries to win over the religious bodies. His having religious backing strengthens his position before the common people, if it does not also salve his own conscience as well as the people's. He must dominate the religious systems, making certain that they have clergy leaders that support the totalitarian policies of

35. What nonpolitical bodies does the king of the north try to win over, and whom does he succeed in corrupting by flatteries?

the king of the north. Rather than have a religious system with international or foreign connections, he wants an independent national religious system owing allegiance to only the national government. Whom can he, whom will he seduce and corrupt by his flatteries into supporting the totalitarian king of the north? Only "such as act wickedly against the covenant." That is why the religious organizations of Christendom under domination by the king of the north have yielded to him. Thus they get seeming advantages from him, so that they are free from persecution and keep operating their churches openly.

³⁶ Not so with the sanctuary class, the people that do know their God by his name and by his revealed Word. They will not deal wickedly with Jehovah's covenant for the kingdom, into which they have been taken as "joint heirs with Christ." Their "citizenship exists in the heavens." They are not part of this world as Jesus himself was not. They refuse to make this world their friend and by doing so make God their enemy and lose the Kingdom. They know the command of the reigning King, Jesus Christ, for the "time of the end" of this world: "This good news of the kingdom will be preached in all the inhabited earth for the purpose of a witness to all the nations, and then the accomplished end will come." Hence they resist the flattering offers of the king of the north and keep strong in faith and in exclusive devotion toward Jehovah God. As His witnesses to all nations they continue preaching the good news of the established kingdom of God.—Romans 8: 17; Philippians 3:20; Matthew 24:14.

³⁷ The sanctuary class are "intelligent," discreet, discerning the principle of godly devotion that should be their rule of conduct. They act with

36. Whom does the king of the north not succeed thus in corrupting?
37. In what way are the sanctuary class intelligent, and how do they impart understanding to many?

insight and keep walking in their integrity or blamelessness toward God. Realizing their being anointed with Jehovah's spirit to preach, they do preach, that they may "impart understanding to many." They help many to see that it is the supreme question of universal sovereignty that has to be decided in favor of Jehovah God. They thus help many to take the side of his kingdom and to quit working in vain for the world domination by either the king of the north or the king of the south.

[38] This uncompromising stand for God's universal sovereignty and this proclamation of the kingdom of his reigning Son Jesus Christ within the domain of the king of the north, whether Nazi or Communist, has meant suffering. Jesus foretold such suffering of persecution during this "appointed time of the end" of Satan's world. (Matthew 24:7-13) So because the sanctuary class refuse to worship the political State, the king of the north under both Nazi and Communist guise has mercilessly persecuted them. He has caused them to "stumble." How? "Through the sword" of execution to death; "through flame" of hot public condemnation, bans, critical publicity, and scorching expressions of official anger; "through captivity" in prisons, in slave labor, concentration and deportation camps, in exile and in underground quarters; and "through being plundered for some time" by invasion of homes, Kingdom Halls and assemblies without proper legal warrant, along with the seizing of Bible literature and even of God's own Word itself, since the sanctuary class feeds on His Word and preaches its good news of salvation to the lovers of truth and righteousness. "For some time" this has kept up, particularly from when the Nazi Fuehrer took dictatorial power in 1933 and also beyond Hitler's death and through Communist Stalin's dictatorial rule and

---

38. How have they been made to "stumble," and why?

down to the present time. In eastern Europe some of Jehovah's witnesses have gone through years of Nazi persecution and then quickly came under Communist oppression.

[39] The God of mercy has helped his intelligent sanctuary class to stagger through this persecution by the king of the north in his domains and also any persecution that he can stir up against them through his propaganda and secret agents in other lands. Jehovah has lovingly fulfilled his word through his angel: "But in their stumbling will they be aided with a little help; but many will join themselves to them with deceptive flatteries. And some of the intelligent will stumble, to make a purification among them, and to select and to cleanse them, until the time of the end; because it is yet for the time appointed." (Daniel 11:34, 35, Le) This persecution is foretold to continue until the king of the north comes to his "time of the end" at Armageddon. When the Devil in his role of Gog of Magog makes his final, full-strength attack "from the uttermost parts of the north," he will be certain to have the Communist king of the north among his assault forces. (Ezekiel 38:1-9; 39:1, 2, AS) So till then Jehovah's sanctuary class may expect to have to stumble and stagger under the totalitarian, dictatorial "king."

[40] Till now as they have thus stumbled along, they have indeed been "helped with a little help." (JPS) This has come about by the defeat of Nazi Germany and Fascist Italy and Imperial Japan, the Axis partners, the democratic "earth" thus opening its "mouth" and swallowing up the "river" belched out by Satan the Devil through that Nazi type of king of the north. (Revelation 12:15-17) Their defeat helped to bring about a liberation of Jehovah's sanctuary class along with others

---

39. Such stumbling is foretold to continue till when?
40. How, though, have they been "helped with a little help"?

in lands that had fallen under the Nazi king of
the north and his allies, in Western Germany,
Norway, Denmark, Holland, Belgium, France,
Italy, Philippine Islands, Korea, Burma, Siam,
Indonesia, Malaya, Singapore, Wake Island, Hong
Kong, Greece, but not in Russia itself. In a number of lands, also, the judicial courts have rendered decisions favorable to Jehovah's witnesses
and relieved them of restrictions and oppressions
by the king of the north or by those who partake
of his spirit. In large assemblies held in 199 cities
around the globe from June 30, 1956, to March
1, 1957, Jehovah's witnesses to the total number
of 462,936 adopted a stirring petition to Nikolai
A. Bulganin, then Premier of the Soviet Union at
Moscow, asking some relief for thousands of their
spiritual brothers cruelly persecuted in Russia
and Siberia. This won no favor or help from Soviet
government officials or courts. Yet it did give
great moral support to the persecuted victims of
the king of the north, and also much encouragement.*

[41] The greatest help to the sanctuary class stumbling under the brutalities of the king of the north
has come from the "sheep" whom Jesus foretold
in his prophecy on the end of this world. In contrast with the "goats," these sheeplike people of
good will have sympathized with Jesus' spiritual
brothers, who are part of Jehovah's sanctuary.
They have come forward in increasing numbers
since 1931, but particularly since 1935, when *The
Watchtower,* as of August, published the explanation of Revelation 7:9-17 to enlighten and encourage these "other sheep" of the heavenly Shepherd. (John 10:16) They have accepted the good
news of God's established kingdom and have
helped the sanctuary class in ways described in

---

* See *The Watchtower* as of April 15, 1957, pages 249-
254.

41. From whom, however, has the greatest help come, and how?

Jesus' parable of the sheep and goats. (Matthew 25:31-46) But most powerfully have they rendered this help by dedicating themselves to the divine Sovereign of the universe and by congregating with the sanctuary class and joining them openly in the field in preaching the good news of God's kingdom that still other "sheep" may be gathered in. They keep worshiping with the sanctuary class, witnessing with them and faithfully suffering with them at the hands of the king of the north as well as the king of the south, even to the death.

⁴² But many who "join themselves to them" do not do so wholeheartedly or with sincere motives, merely in a form of flattery or smooth conduct, for selfish reasons. Some of such ones have turned out to be spies for the king of the north. Others make complimentary remarks about Jehovah's witnesses but go no farther toward worshiping and serving Jehovah himself. Many admire and praise the faithfulness, stanchness and integrity keeping of Jehovah's witnesses but hold back from dedicating themselves to Him and becoming his active, preaching witnesses. This fact brings to light that there is now a test of real devotion to the true God on the part of those who may claim to be "other sheep" or who may for a time receive Bible education by Jehovah's witnesses. They should aim, not to flatter creatures, but to please the Creator.—Galatians 1:10.

⁴³ The God of salvation has been permitting all this persecution of his witnesses in order to test those who profess to seek him and to love him. By the fiery trials from the persecutors and oppressors Jehovah smelts those claiming to be his people in order to expose and skim away those who are mere scummy dross and to manifest,

42. How do many "join themselves to them" with deceptive flatteries?
43. What is Jehovah's purpose in permitting some of his intelligent ones to "stumble," and what are the intelligent determined to do?

purify and retain those who are the pure, precious metal. It is by these genuine ones who lovingly carry out their dedication to him that he receives a vindication of himself as the chosen Sovereign of their lives. Thus Jehovah has permitted thousands of his intelligent witnesses to stumble under persecution, even to a fall into the death of a martyr, to refine the qualities of his surviving witnesses and to reject those not determined to endure to the finish that they may be saved. (Matthew 24:9-13) Down to the bitter end of the king of the north and his fellow persecutors Jehovah's intelligent ones, who see and appreciate the supreme issue of universal sovereignty, are resolved to submit to purification and whitening by persecution. Their reward has no end, but at the "time appointed" their enemy persecutor has his end.

[44] Jehovah's angel gave a true description of the twentieth-century king of the north: "And the king will do according to his pleasure; and he will exalt and magnify himself above every god, and against the God of gods will he speak incredible things, and he will prosper till the indignation be at an end; for that which is determined will be accomplished." (Daniel 11:36, *Le*) Not only in ancient times did the king of the north call himself god or accept the title of god, but his modern successor tries to act the part of god. He wants to know no will or pleasure but his own. To this end he uses conscienceless means to take to himself totalitarian, dictatorial power in government. This was true of him not only in the Nazi and Fascist realm after World War I. It has also been true of him in his Communist fashion since World War II. At least in his own mind he has lifted up and magnified himself over every earthly man-

---

44. Above what has the king of the north exalted and magnified himself, and to what extent?

made "god," although actually he had not yet gained domination over the rival king of the south.

⁴⁵ The king of the north has assailed even *El elim*, the God of gods, who is Jehovah. He does not appreciate that he is on judgment before the real God, the Supreme Judge, of whom Psalm 82: 1, 2 says: "God is stationing himself in the assembly of the Divine One; in the middle of the gods he judges: 'How long will you keep on judging with injustice and showing partiality to the wicked themselves?'" Incredible, wondrous are the things that the defiant king of the north, both in Nazi and in Communist guise, has said against the God of Daniel's people. In fact, if not in word, he denies God's existence. By his declaration of his aims for world domination to the exclusion of God's kingdom in the hands of Christ, he speaks against Jehovah, whose established kingdom Jehovah's witnesses are preaching to all nations. For Jehovah's dedicated people he does not believe in the principle stated by Jesus: "Pay back Caesar's things to Caesar, but God's things to God." (Luke 20:25) He denies God's right to anything. He claims that the political State has the right to everything from its subjects.

⁴⁶ He demands that the citizens shall worship the man-made, Devil-inspired State. To him man is simply a material machine to be worked to death by the State. Since putting man-made sputniks or satellites into space since October 4, 1957, he feels like the lord of the universe, especially since his sputniks have not encountered the person of the invisible God in space between earth and sun. He has prospered to bringing one third of the earth under Communist forms of government, not knowing that God in the heavens laughs and permits this "till the indignation be at an

---

45. Who is the God of gods, and how has the king of the north spoken "incredible things" against him?
46. How has his prosperity made him feel, but till when will he keep on prospering, and then what will be accomplished?

end; for that which is determined will be accomplished." In the "war of the great day of God the Almighty" Jehovah will bring his indignation and denunciation to an end. What will be accomplished there will be, not what the king of the north determined, but what Almighty God determined.

THE KING'S GOD

⁴⁷ In the king of the north Jehovah God does not have to deal with someone whom he did not foresee. Already in ancient times his angel described the king as very modernistic, saying: "And to the gods of his fathers will he pay no regard; and to the desire of women, or to any god whatever will he not pay any regard; for above all will he magnify himself. But in his place will he pay honour to the god of the fortresses; and to a god whom his fathers knew not will he pay honour with gold, and silver, and with precious stones, and costly things." (Daniel 11:37, 38, *Le*) The "gods of his fathers" are the gods of no particular man, like Hitler or Stalin, but are the gods of the fathers of this political office called the "king of the north." During the more than two thousand years that he has been bearing rule, the "king" has undergone changes, from the Seleucid dynasty of the Hellenic kings, through the pagan Roman emperors, the Roman Catholic and Greek Orthodox emperors, the Germanic emperors of the Holy Roman Empire, the Austrian and German Kaisers, the Nazi imperial ruler and now the Communist imperial ruler. However, Satan, who is the "god of this system of things," has in fact been their one continuing god from the start of the king of the north as well as of the king of the south. (2 Corinthians 4:4) So the king of the north regards no paternal "gods" how?

---

47. Who are the "fathers" to whose gods the king of the north at this time pays no regard?

⁴⁸ Not only does he pay no regard to gods of male rulers, but he pays no regard to any special god of the women. The "women" of this prophecy would be the handmaids of the imperial regime of the north or handmaids of the long line of "fathers" of this king. As "women," they would be the weaker vessels. Hence the modernistic king of the north would pay no regard to the god of which these weaker agents are specially fond. Their god is secondary, inferior.

⁴⁹ Nor to any other outside god does he pay regard, for he worships himself as god. He comes first. He is above all. What wonder, then, that he should require all subjects to worship the State or, more narrowly, worship the dictator! How Babylonish, how devilish! For the ancient king of Babylon said against Jehovah God: "Above the stars of God I shall lift up my throne, . . . I shall make myself resemble the Most High." In this the king of Babylon was a prophetic figure of Satan the Devil. (Isaiah 14:4, 12-14) Since Adolf Hitler's suicide upon losing World War II in 1945 the king of the north, now communistic, has not been bound up with Christendom, although he has to do with religious forces of Christendom in Poland, Hungary and elsewhere. Looking at the old-time religions as being the opium that has drugged the people mentally, he has really developed a Red religion for the people. But as for himself, he honors the "god of the fortresses." Nazi Hitler did the same thing.

⁵⁰ In addition to the honor that the king of the north paid to the god of modern, scientific militarism during the Nazi regime, he has gone even farther in his Communist guise. In 1958 he maintained the biggest army in the world, despite any

48. Who are the "women" to whose "desire" the king of the north pays no regard?
49. Whom does the king of the north really worship, Babylonishly, and what religion has he developed for his people?
50. How has the king of the north paid honor to the "god of the fortresses"?

reducing of the number of his conventional troops. Twenty thousand operational warplanes backed up the army. Size of his army was unknown because of the secretive Iron Curtain. His submarines numbered between 500 and 700, the largest undersea fleet in history, greater than that of the German U-boat fleet. When conquering Eastern Germany, he seized as many German experts on rockets and missiles as he could and put these to work in developing rocketry and missilery in Russia. Russian education has specialized on science and the production of engineers, with a view to military and economic domination of the whole earth. In fact, technical science has become his fetish, his idol. He has tried to seize all the "fortresses" or strongholds by making himself strongest in those departments or realms which he needs in order to dominate the world, including the king of the south, the Anglo-American dual world power. The king of the south capped the climax in World War II by dropping two atomic bombs on Japan in August, 1945, but in the course of years the communistic king of the north followed with an atomic bomb of his own. Then he followed the king of the south with his own hydrogen bomb.

[51] However, in his missiles program he forged ahead of the rival king and announced on August 27, 1957, that he had successfully fired an ICBM, an intercontinental ballistic missile, over a huge distance to a target area. Less than two months later, on October 4, he caused great humiliation, consternation and agitation to the American member of the king of the south by rocketing into orbit around the earth the 184-pound Sputnik No. 1. Three days later he spoke from his new fortress or position of strength and accused the United States of America of inciting war between

---

51. How did he forge ahead of the king of the south in missiles and satellites?

the two neighbors, Syria and Turkey. On the third day of the following month he rocketed into orbit his second sputnik, of over half a ton and carrying the dog Laika as passenger. It was first on January 31, 1958, that America rocketed its Explorer satellite of 30.8 pounds into orbit.

[52] The king of the south kept accusing the Communist king of the north of blocking all progress toward international disarmament through the United Nations. On March 31, 1958, the Soviet Union publicly declared that it was halting its tests of atomic and hydrogen bombs, but that it would resume its testing if the other countries, America and Britain, paid no attention to the Communist lead and went on with their bomb testing. Defying that challenge, and for reasons vital to themselves, America began its publicized scheduled series of nuclear tests at the Eniwetok proving grounds in the Pacific Ocean April 28, 1958, and Britain exploded a nuclear device from a jet bomber over the Christmas Island region of the Pacific the next day. All this militaristic preparation has been very expensive. But the king of the north has deprived his subjects of material comforts in order to honor with gold, silver, precious stones and costly things this god of modern scientific accomplishments entirely unknown to his royal "fathers."

[53] With this honored "god" the king of the north has expanded his territories or spheres of influence. Jehovah's angel foretold this, saying: "This will he do for the very strong fortresses together with the strange god: whoever will acknowledge him, him will he give much honour; and he will cause such to rule over many, and he will divide out the land for a price." (Daniel 11:39, *Le*) This

---

52. To what extent has the king of the north paid honor to the god unknown to his fathers with gold, silver, precious stones and costly things?

53. In what way is the god for whom he does such things "strange"?

highly developed, modern scientific "god" is foreign in having been strange and unknown to the "fathers" of the king of the north.

[54] During his aggressions under the form of German Nazism those men in the lands taken over who acknowledged the king of the north were given much honor. He set them to rule over the unwilling peoples. He divided out territories for rulership, if the proper price was paid to him. The Nazi king of the north did find men who would accept areas from him "for a price." These included the Roman Catholic Hierarchy. Historians do not forget that when Hitler took over Austria in 1938 Cardinal Theodor Innitzer of Vienna wrote him and closed his letter with "Heil Hitler!" Also, that when the German Roman Catholic bishops held their Fulda Conference of 1940 they voted their pledge of allegiance to baptized Catholic Hitler.

[55] Later, as a Communist, the king of the north has committed aggressions with his "strange god." He held on to Eastern Germany until he found the men of his price to establish a Communist State there. In Hungary a Communist "people's republic" was set up, unable, however, to get out from under the Soviet's domination, as the suppressing of the people's revolt in 1956 by use of Soviet occupation troops proved. Other European lands were made Communist satellites. Even Korea was arranged to be divided into two parts, with the Communist regime north of the 38th Parallel. But greedy Communists invaded the South Korean Republic in 1950 and the Korean war broke out in which the United Nations, spearheaded by the American member of the king of the south, stepped in to preserve South Korea from being

---

54. Whom did he cause to "rule over many," and whom did he find ready to have areas divided out to them "for a price"?
55. How did the Communist king of the north commit aggressions with his "strange god" and find men to receive areas "for a price"?

devoured. A Communist puppet state was established in Outer Mongolia, which Free China was forced to recognize in the year that World War II ended. Then in 1949 the Chinese Communist forces swept over the vast mainland. By December of that year they had taken possession of the entire mainland of continental China. The Chinese president and his nationalist army took refuge on the island of Formosa or Taiwan. Indeed, the king

COMMUNIST-DOMINATED COUNTRIES (A.D. 1958)

of the north found men to whom to divide the land and give rule.

⁵⁶ The king of the south is determined to hold his dominant place on earth to preserve the "free world," as he claims. He was urged to begin a preventive war before the king of the north became too strong; but he recognizes that nuclear space-age warfare is suicidal. Concerning him Daniel 8:25 (*JPS*) says that he will be "broken without hand" at the universal battle of Armageddon. But many fear that a third world war, a nuclear war, will be touched off by accident or by mistake or by some uncaring madman. Yet the king of the south and the king of the north stand at Armageddon. In due time, prophecy foretells, God Almighty will strike confusion into the ranks of all the earthly opposers of his universal sovereignty, so that at last every man's hand will be against his neighbor.—Ezekiel 38:21, *AV*.

⁵⁷ From this standpoint the further words of Jehovah's angel may be read: "And at the time of the end will the king of the south push against him; and the king of the north will come against him like a storm-wind, with chariots, and with horsemen, and with many ships; and he will enter into some countries, and will overflow and pass along." (Daniel 11:40, *Le*) Down to the "time of the end" at Armageddon there will be competitive coexistence between the "two kings." In some way the king of the south must act, whether preventively or protectively. In the confused fighting between the "two kings" as crazed enemies of Jehovah God and his kingdom, the "kings" will have opportunity and occasion to try out and use their frightful, deadly weapons of all kinds against each other.

---

56. What is the king of the south determined to do, but with self-restraint, and yet what will God cause his enemies to do at Armageddon?

57. How is it, then, that "at the time of the end will the king of the south push against him"?

[58] The prophecy concerning the king of the north in the future says: "He shall enter also into the beauteous land, and many countries shall be overthrown; but these shall be delivered out of his hand, Edom, and Moab, and the chief of the children of Ammon. He shall stretch forth his hand also upon the countries; and the land of Egypt shall not escape. But he shall have power over the treasures of gold and of silver, and over all the precious things of Egypt; and the Libyans and the Ethiopians shall be at his steps." (Daniel 11:41-43, *JPS*) The "beauteous land" into which the king of the north here enters is the key to understanding aright this movement of the king at his "time of the end" at Armageddon. When Jehovah's angel spoke of the "beauteous land" in the earlier part of this prophecy (Daniel 11:16, *JPS*) he foretold that the king of the north in the person of Syrian King Antiochus III the Great would stand in the literal land of Judah, the land of Jehovah's people, and take it all into possession.

[59] In Daniel's earlier vision, Daniel 8:9, 23-25 (*JPS*) speaks of the "beauteous land" toward which the "little horn" or "king of fierce countenance" would extend his power in the latter time of worldly kingdoms, where we are now. In that prophecy the "beauteous land" took on a spiritual meaning. It pictured, not Palestine, but the earthly condition of Jehovah's sanctuary class in their relationship to Jehovah by his new covenant. Likewise, in the final activities of the king of the north, this spiritually "beauteous land" of the sanctuary class is the realm that he invades. He has already tried to profane the sanctuary. (Daniel 11:31, *JPS*) But now at God's appointed time for the Armageddon fight the king of the

north sets out to destroy the "beauteous land" to wipe it off the earth. In this course he acts as an earthly instrument of Gog of Magog, who is Satan the Devil. Ezekiel 38:14-17; 39:1-6 (*JPS*) foretells that Gog with his earthly hordes actually invades this "beauteous land" of restored spiritual Israel. This becomes the time for Jehovah to begin the war of his great day. Consequently, in Daniel 11:41, the sanctuary class are forewarned against the final assault of the king of the north under the unseen leadership of Gog of Magog.

⁶⁰ To balance in a proper way the spiritual meaning of the "beauteous land" of spiritual Israel, the lands of Edom, Moab and the chief of the children of Ammon must take on a spiritual meaning, rather than refer to modern Jordan the capital of which is Amman (ancient Rabbath Ammon). The sanctuary class of Jehovah is not in the Republic of Israel of today, although a few members might be found there. The remnant of the sanctuary class are found all around the earth, and their "land" or earthly condition is flourishing with the beauty of spiritual prosperity. Hence as Edom, Moab and Ammon in ancient times bordered on the land of Jehovah's people, so the symbolic Edom, Moab and Ammon of the prophecy must picture those whose lives touch upon and have to do with Jehovah's sanctuary class of today. Ancient Edom, Moab and Ammon were longtime, unchanging enemies of Jehovah's faithful people. For this reason they came under God's condemnation. (Jeremiah 48:1 to 49:22; Ezekiel 25:1-14; 35:1-15, *AS*) Reasonably, then, they picture the hard-set enemies of Jehovah's sanctuary class, his spiritual Israel, of today.

⁶¹ Naturally the enemies of the sanctuary class

---

60. What meaning, therefore, must Edom, Moab and the chief of the children of Ammon here take on, and so whom do they picture?
61. So why does the king of the north not stretch out his hand upon them, as he does upon other "countries"?

would be the friends or be on the side of the king of the north. So he would not stretch out his hand against those symbolized by Edom, Moab and Ammon. These modern organizations would be delivered or would escape out of his hand, whereas many other "countries" or modern earthly organizations, institutions or situations would "be overthrown."

⁶² Although the symbolic Edom, Moab and Ammon may escape from the hand of the Communist king of the north, they will not be delivered from Jehovah's hand at Armageddon. In ancient time Ammon, Moab and people of Mount Seir (Edomites) marched against Jerusalem in the days of King Jehoshaphat but were thrown into confusion by Jehovah's strange power and were maddened into killing one another off. So at the coming battle of Armageddon, Jehovah will by his irresistible power throw the symbolic Edomite, Moabite and Ammonite enemies of his sanctuary class into disorder and confusion. They will turn their destructive weapons against one another. (2 Chronicles 20:1-24) Any who escape this self-slaughter will be pursued and be destroyed by Jehovah's angelic armies under Christ. His sanctuary class in the "beauteous land" will be protected and survive.

⁶³ Jehovah's angel foretold further aggressions by the Communist king of the north before his end in Armageddon: "And he will stretch forth his hand against some countries, and the land of Egypt will not escape. And he will have control over the treasures of gold and of silver, and over all the costly things of Egypt: and the Libyans and the Ethiopians will follow at his steps." (Daniel 11:42, 43, Le) Back in the days of the Ptole-

---

62. Out of whose hand will symbolic Edom, Moab and the chief part of the children of Ammon not be delivered, and where?
63. Since Daniel 11:42, 43 speaks of the "costly things of Egypt," when was literal Egypt a rich country?

maic kings, Egypt was a rich country. Its seaport and capital, Alexandria, was second city to Rome, and was a great commercial as well as cultural center.

[64] As for modern Egypt, it gained its full independence A.D. 1936 and the erstwhile British High Commissioner was taken away and British troops were withdrawn from the land, except that those guarding the Suez Canal and the British naval base at Alexandria continued. During World War II the British troops prevented the Nazi king of the north from reaching and taking over the Suez Canal and Alexandria and overrunning Egypt. In 1945 Egypt proved to be one of the fifty-one original members of the United Nations. In 1952 King Farouk was expelled and governmental changes took place. Finally Colonel Gamal Abdel Nasser became president of the Republic. The British withdrew from Alexandria and from the Suez Canal by June 13, 1956. The dangerous Suez Canal incident took place later in 1956, but President Nasser came forth with enhanced prestige throughout the Arab world. February 1, 1958, the republics of Egypt and Syria joined together as a unified state called the United Arab Republic. For this union President Nasser thanked Allah. March 8, 1958, the kingdom of Yemen joined the U.A.R. to form the United Arab States, and President Nasser prayed to Allah in behalf of this enlarged union. He strongly proclaimed his determination to steer his country on the course of "positive neutrality" toward the Communist Eastern bloc and the democratic Western bloc.

[65] In the angelic prophecy to Daniel, Egypt was the seat of the king of the south. Hence the attack

---

64. When did modern Egypt gain its independence, and what led up to the formation of the United Arab Republic as a neutral country?
65. Why is Egypt to be viewed symbolically in Daniel 11:42, 43, and in what way is the king of the north selfishly interested in this symbolic Egypt?

upon Egypt from the north, to push back the king of the south. In the fulfillment of the prophecy today this does not have reference to the literal land of Egypt, for the "beauteous land" to the north has taken on a spiritual or symbolic meaning. So, too, Egypt must be viewed spiritually, as in the last book of the Bible, which says of Jehovah's "two witnesses": "Their corpses will be on the broad way of the great city which is in a spiritual sense called Sodom and Egypt, where their Lord was also impaled." (Revelation 11:8) Since Jesus Christ the Lord was actually put to death at Jerusalem in Judea, he could have been impaled in "Egypt" only in the spiritual sense that Egypt symbolized this world of which Jesus said that he and his faithful followers were no part. (Luke 13:33, 34; John 15:18, 19; 17:14-16) It is this world in which the Communist king is bent on winning the dominant position. He now claims that he can capture world domination without general war, but by an ideological, commercial, scientific, cultural campaign. He is out, not only to win over the neutral bloc of nations, but also to pull in or subvert the nations that adhere to the democratic king of the south, the Anglo-American dual world power. So he continues to "stretch forth his hand against some countries [or earthly realms of interest]" by various means.

⁶⁶ During the past he distinguished himself by infiltrating Communist spies and subversive agents, by bribery and corruption, by trade agreements, by offering loans and technical assistance, by threatening retaliation to nations seeking to defend themselves, by taking the initiative in propaganda to put his opponents in a bad light, this by radio, by political conferences on various levels clear to the summit, and by speeches even in the

---

66. Since World War II, how has the king of the north pushed his offensive wherever possible?

United Nations Assembly. He has posed as the champion of the forces of peace and has made peace proposals. He has promised liberation from colonialism, from imperialism and from warmongering capitalism. He has led off in the field of missiles and put up the first and second sputniks into outer space by means of intercontinental ballistic missiles during the 1957-1958 International Geophysical Year.* He has waged a terrific "cold war" and has warred also to capture the minds of men. He has vehemently attacked with words the defense alliances of nations, such as the NATO and the SEATO and the Baghdad Pact. He has paid official courtesy visits to neutral nations and has supplied military equipment to those refused by the king of the south. In all directions he has pushed his offensive.

⁶⁷ How far the king of the north will have got when he reaches his "time of the end" the future alone will tell. But he is predicted to gain control over the treasures of gold, silver and all the precious things of this commercialized, materialistic world, including oil. Those who are neighbors to this world, pictured by Egypt's neighbors, the Libyans and Ethiopians, will be "at his steps," following the king of the north, either by compulsion or willingly for selfish reasons. This turns out to be, of course, with considerable loss to the king of the south in various ways.

⁶⁸ He does not destroy the king of the south, nor does the king of the south destroy him. What, then, causes the king of the north to take the final step

---

* On May 15, 1958, the Soviet Union launched its third sputnik, weighing 2,925.53 pounds (1,327 kilograms).

---

67. Over what does Daniel 11:43 predict the king of the north to gain control, and in what way will the Libyans and Ethiopians be "at his steps"?
68. Does Daniel's prophecy indicate that the king of the north will destroy the king of the south, or that he himself will come to his end by the king of the south?

to his own destruction? Jehovah's angel throws light on this by the prophecy: "But reports out of the east and out of the north will terrify him; and he will go forth with great fury to destroy, and to exterminate many. And he will pitch the tents of his palace between seas and the glorious holy mountain [the beauteous holy mountain, *JPS*]; and he will come to his end, without one to help him."—Daniel 11:44, 45, *Le.*

[69] The terrifying reports out of the east and north could not be reports from the king of the south. Neither are they from his own kingdom in the north. The reports must come from outside the realms of the king of the north and the king of the south, between whom this earth is divided. Neutral nations do not count much, because of not being nuclear nations. Although the symbolic Gog of Magog is prophesied to come down from the "farthest ends of the north" (Ezekiel 39:2, *Le*), yet the terrifying reports do not come from Satan the Devil, for this symbolic Gog of Magog leads both the king of the north and the king of the south in his train. From whom, then, do the reports come with terrifying effect?

[70] In the prophecy of Daniel, the king of the north had pushed south, penetrated into Egypt, grabbed control over its precious things and influenced the southern peoples, the Libyans and the Ethiopians, to follow at his steps. From this strategic southern location of the king of the north, the "beauteous land" or land of Judea was to his north and east, or northeast, just as ancient Judea was northeast of Egypt. The terrifying reports must therefore come from Jehovah's sanctuary class in the "beauteous land" of spiritual prosperity. Up to now the sanctuary class, supported by the great crowd of "other sheep," have

69. From whom could those terrifying reports not come to the king of the north?
70. In coming from the east and the north, from whom, then, must the terrifying news come, and what does the news contain?

been reporting on Jehovah's universal sovereignty, on the establishment of his kingdom by Christ at the close of the "appointed times of the nations" in 1914, and on the coming "war of the great day of God the Almighty," commonly called the battle of Armageddon. What contents the reports will finally bear so as to infuriate him to go forth to bring the sanctuary class and their fellow worshipers to ruin and to devote them to destruction, Jehovah now knows and will yet determine.

[71] Since the reports really issue forth from Jehovah and through his reigning King Jesus Christ, it is Scripturally well said that the reports are out of the north and the east. The Scriptures locate Jehovah God relatively in the north. (Psalm 75:6, 7; 48:2) He the King of eternity and his reigning King Jesus Christ are symbolically spoken of as the "kings from the rising of the sun" or from the east, who move against the organization foreshadowed by Babylon on the Euphrates River. (Revelation 16:12) Jehovah speaks of calling his reigning King from the east or sunrising. (Isaiah 46:10, 11) So, not merely the reports, but also the forces of destruction will come from those directions upon the king of the north. As the reports must reach this king by means of Jehovah's visible earthly channel of newsreporting, so as to infuriate the king to his ruinous course, this prophecy makes one thing clear: Jehovah's sanctuary class and their great crowd of fellow worshipers will persist in obeying Matthew 24:14 by preaching "this good news of the kingdom" in all the inhabited earth down to the "time of the end" of the king of the north. He will not stop them!

[72] The king of the north will sally forth to destroy and to exterminate many, but how far will

71. Besides the news, what else will come from the north and the east against the king of the north, and so how long will the news keep coming to him?
72. In his purpose to destroy, where will he pitch his palatial campaign tents, according to Jehovah's angel?

he get with his destructive purpose? Where does he establish his base of operations? Jehovah's angel prophesied that the king would pitch his palatial campaign tents "between the seas and the beauteous holy mountain."—*JPS*.

[73] From Daniel's viewpoint, this tent location would be between the Mediterranean, the Great Sea, and the holy mountain of Jehovah's sanctuary or temple. Because of its excelling greatness in comparison with the Palestinian Dead Sea and the Sea of Galilee, the Mediterranean could, in Hebrew, be spoken of as "seas." The king's camp would therefore be in the land of Jehovah's dedicated people, the "beauteous land," and the king's main point of attack would be against the "beauteous holy mountain," where Jehovah's sanctuary is and where his "holy nation" together with aliens of good will worship him. Plainly the king of the north is set to wipe out Jehovah's worship, the sanctuary of which the king of the north profaned and trampled upon in times past. Its persistent survival and its unchecked growth, even in underground ways, irritates the king. The reports that the sanctuary class and the worshiping "other sheep" announce from house to house and publicly and unpublicly underground disturb the Communist dictatorial power. A campaign against these Kingdom publishers becomes more important than the king's aggressive campaign against the king of the south. The relations between the king of the north and the king of the south are not so serious and threatening. In fact, the unseen mastermind, the symbolic Gog of Magog, maneuvers both kings into joining him in a final, full-scale assault upon Jehovah's "beauteous land."

[74] The mountain upon which Jehovah's material

---

73. According to this campaign base, what would be the main point of attack by the king of the north, and by whom will he be finally joined in this attack?
74. Why is the goal of his attack the "beauteous holy mountain," and what does prophecy say about the success of his attack?

temple stood till A.D. 70 and which the kingdom of Jordan held fast because the Mohammedan Dome of the Rock has stood there is no longer holy to Jehovah God. Hence this earthly mountain in the Middle East is not the real goal of the infuriated king of the north. It is Jehovah's remnant of the sanctuary class and the great crowd of "other sheep." These worship Jehovah and refuse to worship the "image of the beast" or the self-deifying king of the north or the political State or the "god of the fortresses." Will the king of the north succeed? Will he put an end to this disapproved, condemned banned worship? The voice of prophecy answers: "And he will come to his end, without one to help him." He reaches his "time of the end," and it comes at the "time appointed."

⁷⁵ He has not believed the "reports out of the east and out of the north" warning him of his destruction for fighting against Jehovah God and his kingdom. He carries his fighting too far in making his attack under God's leadership upon Jehovah's sanctuary at his "beauteous holy mountain." He meets his end, his Armageddon, at Jehovah's appointed time for it. He has none to help him, not even the king of the south, for this king also is destroyed at Armageddon: "he shall be broken without hand." (Daniel 8:25, *JPS*) The demonic Gog of Magog, Satan the Devil, together with all his demons, will prove unable to help the king of the north in his last fight of history, for Gog himself will be crushed in defeat.

⁷⁶ Why will this two-thousand-year-old "king of the north" thus "come to his end" there in utter helplessness? The continuing angelic prophecy gives the grand, inspiring answer.

75. Why does he carry his fighting too far, and why will he have none to help him?
76. How do we learn why he must "come to his end" at Armageddon in utter helplessness?

CHAPTER 12

The "Prince" Of The Sanctuary Stands Up

7HIS generation of mankind is living in a marked time. Mankind's Creator has marked it, He who thousands of years ago said: "Let luminaries come to be in the expanse of the heavens to make a division

between the day and the night, and they must
serve as signs and for seasons and for days and
years." (Genesis 1:14) He wanted man on earth
to keep time. He himself keeps time with relation
to man, according to His own unerring, unchangeable time schedule that is just as accurate as the
sun, the moon and the stars in marking off time
for the earth.

[2] By studying God's written Word, the Bible,
man can find out God's time under the guidance
of God's unseen active force, his holy spirit. To
reassure his spiritual brothers of this, the Christian apostle Paul wrote: "Now as for the times
and the seasons, brothers, you need nothing to be
written to you. For you yourselves know quite
well that Jehovah's day is coming exactly as a
thief in the night. Whenever it is that they are
saying, 'Peace and security!' then sudden destruction is to be instantly upon them just as the pang
of distress upon a pregnant woman, and they will
by no means escape. But you, brothers, you are
not in darkness, so that that day should overtake
you as it would thieves." (1 Thessalonians 5:1-4)
In this nuclear space age, when international peace
and security are being so frantically urged, for
what event is it that the Creator has marked the
time of this generation?

[3] This marked time began in the year 1914
(A.D.). In that important year the "appointed
times of the nations," 2,520 years long, ran out.
If we measure back that many years from 1914
we come to the ancient date of 607 B.C. That year
was marked for the overthrow of the earthly

---

1. How is it that the time in which this generation is living is
a marked one?
2. If it is possible to find out God's time, how can it be done, and
what would we want to know about marking the time of this
generation?
3. Why did this marked time begin in 1914, and how does this
lead us to want to know what Jesus' name was formerly in
heaven?

"throne of Jehovah" and for the destruction of the throne city of Jerusalem and its sanctuary and for the total desolation of the land of the kingdom of Judah. Nineteen hundred years ago the natural descendant of Jerusalem's first king of Judah came to earth as the rightful Heir to the overturned throne. He was Jesus. He came to be called Christ because he was anointed with Jehovah's spirit to reign in the kingdom of God. He had come down from heaven, to be born as a man who worshiped Jehovah God. First on earth it was that he was called Jesus. What was his name in heaven before becoming man? Can we know? We can, and we will.

[4] Although he was King David's permanent Heir and was anointed with spirit instead of with holy anointing oil, he was not asked to sit on that overturned "throne of Jehovah," even when he rode triumphally into the throne city of Jerusalem in the spring of the year 33. The Jewish high priest and underpriests and other religious leaders had him put to death on Passover day. On the third day he was raised from the dead and, forty days later, ascended back to heaven. What is his name in heaven since then? With his proper name up there, he waited at God's right hand till A.D. 1914. Then at the end of the "appointed times of the nations" God enthroned him as king.

[5] The prophecy of Jehovah's angel pointed to this enthronement of the anointed Son of God in heaven in 1914, saying to Daniel: "And at that time shall Michael stand up, the great prince who standeth for the children of thy people; and there shall be a time of trouble, such as never was since there was a nation even to that same time; and at that time thy people shall be delivered, every

---

4. How was it that he got back to heaven, and since then what is there of interest about his identity?
5. In what words did Daniel 12:1 refer to this enthronement of God's Son?

one that shall be found written in the book."
—Daniel 12:1, *JPS*.

⁶ Where, though, does Daniel 12:1 mention the
name of Jesus? It does not do so, because this
prophecy was spoken and written down over five
hundred years before King David's Heir was born
at Bethlehem and named Jesus. Yet a son of God
is mentioned in Daniel 12:1. Who? Michael. In
the conversation that preceded or introduced this
verse the angel spoke to Daniel of this heavenly
son of God as "Michael, one of the chief princes,"
and as "Michael your prince." And in Daniel 12:1
itself the angel called him the "great prince who
standeth for the children of thy people." He was
a Prince of God and Prince over the people of God,
Daniel's people. Hence he was a son of God. Jehovah God included him as a son when He talked of
earth's creation as the time "when the morning
stars joyfully cried out together, and all the sons
of God began shouting in applause." (Job 38:7)
When Jesus Christ was on earth as a member of
Daniel's people and was anointed to be prince or
king over Daniel's people, was Michael then up in
heaven and was he then prince in heaven over
Daniel's people, including Jesus? How can we
know?

⁷ To determine this, the question must be asked:
What does Daniel 12:1 say about Michael up in
heaven? This: "At that time shall Michael stand
up." What does this mean? That Michael becomes
king in heaven. Repeatedly in Daniel, chapter 11,
the expression "stand up" is used to mean taking
power and beginning to reign as king: "There
shall stand up yet three kings in Persia; . . . And
a mighty king shall stand up, that shall rule . . .
But one of the shoots of her roots shall stand up

---

6. (a) Why is the name Jesus not mentioned in this verse, and
yet how is a son of God here named? (b) What question arises as
to Michael's location five hundred years later?
7. What does Michael's standing up in fulfillment of Daniel 12:1
mean, and at what time did he thus stand up?

in his place, . . . Then shall stand up in his place one that shall cause an exactor to pass through the glory of the kingdom; . . . And in his place shall stand up a contemptible person, upon whom had not been conferred the majesty of the kingdom." (Daniel 11:2, 3, 7, 20, 21; also 8:22, 23, *JPS*) Michael begins to reign as king in heaven during the final years of the king of the north, or, "at that time." That time God has marked as A.D. 1914.—Daniel 11:29, *JPS*.

[8] Since Michael stands up to reign during the conflict between the king of the north and the king of the south, Michael stands up to rule, to go subduing in the midst of the enemies of the people over whom he is "prince." Hence he stands up in the midst of his own enemies. More than 530 years before Jesus' birth, or more than 2,440 years before A.D. 1914, Michael was foretold to do this. In 1914, at the end of the "appointed times of the nations," who must begin ruling as king according to other Bible prophecies? King David's Heir, the One whose right it is to reign in the restored kingdom of God. Who, according to earthly name, is this One? It is Jesus Christ, glorified in heaven at God's right hand. He is the Son of man who, in Daniel 7:13, 14, is brought to the throne of the Ancient of Days and to whom are given dominion, glory and a kingdom.

[9] Furthermore, who is the One whose rod of strength Jehovah sends out of the heavenly Zion with the command: "Go subduing in the midst of your enemies"? (Psalm 110:1, 2) It is Jesus Christ. "This man offered one sacrifice for sins perpetually and sat down at the right hand of God, from then on awaiting until his enemies should be made

---

8. (a) Why did Michael stand up or proceed to reign? (b) How long ago was it that Michael was foretold to do this, and in other prophecies who was foretold to do this in 1914 (A.D.)?
9. Who is the one that was to be commanded to go subduing in the midst of his enemies, and his identification with whom is therefore unavoidable?

a stool for his feet. For it is by one sacrificial offering that he has made those who are being sanctified perfect perpetually." (Hebrews 10:12-14) Michael's identification is thus unavoidable. The Michael that stands up as the "great prince" to fulfill Daniel 12:1 is the Lord Jesus Christ at God's right hand.

[10] The rest of Daniel 12:1 (*JPS*) supports this identification, for it says: "And there shall be a time of trouble, such as never was since there was a nation even to that same time; and at that time thy people [Daniel's people] shall be delivered, every one that shall be found written in the book." Michael's standing up to reign in the midst of his enemies and to go subduing in their midst calls for a war the like of which there had never been before, a time of trouble more distressing than anything previous. This must be so, not just because the war that flamed up in 1914 was earth-wide, but because this trouble embraced heaven as well as earth.

[11] Since Jesus Christ glorified is Michael the great prince of Daniel's people at the outbreak of this trouble, it was only fitting that Jesus on earth in prophesying on the end of this world should also predict this world trouble and do so in the language of Daniel's prophecy. In Jesus' prophecy he twice quotes from the book of Daniel and says: "Therefore, when you catch sight of the disgusting thing that causes desolation, as spoken of through Daniel the prophet, standing in a holy place, (let the reader use discernment,) then let those in Judea begin fleeing to the mountains. . . . for then there will be great tribulation such as has not occurred since the world's beginning until now, no, nor will occur again. In fact, unless those days

10. Daniel 12:1 foretells that Michael's standing up would mean what outbreak, on what scale?
11. Why was it fitting that Jesus, when prophesying on the world's end, should quote from Daniel's prophecy?

were cut short, no flesh would be saved; but on account of the chosen ones those days will be cut short."—Matthew 24:15-22.

¹² Jesus said this as part of his answer to his apostles' question: "Tell us, when will this happen; and what will be the sign of your coming, and of the conclusion of this state?" (Matthew 24:3)* Or, in the New World Translation of the Holy Scriptures: "Tell us, When will these things be, and what will be the sign of your presence and of the consummation of the system of things?" The beginning of this world tribulation is part of the evidence that Jesus Christ, who is Michael the great prince in heaven, is present in the throne of God's restored kingdom. This fact betokens that "this state" or this "system of things" must conclude.

¹³ The last book of the Bible, The Revelation given to John by Jesus Christ, makes more than forty part-quotations from the book of Daniel. In picturing by signs the birth of God's kingdom by the crowning and enthroning of Jesus Christ in heaven, Revelation foretells that the trouble the like of which had never occurred would include heaven. Telling of the successful birth of the Kingdom like a male baby, the revelation of unseen

---

* Quoted from *The Sacred Writings of the Apostles and Evangelists of Jesus Christ, commonly styled the New Testament*. Translated from the Original Greek by Doctors George Campbell, James MacKnight, and Philip Doddridge. With prefaces, various emendations, and an appendix. By Alexander Campbell. Fourth Edition. Bethany, Brooke County, Virginia. Printed and published by M'Vay & Ewing, 1835. In Matthew 13:39, 40 this translation says: "The harvest is the conclusion of this state. . . . so shall it be at the conclusion of this state." In Matthew 28:20: "the conclusion of this state."

12. In answer to what question by his apostles did Jesus say the above, and so of what does the beginning of that tribulation give evidence?
13. How many part-quotations from Daniel does the Revelation to John make, and whom does the Revelation picture as leading the war in heaven against Satan the Devil?

things in heaven says: "And her child was caught away to God and to his throne. . . . And war broke out in heaven: Michael and his angels battled with the dragon, and the dragon and its angels battled but it did not prevail, neither was a place found for them any longer in heaven. So down the great dragon was hurled, the original serpent, the one called Devil and Satan, who is misleading the entire inhabited earth; he was hurled down to the earth, and his angels were hurled down with him. And I heard a loud voice in heaven say: 'Now have come to pass the salvation and the power and the kingdom of our God and the authority of his Christ, because the accuser of our brothers has been hurled down, who accuses them day and night before our God!'" (Revelation 12:5-10) In this war against Satan the Devil, Michael leads.

[14] Is this Michael the resurrected, glorified and enthroned Jesus Christ? Yes. He is here the same as the Michael who helped the angel that brought the prophetic vision to Daniel. (Daniel 10:13, 21, *JPS*) Before 2 B.C. God's only-begotten Son in heaven was called Michael, this name meaning "Who is like God?" When he emptied himself of his heavenly powers and his life was miraculously transferred to the womb of the virgin Jewess Mary and he was born and called Jesus, did he forfeit his heavenly name Michael? No! Before the birth of Jesus there are ten men in the nation of Israel who were listed with the name Michael,* yet the Son of God was not to be known on earth by that name. "You are to call his name Jesus," said the angel Gabriel to Mary his mother. (Luke 1:26-31; 2:21) So on earth it was not even hinted at that he had been Michael in heaven and "one

---

* Numbers 13:13; 1 Chronicles 5:13, 14; 6:40; 7:3; 8:16; 12:20; 27:18; 2 Chronicles 21:2; Ezra 8:8.

14. When he was on earth as a man, how was it not to be hinted at that he had been Michael and one of the chief princes in heaven?

of the chief princes." Daniel 8:11, 25 (*JPS; AS*) speaks of Jehovah God as "the prince of the host" and "the prince of princes." Jehovah is the chiefest Prince, and with Him his Son Michael is "one of the chief princes." He has become Prince of Peace.—Isaiah 9:6.

[15] When he died as the man Jesus Christ and was resurrected and went back to heaven, what was his proper name? Was it still or was it only Jesus Christ? No; it was not just his earthly human name. He resumed his heavenly name Michael. The name Jesus Christ was retained in order to show his identicalness with the human-born Son of God on earth. The name Michael was resumed in order to tie him in with his prehuman existence. As Michael, he was the heavenly member whom Jehovah's wifely organization of holy angels, Jehovah's symbolic "woman," provided in order to be the Seed that should be bruised in the heel by the great Serpent and that should, in turn, bruise the Serpent in the head. (Genesis 3:15) Hence it was a just thing that the glorified Jesus Christ, who had been bruised in the heel on earth, should, as Michael once again, battle against Satan and his demons and hurl them out of heaven to beneath his feet at the earth. Jude 9 calls him "Michael the archangel" who had had a dispute once before in heaven with Satan the Devil, and had won.

[16] Since Jesus Christ glorified is Michael the great prince who stands for the children of Daniel's people, he is the Prince of the sanctuary. Daniel's people today are, like Daniel, witnesses of Jehovah. They are Jehovah's sanctuary class, His temple of "living stones," his "spiritual house," in which he dwells by his spirit. The glorified Jesus

---

15. After he returned to heaven, what was his name, and why was it a just thing for him to be the one to hurl Satan out of heaven?
16. How is he the "Prince" of the sanctuary, and what was his duty toward the remnant of the sanctuary class?

Christ, or Michael, is the Chief Cornerstone of this living sanctuary. So he is the Prince of this sanctuary and upon his own self as the rock-mass he builds this sanctuary. Hence it is his duty to stand up for the remaining members of this sanctuary class and to deliver them from their oppressors.

[17] More than ever before as Michael he should be their Prince. Why? Because now he is Jehovah's Right Shepherd who laid down his human life for his "little flock" of Kingdom joint heirs. "You must call his name 'Jesus', for he will save his people from their sins." (Matthew 1:21; John 10:11-15; Luke 12:32; Romans 8:16, 17) As Prince he now has more power than ever, because he "humbled himself and became obedient as far as death, yes, death on a torture stake. For this very reason also God exalted him to a superior position and kindly gave him the name that is above every other name, so that in the name of Jesus every knee should bend of those in heaven and those on earth and those under the ground, and every tongue should openly confess that Jesus Christ is Lord to the glory of God the Father." (Philippians 2:8-11; Matthew 28:18) In 1914 he was made reigning King in Jehovah's capital organization over all the universe. He will prove himself to be Prince of Peace.—Isaiah 9:6.

[18] Michael in heaven was associated with the angel that brought the vision to Daniel. Thus he was acquainted with the prophecies of the book of Daniel. When on earth as the man Jesus, anointed with Jehovah's spirit, he showed familiarity with Daniel's book. He foreknew that the great Prince of Jehovah's people must stand up in Kingdom power in the thick of the fight be-

17. Why now more than ever before should he be their Prince?
18. For having been Michael in heaven, what familiarity with Scripture did Jesus show, and in the midst of what fight did he know that he had to come into his kingdom?

tween the symbolic king of the north and the king of the south. Hence when the apostles of the sanctuary class asked Jesus for the visible evidence of his being present in the Kingdom at the consummation of the system of things, Jesus answered in harmony with the book of Daniel. He said: "Nation will rise against nation and kingdom against kingdom, and there will be food shortages and earthquakes in one place after another. All these things are a beginning of pangs of distress. Then people will deliver you up to tribulation and will kill you, and you will be hated by all the nations on account of my name. . . . But he that has endured to the finish is the one that will be saved. And this good news of the kingdom will be preached in all the inhabited earth for the purpose of a witness to all the nations, and then the accomplished end will come. Therefore, when you catch sight of the disgusting thing that causes desolation, as spoken of through Daniel the prophet, standing in a holy place, (let the reader use discernment,) . . . " (Matthew 24:7-15) By these events that started in 1914 with the first world war between the king of the north and the king of the south, Jehovah's sanctuary class were to know that Jesus their Prince was present in the heavenly kingdom and that the good news of this was to be preached earth-wide as a witness to all the nations before their end.

[19] In 1919 the "disgusting thing that causes desolation" was set up in the form of the League of Nations and was idolized as the political expression of the kingdom of God on earth. By this the Christians had further evidence that Michael had stood up and that we were in the "appointed time of the end." Even the persecution that they began to undergo in a special way for refusing to idolize this "image of the wild beast" and for standing

---

19. To the Christians, of what was the setting up of the "disgusting thing" and their own persecutions still further evidence?

loyal to the established kingdom of God and for preaching it everywhere was more evidence of our being in the last days of this system of things.

[20] When they saw the darkness and distress of the nations increase after that "beginning of pangs of distress" between 1914 and 1918, these intelligent ones appreciated that it was the fulfillment of Daniel's prophecy and of Jesus' prophecy: "Immediately after the tribulation of those days the sun will be darkened, and the moon will not give its light, and the stars will fall from heaven, and the powers of the heavens will be shaken. And then the sign of the Son of man will appear in heaven, and then all the tribes of the earth will go to wailing and they will see the Son of man coming on the clouds of heaven with power and great glory." (Matthew 24:29, 30) When stars fall from heaven, where do they drop? Down on this earth? This earth could not endure that; it could not accommodate them all. So that is not to be expected. Yet, if they fell from heaven, they would no longer be lights in heaven for men but would all disappear. This would add to the continual darkness caused by the sun's being darkened during the day and the moon's not giving its light by night. The old world becomes all dark.

[21] The Christian disciple Luke gives further details of Jesus' prophecy concerning the evidences of his kingdom and of the "appointed time of the end" of this world: "Nation will rise against nation, and kingdom against kingdom, and there will be great earthquakes and in one place after another pestilences and food shortages, and there will be fearful sights and from heaven great signs. Also there will be signs in sun and moon and stars, and on the earth anguish of nations, not knowing

20. (a) The increase of international darkness and distress after the "beginning of pangs" fulfills what further prophecy of Jesus? (b) What is the result of the falling of the stars from heaven? 21. With what further details does Luke record Jesus' prophecy, and their fulfillment is witnessed to by what reports?

the way out because of the roaring of the sea and
its agitation, while men become faint out of fear
and expectation of the things coming upon the
inhabited earth; for the powers of the heavens
will be shaken. And then they will see the Son
of man coming in a cloud with power and great
glory." (Luke 21:10, 11, 25-27) The news reports
from all over the world since 1914 bear witness
to the undeniable fulfillment of Jesus' prophecy,
to prove that Michael, the Son of man, stood up.

[22] Not to be dismissed from consideration as
"fearful sights" and "great signs" from heaven
are new things that modern science is discovering
and bringing to the people's attention, to their
own and the people's mental agitation and rising
fears. The so-called cosmic rays are more and more
commanding scientific study. Only as far back as
1911 scientific experiments on the absorbing of
penetrating gamma rays from radium in the air
led a Dr. V. F. Hess to suspect that not all the
ionization in air was due to this alone. Experiments later with balloons developed the right conclusion, that there was some extremely powerful
radiation coming from above; there were cosmic
rays. With the speed of light the cosmic rays are
carried along through earth's atmosphere and
finally hit the earth with still enough energy to
penetrate and be measurable to a depth of two
hundred feet underground. Cosmic rays reach an
energy of many billions of electron volts. The sun
of our solar system plays its part in these cosmic
rays.

[23] It has been observed that there has been an
intensifying of cosmic ray showers during what
appear to be patches of something on the face of
the sun. What? Patches of darkness, to us. Sun-

22. As "fearful sights" and "great signs" from heaven, what
things of recent discovery are not to be left unconsidered, and
what rays are of increasing interest?
23. According to reports, how does the sun of our solar system
play its part in these cosmic rays, and with what effects?

spots, we call them. They are in actuality great flares of energy on the surface of the sun. In December, 1957, during the International Geophysical Year, it was reported that "in recent months" the sun had co-operated with the scientific studies being made. How? By "displaying what is regarded here as the greatest number of flares in its recorded history. . . . In recent months the sun has been at the peak of its eleven-year sunspot cycle. This has produced an unusual number of flares. These are thought to spray out particles, which strike the earth's atmosphere a day or two later and cause magnetic storms and other phenomena."* The sunspot activity was reported as having "disrupted radio and television waves." Studies have shown that, accompanying a solar flare, there is a sudden increase of cosmic radiation and radio fade-outs. About a day after the appearance of the flare a magnetic storm is felt all over the world. During the period of greatest cosmic ray intensity some areas of the earth are almost completely blacked out with respect to radio communication. Lead-encased cables for communication and for transmitting power have also been burned completely through, and unexposed X-ray film has been rendered useless.

[24] What is the source of these cosmic rays? Not the stars. It has been scientifically established that the total energy carried by all cosmic ray particles is much more than all the energy ever emitted by stars. Cosmic rays seem to come from all directions with such great energies that scientists have not arrived at any satisfying explanation of their origin. Those of highest energy evidently come from beyond our Milky Way.

---

* According to a special dispatch, dated Boulder, Colorado, December 14; published in the New York *Times* of December 15, 1957.

---

24. What has been observed concerning the source of these cosmic rays?

²⁵ Studies have been made of the effect of cosmic rays on living cells in animal bodies, particularly with respect to disorders of the mind. What effect do they have or will they have on the way men behave here on earth? Certainly the Creator of cosmic rays, Jehovah God, could use these to affect the minds of his enemies, including the king of the north and the king of the south, and could drive them to mutual slaughter: "every man's sword shall be against his brother." (Ezekiel 38: 21, *AS*) In this prophecy God warns that he will also use other natural forces that are at his disposal, possibly a rain of anti-matter that has the property of annihilating any material thing that it meets. He warns all scoffers that he will do an 'unusual work.'—Isaiah 28:21.

²⁶ The moon also has come in for scientific interest. The missile experts would transform it from being the gently beaming luminary of the night to being an object of fearsome possibilities. The conquest of the moon has become a serious aim. Not only "sterilized" rockets to the moon and satellites to go around and inspect the moon on both sides, but also the establishing of a manned base on the moon for observing and dominating all the earth! One Swedish scientist warned fellow scientists to study the possibility that the explosion of a hydrogen bomb on the moon might create disastrous tides of the oceans on the earth. Such an explosion would also create radioactivity on the moon and make the future exploration of it by scientific visitors hard. What with mysterious "flying saucers" being reported, even though the reports may be proved to be largely unfounded, man on earth since A.D. 1914 is indeed feeling

25. How could Jehovah God use these cosmic rays to affect the king of the north and the king of the south, and what other natural force might he use in his work?
26. How is the moon becoming an object for fears to man, and what is man feeling more and more with regard to space and the visible heavenly bodies?

horrors with respect to cosmic space and the sun, the moon and the stars.

[27] Should the "people that do know their God" share in the anguish of nations and in the fear of men in view of all the things coming upon the earth? Not at all! They know that Jesus foretold this present world situation and said to them: "But as these things start to occur, raise yourselves erect and lift your heads up, because your deliverance is getting near. . . . when you see these things occurring, know that the kingdom of God is near." (Luke 21:28, 31) Today, while the doomed world is in spasms of fear, Jesus' followers, the sanctuary class and the great crowd of "other sheep," do straighten up with confidence and lift up their heads with joy. They understand the glorious meaning of these things which they see occurring. They know that Michael their great Prince has stood up in the kingdom of God now established. He has stood up both to deliver them and to vindicate the universal sovereignty of Jehovah.

27. At the sight of such things occurring, what do Jesus' followers do, and why?

CHAPTER 13

The Present Happiness At The Sanctuary

THERE was a short period of sorrow and captivity before the heavenly Michael, standing up in his kingdom power, delivered Jehovah's sanctuary class.

Michael, when on earth as the man Jesus Christ, had foretold this in the prophecy on the end of this wicked system of things. He predicted the first world war and said that his faithful followers would be persecuted and be hated by all the nations on account of his name. Some followers would even be stumbled by this persecution and would fall away. (Matthew 24:7-12) This took place while the war in heaven was being fought by Michael and his angels against Satan the Devil and his demons. The people, for whom the reigning Michael was the great Prince, came into a forced captivity to the Devil's visible organization on earth.

[2] Michael their Prince permitted the persecution and sorrowful captivity of them for a test to them, to make two classes among those claiming to follow him become manifest. What a happiness followed when Michael, having fought a victorious war in heaven, delivered his people from the power of the king of the north and the king of the south! He delivered the sanctuary class, that is, the remnant of it that was then alive on earth, "every one that shall be found written in the book."—Daniel 12:1, JPS.

[3] Jesus once told his disciples: "Rejoice because your names have been inscribed in the heavens." (Luke 10:20) Being anointed to serve as the symbolic "twenty-four elders" before the throne of God in heaven, they were spoken of as the "congregation of the firstborn who have been enrolled in the heavens." (Revelation 4:4, RS; Hebrews 12:22, 23) When the persecution and the captivity came, they endured it in a faithful way that kept their names from being blotted out of the book of

1, 2. (a) As foretold by Jesus, what period of sorrow and captivity took place before Michael brought deliverance? (b) Why did Michael their Prince permit that, and who were the ones delivered? 3. Because of what had their names been inscribed, and why had they not been blotted out of the book?

God's record. At the happy time marked in Daniel's prophecies they were furnished with escape.

⁴ Jehovah's angel told Daniel of the result of the deliverance furnished by Michael the heavenly Prince: "And many of them that sleep in the dust of the earth shall awake, some to everlasting life, and some to reproaches and everlasting abhorrence." (Daniel 12:2, *JPS*) Because of the unjust oppressions during World War I, the sanctuary class and their associates were beaten to the dusty ground, as the symbolic "little horn," the "king of fierce countenance," cast them down and trampled upon them, took away the continual burnt offering of praise to God and cast down the place of his sanctuary. (Daniel 8:9-11, 23, 24, *JPS*) They were not actually dead and buried, but Revelation 11:1-12 pictures these witnesses of Jehovah God as lying dead in the very street of this worldly organization. They were as asleep in death. Yet there was a postwar work to do, as Michael himself had foretold in Matthew 24:14. For this witness work it was necessary to use the remnant of the sanctuary class. At the marked time in 1919 Michael, the reigning Jesus Christ, delivered his people, spiritual Israel, for he was their great Prince. With an "archangel's voice" he issued a "commanding call" to them to awake from their sleep in that abased, captive condition. (1 Thessalonians 4:16, 17) What was the result?

⁵ In that first postwar period there was an awakening from the inactive deathlike state. The faithful remnant of the sanctuary class wanted to be alive and expend their strength, time and means in giving the world-wide witness to God's established kingdom. This was the line of activity that would lead to everlasting life in the heavenly

---

4. In what way were many sleeping "in the dust of the earth," and when and why was there a command to awake?
5. How did some awake "to everlasting life," and with what happiness resulting?

kingdom in God's new world. By awaking and rousing themselves to the Kingdom witness-work they were those out of the "many" who awoke to everlasting life. Because of their willingness to accept the care of the earthly interests of God's established kingdom, Michael as the reigning King appointed them to be the "faithful and discreet slave" with oversight "over all his belongings." Happy indeed was this slave class at such an honored appointment to Kingdom service.

⁶ But out of the "many" there were some that awoke and put themselves into postwar action, but it was to "reproaches and everlasting abhorrence" that these awoke. These included many democratically elected "elders" of congregations. These refused to take upon themselves the responsibility of the Kingdom interests, to deliver a world-wide witness to the established Kingdom; and they abused those of the "faithful and discreet slave" class who did. They tried to lead others to oppose the work of witnessing from house to house as well as publicly. (Acts 20:20, 25) The names of all these who went over to the opposition were blotted out of the book. They were found guilty of being an abusive, self-indulging "evil slave" class and were cast out into the darkness outside in this doomed world and were assigned their part with the religious hypocrites, to weep and gnash their teeth in bitterness out there. They earned reproaches, not recommendations. They became something ever abhorrent, something ever repulsive to God.—Matthew 24: 45-51.

⁷ Foretelling of those who awoke to everlasting life as Kingdom witnesses, Jehovah's angel went on to say: "And the intelligent shall shine bril-

---

6. How did some awake "to reproaches and everlasting abhorrence," and with what effect upon their names?
7. How did the "intelligent" ones then shine, and how did they "bring many to righteousness"?

liantly like the brilliance of the expanse of the sky; and they that bring many to righteousness shall be like the stars, for ever and ever." (Daniel 12:3, *Le*) These spiritually intelligent ones began shining with heavenly light, because Jehovah's glory had shone forth upon them and they obeyed his command to arise and shed forth light. (Isaiah 60:1, 2) With the good news of the newborn kingdom of God they shone like the sun, which lets nothing be concealed from its heat all around the globe. In the midnight darkness of this world they were like stars of light, for they engaged in an educational work that brought the Bible and its Kingdom truths directly into the homes and private lives of the lost "other sheep" and turned them to righteousness, which is the worship and the ministry of the true God, Jehovah. They turned these from worshiping the abominable "image of the wild beast" or worshiping the self-deifying king of the north and his State.

[8] Living as we do in this time of the end since Michael the great Prince stood up in heaven, we are living in a time more highly favored than that of the prophet Daniel. As Daniel came near to the end of his prophetic book, Jehovah's angel said to him: "But you, Daniel, shut up the words, and seal the book, until the time of the end. Many shall run to and fro, and knowledge shall increase." (Daniel 12:4, *RS*) To us in this "time of the end" Daniel's book has been opened and unsealed. It was the meaning of the words in it that was shut up within God's power. It was the explanation of the book that was sealed off till God should give it as the great Interpreter of his own prophecies. Sincere seekers after God's will who go running to and fro through the words of Daniel's book that they may know God's will and do it are rewarded. Their knowledge of the Holy

---

8. In running to and fro, as foretold in Daniel 12:4, how do we find ourselves living in a time more highly favored than Daniel's?

Scriptures increases. With their increased knowledge there goes a better understanding of God's will and purpose. This enables them to impart understanding to many other sheep.

PROPHETIC "TIMES" AND "DAYS"

[9] When Daniel received the final vision in the third year of Cyrus the king of Persia he was alongside the Mesopotamian river Tigris, anciently called Hiddekel. (Daniel 10:4) After the vision he received time measurements that are of high interest to us who are seeking happiness during this world's "time of the end." Says he: "Then I Daniel looked, and behold, there were two others standing, the one on this side of the bank of the stream, and the other on that side of the bank of the stream. And one said to the man clothed in linen, who was above the waters of the stream, How long shall it be to the end of these wonders?" (Daniel 12:5, 6, Le) The angel that appeared like a man clothed in linen and was miraculously above the waters of the Tigris River was Michael's associate, the angel that had brought the vision to Daniel in answer to his prayer. Two other angels appeared, one on the same bank of the river where Daniel was. For Daniel's benefit, but particularly for ours today, one of these asked the angel that had brought the vision to Daniel just how long it would be to the "end of these wonders," that is, how long till the wonderful details of the vision should be accomplished in completeness. Here we listen in with Daniel:

[10] "Then heard I the man clothed in linen, who was above the waters of the stream; and he lifted up his right hand and his left hand unto the heavens, and swore by the Everliving One that after

9. Where was Daniel when he had this vision, and what question did he hear asked?
10. What answer did Daniel hear to the question, and how was the answer made more certain as to its fulfillment?

a time, times, and a half, and when there shall be
an end to the crushing of the power of the holy
people, all these things shall be ended." (Daniel
12:7, Le) This prediction of time is sworn to in
the name of the Immortal God, the King of eternity, Jehovah. Its being sworn to with both hands
lifted heavenward would seem to make the sworn
oath doubly strong. However, this raising of both
hands in oath enabled one on either side of the
Tigris River to see an upraised hand. Being thus
sworn to, the coming true of this time prophecy
is just as certain as that Jehovah lives immortal.

[11] The count of a "time, times, and a half" must
be taken into consideration here. The Hebrew
word translated "time" here is translated "appointed time" earlier, in Daniel 8:19, and means
a space of time. How long a space? *An American
Translation* renders the entire Hebrew expression
"a year, years, and half a year"; James Moffatt's
translation, "three years and half a year." This
entire time period falling inside the "appointed
time of the end" that began in 1914 (A.D.), the
period must be a literal three years and a half.
It could begin counting no earlier than the start
of the "appointed time of the end" in the fall of
that year 1914.

[12] When these three years and a half end, there
should be an end to the crushing of the power of
the holy people of Jehovah God, his saints, his
sanctuary class.* This time period doubtless corresponds with the time period of equal length

---

* It is only by changing the vowel pointing of the
Hebrew Bible text of Daniel 12:7 and by rearranging
the Hebrew words that the translation is forced: "after
the power of him who shattered the holy people should
be ended, all these things should be ended."—*AT; Mo.*

---

11. What count of time must here be considered, and is it literal
or symbolic, and before when could it not start?
12. With what time period in Daniel 7:25 does the time period
here correspond, and how at the culmination of it was the organizational work crippled in a way not duplicated?

given in Daniel 7:25 (*JPS*) concerning the symbolic horn, the Anglo-American dual world power, and its abuse of the sanctuary class: "He . . . shall wear out the saints of the Most High; . . . and they shall be given into his hand until a time and times and half a time." These three years and six months were found to begin in the first half of November, 1914, and to end on May 7, 1918.* On this latter date the king of the south, comprising Britain and America as war allies, went to the limit in dealing Jehovah's sanctuary class a shattering blow by striking at the very summit of Jehovah's consecrated visible organization, the central headquarters in Brooklyn, New York, and laying hold of the president of the Watch Tower Bible & Tract Society together with its secretary-treasurer, and breaking up the relations of the Society's Brooklyn headquarters with its branch offices and agencies in foreign countries. On June 20, 1918, the said officers, together with six others prominent in the Bible publication work, were sentenced to eighty years' imprisonment. All their brothers in the sanctuary class around the earth were shocked, grieved and benumbed. This crippled the organizational work of Jehovah's sanctuary in a way that has never been duplicated since then, not even during World War II.

[13] The main one behind this shattering of Jehovah's holy ones was Satan the Devil, who claims possession of all the kingdoms of this world and their glory. (Matthew 4:8, 9; Luke 4:5, 6) In 1914, when Michael stood up, the war in heaven was begun to oust the Devil and his demons. He was defeated by Michael, and there is Scriptural reason to believe that by the time of the annual cele-

---

* See chapter 8, pages 180, 181, paragraphs 25-27; chapter 9, pages 201-206.

---

13. Who was behind this shattering work, and what now indicates that his power to shatter has come to an end?

bration of the Lord's evening meal on March 26, 1918, Satan the Devil was hurled down to the earth. For the reason that he now knows that he has yet a "short period of time" before he is bruised in the head in the battle of Armageddon, he has great anger, especially against the remnant of the sanctuary class. On these he has waged war by all means at his disposal. (Revelation 12:7-17) But to this date he has failed to show the power to shatter that he was permitted to show in 1918. Neither will he shatter Jehovah's sanctuary in their "beauteous land" when he plays the part of Gog of Magog and comes down from the north with all his visible and invisible hosts to destroy the holy remnant and the "other sheep." He himself will be bruised. His power to shatter has come to an end.—Ezekiel 38:1 to 39:16.

¹⁴ The period of three times and half a time having ended in 1918, the other important things of the vision must "be ended" or be brought to accomplishment at their appointed time. The prophet Daniel away back there could not decipher the meaning of the things seen in vision. He confesses: "And I heard, but I understood not; then said I: 'O my lord, what shall be the latter end of these things?' And he said: 'Go thy way, Daniel; for the words are shut up and sealed till the time of the end. Many shall purify themselves, and make themselves white, and be refined; but the wicked shall do wickedly; and none of the wicked shall understand; but they that are wise [the intelligent, Le] shall understand." (Daniel 12:8-10, JPS) Daniel did go his way into death sometime after the writing down of the vision about 537 B.C., shutting up the words and sealing the book.

---

14. The three times and half a time having ended, what other things must be ended in due time, and why has Daniel not received an understanding of the things heard, even till now?

[15] Great understanding of the book of Daniel was displayed by Jesus Christ on earth. In this "time of the end" since 1914 he is the one whom God uses to open or unstop the words like a well of knowledge and information and to unseal the book in all its meaning. (Revelation 5:1-5) Do we want to understand the book with its marvelous references to our day? Then with Jehovah's help through Christ we must purify ourselves from this world, we must make ourselves white with righteousness through the Lamb's blood, and we must be refined in our sincere devotion to Jehovah God and his kingdom. Only the Scripturally intelligent ones will be allowed to understand the book of Daniel and all the rest of the Bible. However, none of the wicked can and will understand it and gain salvation. In these critical times hard to deal with they will go on in their wickedness, especially against Jehovah's witnesses, until they are destroyed as unhappy fighters against God.—2 Timothy 3:1-5.

1,290 DAYS

[16] The shattering or crushing of the power of Jehovah's holy people in 1918 did not make an end of them. This is the "time of the end," not of the holy sanctuary class, but of the king of the north and of the king of the south and of all the neutral nations. It is a time of deliverance for the sanctuary class and for the "other sheep" who worship with them. After saying that these spiritually intelligent ones would understand, Jehovah's angel added: "And from the time that the continual sacrifice will be removed, even to set up the desolating abomination, there will be a thousand two hundred and ninety days."—Daniel 12:11, *Le.*

---

15. Who has been used to unstop the words and unseal the book for us, and what must we do in order to be among the intelligent who will understand?
16, 17. (a) For whom is this the "time of the end"? (b) From when is it the time to begin counting the 1,290 days?

[17] This taking away of the continual sacrifice of praise to God was already foretold in Daniel 8:11. It took place in 1918, when the time, times and half a time were fulfilled.* The taken-away condition of the daily or continual sacrifice lasted into the following year, until March 26, 1919, on which date the release occurred for the Watch Tower Society's president, secretary-treasurer and six fellow prisoners, under bail. The setting up of the "desolating abomination" occurred when the worship of the "image of the wild beast," that abominable makeshift for God's kingdom, the League of Nations, was set up by the religious organizations of Christendom. By action of the Federal Council of the Churches of Christ in America this was dated from the close of January, 1919.† By the time of this latter date both of these two mentioned things had taken place. Consequently this is the point of time from which to count.

[18] After the 1,290 days had begun to count, Michael their great Prince delivered his people, in March of 1919. On April 13, 1919, there were more than 17,961 that celebrated the Lord's evening meal earth-wide.‡ During the rest of the 1,290 days the work of God's holy organization was reorganized, improved and strengthened for the global witness that had to be given before the complete end should come upon this old system of things. In due time, what happened that out-

---

* See chapter 9, pages 201-206. During the Nazi regime from 1933 to 1945 the king of the north tried to take away the continual burnt offering, but it was not with the same results as in 1918.—Daniel 11:31, *AS*.

† See chapter 9, pages 206-210.

‡ See *The Watch Tower* as of May 15, 1919, page 151. The figures there given do not include groups of less than thirty in attendance.

---

18. With relation to the 1,290 days, when did Michael deliver his people, and how long a period in solar time do those 1,290 days equal?

standingly marked the end of those divinely numbered days? The 1,290 days must be treated from
the standpoint of the lunar calendar. Hence divine
prophecy treats a month as being thirty days long,
on the average. The 1,290 days are just thirty days
or one lunar month longer than 1,260 days in
prophecy. Revelation 11:2, 3 definitely shows that
1,260 days equal forty-two months. Forty-two
months amount to three years and six months.
In prophecy these three years and six months are
not affected by any leap year or by any Jewish
Veadar year in which a thirteenth lunar month
is added to the Jewish calendar to bring the series
of lunar years up to the length of the series of
solar years. Since 1,260 days in prophecy equal
three years and six months, then 1,290 days equal
three years and seven months. Counted from the
close of January, 1919, where do those three years
and seven months end?

¹⁹ They bring us to the end of August and the
beginning of September of 1922. It was in the
first half of September, 1922, that the electrifying
words rang out: "Be faithful and true witnesses
for the Lord. Go forward in the fight until every
vestige of Babylon lies desolate. Herald the message far and wide. The world must know that Jehovah is God and that Jesus Christ is King of kings
and Lord of lords. This is the day of all days.
Behold, the King reigns! You are his publicity
agents. Therefore advertise, advertise, advertise,
the King and his kingdom." This came on The
Day (September 8) of the nine-day international
convention of Jehovah's witnesses at Cedar Point,
Ohio, at the conclusion of the address of the president of the Watch Tower Society on the subject
"The Kingdom." In this address J. F. Rutherford
proved from Scripture and fact that Jehovah's

19. Toward the end of those 1,290 days, what electrifying message
was delivered, and what judgment work was called to our attention?

"messenger of the covenant" had come to the temple, the spiritual sanctuary, in the spring of 1918 for judgment work. The judgment that was to "start with the house of God" was now in progress! (1 Peter 4:17; Malachi 3:1-5, *AS*) In expression of this judgment upon Christians a resolution was adopted.

[20] Sunday afternoon, September 10, President Rutherford delivered his public address on the challenging subject "Millions Now Living Will Never Die." At its conclusion he introduced a resolution entitled "A Challenge to World Rulers," which was adopted with acclaim by the 18,000 to 20,000 present. This notified the nations that the "appointed times of the nations" had run out in 1914; that God's kingdom by Christ had then been set up in heaven; that the League of Nations was a fraud and "must fail, because God has decreed it thus"; that the kingdom of Jehovah's Messiah was the complete cure-all for the ills of humankind; and that by obeying the laws of that righteous kingdom men will continue to live and never die off the earth.* This bold resolution was the first in a series of seven resolutions adopted at annual general assemblies of Jehovah's witnesses from 1922 to 1928. Like plagues, these resolutions were poured out upon apostate Christendom. Of the initial resolution, "The Challenge," there were eventually 45,000,000 copies distributed worldwide in many languages.

1,335 DAYS

[21] Unquestionably that Cedar Point convention (September 5-13, 1922) was an impressive marker

---

* See the issue of November 1, 1922, of *The Watch Tower;* also the issue of October 11, 1922, of *The Golden Age,* pages 22-26.

20. What expression of judgment upon professed Christians was then sent forth, and thus the series of what things began?
21, 22. (a) What still further time period did God mark in his Word? (b) When did this time period begin, and what happened to the waiting ones during this period?

of the climax of the 1,290 days for the sanctuary class. But inspiriting as it was, Jehovah God foresaw something still further that deserved timing in his prophecy, because of what it would mean to his consecrated people. To put them in further expectation, he inspired his angel to say to Daniel: "Happy is he who waits till he reaches the thousand three hundred and thirty-five days!" (Daniel 12:12, *AT*) This period would be in addition to the 1,290 days and would be forty-five days or a month and a half longer in prophetic time. It would equal three years eight months and fifteen days. This time period would count from the end of the previous 1,290 days, which had culminated at the second Cedar Point convention in September, 1922. The following period of 1,335 days would therefore end in the month of May, 1926.

²² During this period Jehovah God helped his people to wait or endure, carrying on his Kingdom preaching on a widening scale. This resulted in bringing into the sanctuary many more to be members of this remnant consecrated by Jehovah. This was evident from the increasing attendance at the annual celebrations of the Lord's evening meal, 32,661 participating in 1922; 42,000 in 1923; 62,696 in 1924; and 90,434 in 1925.* Evidently, however, there were some who did not 'wait' till the end of the announced time, for in 1926 there was a reported decrease in the attendance on March 27 at the Lord's evening meal to 89,278. The year 1925 especially proved to be a year of great trial to many of Jehovah's people. Some stopped waiting and went with the world.

²³ Came the month of May, 1926. May 1-3 there was a general assembly at Basel, Switzerland. On

---

* These total attendance figures earth-wide do not count in groups of less than twenty celebrators of the Lord's evening meal, excepting some foreign reports.

23. How was the month of May, 1926, marked, and where did the grand climax of this month come?

May 13-16 another general assembly was held at
Magdeburg, Germany, at which President Rutherford gave the public address on "Comfort for the
People," attended by 25,000. But the grand climax
in assemblies that marked month was in London,
England, the capital of history's greatest empire,
the British Empire. The convention was thus at
the seat of the chief backer of the League of
Nations, the abominable "image of the wild beast,"
the political-religious makeshift for the true kingdom of God. From May 24 to 31 the conventioners
held their joyous sessions; and strait-laced, sanc-
timonious, traditional religious restrictions upon
God's people were exposed and discarded, to their
great relief. On May 28 President Rutherford submitted for adoption by the convention the fifth
of the series of annual resolutions, this one being
entitled "A Testimony to the Rulers of the World."
The thrilling new book entitled "Deliverance" was
also released that same day.

²⁴ Sunday night, May 30, in London's then
greatest auditorium, Royal Albert Hall, came the
climax. World powers were then addressed indeed,
when President Rutherford spoke to the packed
Hall on "Why World Powers Are Tottering—The
Remedy" in support of the Resolution that had
been submitted to them. In consequence of this
putting the seventh world power on notice, the
Anglo-American dual world power committed the
"transgression of desolation,"* and the 2,300 prophetic days began to count, to mark off when Jehovah's sanctuary should be restored to its rightful state.—Daniel 8:13, 14, *RS*.

²⁵ With this London international convention
there began a period of happiness that has not

---

* See chapter 9, pages 210-219.

---

24. On Sunday night, May 30, 1926, who were indeed addressed,
and what did these commit, to begin the counting of what time
period?
25. For those who had waited, what period began with that
London convention, and on what account particularly?

ended and will never end. How happy those of the sanctuary class were that they had waited till the close of the 1,335 days! They were taking on a newer happiness because of appreciating more their privilege of being the witnesses of the Most High God, whose name is Jehovah. At the beginning of the year the issue of January 1, 1926, of *The Watch Tower* confronted them with the leading article "Who Will Honor Jehovah?" On Service Day (May 29) at London the conventioners went out on the streets as witnesses of Him and put in the hands of the people 110,000 copies of the new booklet *The Standard for the People*. Reporting on this successful witness effort, the *Watch Tower* report (as of July 15, 1926) on the London convention concluded with these meaningful words: "Nothing like this has ever been known on Service Day at a convention. The friends were bubbling over with enthusiasm. They felt that they had done their best to obey the command of Jehovah: 'Ye are my witnesses that I am God.'" (Isaiah 43:12, *AS*) With still greater happiness the sanctuary class embraced the very name "Jehovah's witnesses" in international assembly at Columbus, Ohio, July 26, 1931.

²⁶ Some day in the not distant future the faithful pre-Christian witness of Jehovah, the prophet Daniel, will know how the time periods that the angel foretold were fulfilled upon the sanctuary class in this twentieth century. Jehovah's angel indicated how it will become possible for Daniel to know, saying: "But thou, go thy way toward the end; and thou shalt rest, and arise again for thy lot at the end of the days." (Daniel 12:13, *Le*) When Daniel reached the end of his way in death, he rested in Sheol, mankind's common grave, in the sleep of death. He did not go to heaven. Jesus,

---

26. (a) How will Daniel in a future day be able to know how the time periods that the angel foretold were fulfilled? (b) For what lot will Daniel arise again, and what may he become?

who had come down from heaven, said so. (John
3:13) As a witness of Jehovah, who "did good
things," Daniel awaits the fulfillment of Jesus'
words: "The hour is coming in which all those
in the memorial tombs will hear his voice and
come out, those who did good things to a resurrection of life, those who practiced vile things to
a resurrection of judgment." (John 5:28, 29)
Daniel's lot will be an earthly one in God's new
world after Armageddon. He will be resurrected
and stand up for his blessed lot under Christ's
rule of a thousand years. He will have everlasting
life in view. By accepting the ransom sacrifice of
his King, the Right Shepherd, Daniel will become
a son of the Father for eternity. (Isaiah 9:6) Because he displayed faithfulness as an earthly
prince over Jehovah's people long ago he will no
doubt be assigned among those whom Christ the
King will "appoint as princes in all the earth."
—Psalm 45:16.

CHAPTER 14

Earthly Blessings When His Will Is Done

JESUS Christ was on earth when he taught his disciples to pray to his heavenly Father Jehovah: "Let your kingdom come. Let your will come to pass, as in heaven, also upon earth." (Matthew 6:9, 10) At that time his disciples were all natural Jews. Their earthly forefathers had known Jehovah's rule as King during the days when he raised up judges to rule over Israel, such as Joshua, Gideon, Barak, Samson and Samuel, and also when King David and his successors ruled, sitting upon the "throne of Jehovah." In 607 B.C. that typical kingdom of Jehovah God was overturned in harmony with his own decree; and in Jesus' day the "contemptible person," Emperor Tiberius Caesar, ruled the land of the Jews through the Roman procurator, Pontius Pilate. Jesus' Jewish disciples could keenly appreciate praying for the kingdom of Jehovah God to come back and exercise its power over earth, that here on earth the heavenly Father's will might be done just as up in heaven. That kingdom must come, not to destroy man's home, the earth, but to see that God's will is done on earth as well as in heaven.

² In 1914 (A.D.) Michael stood up in Kingdom power and authority. Or, according to the vision of Daniel 7:13, 14, the glorified Son of man in heaven was brought before the Ancient of Days and was given the everlasting kingdom to which he was the rightful, sworn Heir. Because he was the one that had the "right" to it, Jehovah, the Ancient of Days, gave it to Jesus Christ. (Ezekiel 21:27, *RS*) At once that kingdom battled against Satan and his demons and cast them down to earth, to await here the universal "war of the great day of God the Almighty." The Kingdom also directed its power toward the earth in particular behalf of the sanctuary class and the great

---

1. (a) Why could the disciples whom Jesus taught the model prayer appreciate praying for God's kingdom to come? (b) Why must that kingdom come?
2. (a) In 1914, what was given to the Son of man, to fulfill Daniel 7:13, 14, and what was its action toward heaven and earth? (b) Why did it not proceed against the king of the north and the king of the south?

crowd of "other sheep" who were to be gathered. (John 10:16) Yet that kingdom did not "come" against the king of the north and the king of the south in an Armageddon battle to destroy all the kingdoms of this world. Like the symbolic stone that was cut out of the mountain without human hands, that kingdom, set up by the God of heaven, did not then strike the metallic image of Nebuchadnezzar's dream upon its iron and clay feet and destroy all the earthly governments pictured by the image. There were other parts of God's will that needed to be done on earth first before the destruction of this system of things at Armageddon.

³ Much as Satan the Devil would like to do so in his insane purpose of "rule or ruin," it is not the purpose of Jehovah God to depopulate the earth by his war between his kingdom and Satan's world. Satan's four-thousand-year-old world must be cleared out, in order to make way for Jehovah's righteous new world under the Seed of his "woman," Jesus Christ. Since it is a world that has to be destroyed in that universal war, the people on earth will be unable to escape that war by space travel or by long-submerged atomic-powered submarines but face destruction. Since 1914 they needed to be warned of what is ahead and to be informed of any God-given way of escape. This required a global witness to be given in all the inhabited earth, to all races and nationalities, before the end should come upon Satan's world in both its parts, visible and invisible.

⁴ It is not obligatory upon Almighty God to do this, but it has been his loving course of mercy to send advance warning before his unusual work of destruction upon his enemies. To serve this

---

3. Contrary to Satan's liking, what is it Jehovah's purpose not to do by his coming universal war, and hence what does this require in behalf of the people?
4. Was that obligatory upon God, and whom would he raise up for the lifesaving work, and who would be spared at Armageddon?

warning notice and this guidance to a safety shelter, there was a need of notice servers and safety guides. Whom would Jehovah provide for this lifesaving work? Angels from heaven? No; but his sanctuary class, a remnant of which was on earth. Hence God's symbolic stone, the kingdom of his Son, did not strike the symbolic image of Satan's visible earthly organization and crush it in 1918 when the "place of his sanctuary was cast down" and the sanctuary class were "trampled under foot." But the heavenly Michael had stood up in Kingdom power, and he delivered these faithful ones, because they were "found written in the book." These he awakened to activity in giving the foretold Kingdom witness everywhere. (Matthew 24:14) Let reject the "good news of the kingdom" whoever wanted to, but those who took to heart the witness and made the Kingdom their only hope of salvation would be spared at the battle of Armageddon.

⁵ At an ascertainable date, at the end of the "appointed times of the nations," God's kingdom was born in 1914 and Michael and his angels commenced battle against the invisible part of Satan's world up in heaven. The demonic part of Satan's world was hurled down to the unseen vicinity of this earth in the outer space through which the king of the north and the king of the south are rocketing their earth-moons or satellites or spaceships. But the day and the hour when Michael, the Son of God in Kingdom power, again takes up the battle at Armageddon is not known, which leaves also the year of it unknown to us in advance. In the year that Jehovah wiped out the "ancient world," the "world of ungodly people," Noah, having finished the three-story ark for survival for his family and animal species, was

5, 6. (a) At what ascertainable date was God's kingdom by his Son brought to birth, and at what ascertainable date did the flood come in Noah's day? (b) What did Jesus say concerning knowing when he in his kingdom comes against Satan's world at Armageddon?

told of the day that the deluge would come down upon the earth. (2 Peter 2:5; Genesis 7:1-11) The "ungodly people" were not told the day, but they had had enough hearable and seeable evidence in Noah's preaching, in his completing the ark and in his gathering the animals and birds in it to know that the globe-engulfing flood was near at hand. Can we today know when the Son of God comes in his kingdom against Satan's world at Armageddon? Jesus' prophecy on the world's end says:

⁶ "Concerning that day and hour nobody knows, neither the angels of the heavens nor the Son, but only the Father. For just as the days of Noah were, so the presence of the Son of man will be. For as people were in those days before the flood, eating and drinking, marrying and giving in marriage, until the day that Noah entered into the ark; and they took no note until the flood came and swept them all away, so the presence of the Son of man will be. . . . On this account you, too, prove yourselves ready, because at an hour that you do not think to be it, the Son of man is coming."—Matthew 24:36-44; Luke 21:26, 27; 2 Peter 2:5.

⁷ Let it here be noted that the world-destroying flood did not rush in upon the unheeding people until Noah had got his family and the submissive birds and beasts into that flood-worthy ark. As a happy result there were eight humans besides the birds and animals that lived through the destruction of the ancient world and that started living on a washed earth in the world that has continued till this "appointed time of the end." Happy were Noah's family for having heeded and joined in his preaching and in his building of the ark and gathering in the lower creatures! In like

7. (a) That flood did not rush in until what had taken place, and for what similar reason did Jehovah's destruction not rain down on the people in 1918? (b) In illustration, what did Jesus say regarding the "days of Lot"?

manner now, Jehovah's destruction was not rained down upon wicked, heedless people in 1918. Those upon whom He has mercy must be got out of the danger zone. "Likewise," said Jesus in prophesying about the end of this world, "just as it occurred in the days of Lot [the nephew of faithful Abraham]: they were eating, they were drinking, they were buying, they were selling, they were planting, they were building. But on the day that Lot [with his family] came out of Sodom it rained fire and sulphur from heaven and destroyed them all. The same way it will be on that day when the Son of man is to be revealed."—Luke 17:28-30; Genesis 19:1-26; 2 Peter 2:6-9.

[8] One of the two angels who helped Lot and his daughters to get out of the doomed city and the danger zone said to Lot: "Hurry! Escape there, because I am not able to do a thing until your arriving there [at Zoar]!" (Genesis 19:22) True to this informative picture, Michael the great Prince and his angels will do nothing to destroy Satan's Sodomlike world until those pictured by Lot and his daughters, that is, the "other sheep," have been got out of this doomed system of things by Jehovah's sanctuary class, his chosen ones still in the flesh. Jesus foretold how Jehovah would provide an interruption of the tribulation upon Satan's organization to allow for Jehovah's chosen ones in the flesh to do this lifesaving work toward the "other sheep." Jesus said: "Those days will be days of a tribulation such as has not occurred from the beginning of the creation which God created until that time and will not occur again. In fact, unless Jehovah had cut short the days, no flesh would be saved. But on account of the chosen ones [yet in the flesh] that he has chosen he has cut short the days."

---

8. (a) What did one of the angels say to Lot about his inability to act? (b) In what words did Jesus say there would be an interruption of tribulation for a similar reason?

⁹ True to those words of Mark 13:19, 20, Michael delivered the members of the sanctuary class in 1919. Why? That they might renew the "continual sacrifice" of praise to God for their own salvation, as well as for helping the many "other sheep" to take refuge under God's kingdom. There, under divine protection with the remnant of the spiritual sanctuary, these "other sheep" will not be destroyed with this modern Sodom when destruction flames down upon it in a tribulation such as mankind has never known since creation.

¹⁰ Like Noah's wife, who survived with her sons and daughters-in-law, the remnant of the sanctuary class expect to survive the delugelike destruction at Armageddon along with the great crowd of sheeplike worshipers of Jehovah God, who fully dedicate themselves to Him through the Greater Noah, Jesus Christ. They have in mind the apostle Peter's consoling words. Peter described the ending of the ancient world and then likened the firelike consuming of the Devil's organization to the burning up of heaven and earth. He said: "By those means the world of that time suffered destruction when it was deluged with water. But by the same word the heavens and the earth that are now are stored up for fire and are being reserved to the day of judgment and of destruction of the ungodly men." To show that the sanctuary class will survive by not turning ungodly but by keeping clean and holy as a sanctuary, Peter added:

¹¹ "The heavens being on fire will be dissolved and the elements being intensely hot will melt! But there are new heavens and a new earth that we are awaiting according to his promise, and in these righteousness is to dwell. Hence, beloved

9. True to those words, what did Michael do in due time, and hence who will not be destroyed when modern Sodom gets burned down?
10, 11. (a) Who expect to survive Armageddon along with the great crowd of "other sheep"? (b) In favor of this expectation, what consoling words of Peter do they have in mind?

ones, since you are awaiting these things, do your utmost to be found finally by him spotless and unblemished and in peace. Furthermore, consider the patience of our Lord as salvation."—2 Peter 3:6, 7, 12-15.

[12] With this remnant of the sanctuary class as fellow survivors, the great crowd of "other sheep" will be in excellent position to renew Jehovah's worship on the purged globe, just as Noah's sons and their wives joined in with their father and mother in offering thanks and sacrifice to Jehovah God right after the flood.

[13] That the heavenly Father's will may come to pass and be done on earth as well as in heaven, he creates and establishes the promised new heavens and new earth. The heavenly kingdom for which Jesus taught his followers to pray is the promised new heavens, composed of Jesus Christ and the 144,000 other members of the sanctuary class. True, the remnant of the "spiritual house" expect to survive Armageddon and to dedicate the "new earth" to Jehovah's worship after the old world's destruction. However, they also look forward to finishing their earthly course in the new world and dying as a sacrifice of praise and vindication to God. They do not expect to sleep in death but expect to experience instantaneously a spiritual resurrection to life immortal in the heavens with their chief Joint Heir, Jesus Christ. There they will be among the "twenty-four elders" clothed in white, crowned and enthroned around Jehovah's throne. (Revelation 2:10, 11; 20:6; 4:4; 1 Corinthians 15:42-54) They will leave the "new earth" where God's will is being done.

---

12. With such fellow survivors, what will the great crowd be able to do like what Noah and his family did right after the flood?
13. (a) That his will may be done on earth as well as in heaven, what does Jehovah create and establish? (b) Although they will survive Armageddon, how do they expect to become part of the "twenty-four elders" around God's throne?

¹⁴ The new earth will be composed of the dedicated "other sheep" for whom the Right Shepherd sacrificially died. (John 10:14-16) Those other sheep who survive the end of the old world and its bad heavens and earth will be members of this post-Armageddon new earth. By continued, unswerving obedience to the royal new heavens they will gain the right to endless life on earth and will never die.

¹⁵ These Armageddon survivors are not all the "other sheep" yet to be. There are many of these other sheep who will have died before Armageddon and will be resting in the memorial tombs. Such other sheep include the just ones like Daniel and other pre-Christian witnesses of Jehovah, from John the Baptist all the way back to the first martyr Abel. For all of these also the Right Shepherd surrendered his soul or laid down his life. In due time under the Kingdom they will be restored to earthly life when there comes the "resurrection of both the righteous and the unrighteous." (Acts 24:15) These righteous ones like Daniel, David and Abel will quickly become a dedicated part of the new earth of God's new world.

¹⁶ Under entrancing symbols the apostle John saw in vision the coming into being of the new world and its capital city under Christ the spiritual Bridegroom. John says: "And I saw a new heaven and a new earth, for the former heaven and the former earth had passed away, and the sea is no more. I saw also the holy city, New Jerusalem, coming down out of heaven from God and prepared as a bride adorned for her husband." (Revelation 21:1, 2) That the will of the Father in

heaven may be done on earth, the "sea is no more."

[17] We must not misunderstand by this that the great bodies of water so vital to creature life and that mark our globe as different from the other planets of the solar system will be no more with all the exciting variety of plant and animal life that grow in the seven seas! No; but that wicked element of mankind will be no more, out of which the four wild beasts of Daniel's vision arose to prey upon mankind or out of which the seven-headed, ten-horned wild beast arose to act as the entire visible ruling organization empowered by Satan the Devil. (Daniel 7:2, 3, *RS;* Revelation 13:1, 2) No more a peaceless body of peoples that is commercialized by the Devil's organization Babylon and that tosses up messy stuff like seaweed and mire!—Isaiah 57:20, 21; Revelation 17:1, 2, 15.

[18] The symbolic "new earth" will be peaceful because it has God's approval. There will be "upon earth peace among men whom he approves." (Luke 2:14, *margin*) The Prince of Peace, together with his 144,000 happy peaceable ones, will be reigning in the new heavens and preserving the peace on earth. At the climax of Armageddon he will have bruised the original Serpent, Satan the Devil. He will have cast him and his demons into the abyss for a thousand years, to keep him out of ruinous, peace-disturbing mischief.

[19] What, though, was God's original purpose for this earth? It was that his earthly children, Adam and Eve at that time, should fill the earth with their perfect human kind and should subdue the earth and have all the lower animal creation in subjection. (Genesis 1:26, 28) After the coming of His kingdom this unchanged part of God's will must be done on earth. By means of the great

---

18. Why will the new earth be peaceable?
19. (a) What was God's original purpose for this earth? (b) Under whom and how will this begin to be carried out after Armageddon?

crowd of "other sheep" who have survived the battle of Armageddon, God will begin to fill the earth with a righteous race. Married survivors of Armageddon and the single survivors that will marry will bring forth children conceived in righteousness, not to die but to take advantage of the opportunities of everlasting life on earth that the Kingdom offers. Such bringing forth of righteously disposed children in the "new earth" will be carried on under the Father for eternity. He is the "last Adam," the glorified Son of man. The "inhabited earth to come" will be subjected to him. (Isaiah 9:6; 1 Corinthians 15:45; Hebrews 2:5; Psalm 8:4-8) He is the Greater Noah, in whose symbolic ark the great crowd of "other sheep" from the three great branches of the human family have survived the end of this wicked world.—1 Peter 3:20, 21.

[20] In all parts of the globe will the "other sheep" and their righteously trained offspring be found. They will set themselves to the carrying out of God's will, to subdue the earth as well as to have the lower animal creatures in subjection. At man's beginning Adam and Eve were to start with their Paradise, their garden of Eden, and subdue all the earth outside to a Paradise development and beauty. After Armageddon all "those ruining the earth" will have been brought to ruin. Only those eager to upbuild the earth and to "cultivate it and to take care of it" will remain. (Revelation 11:18; Genesis 2:15) Under the "last Adam" in heaven and in collaboration with their "princes in all the earth," the other sheep and their sheeplike children will proceed to subduing the earth.

[21] In progress of time, under the blessing and guidance of the kingdom of God, all the earth will be "like Eden," even "like the garden of Jehovah."

20, 21. (a) How will the Armageddon-surviving great crowd proceed to subdue the earth? (b) As for whom of ancient times will Jehovah do for them, that his will may be done on earth?

(Psalm 45:16; Isaiah 51:3) God will do for these dedicated sheep as he agreed to do for ancient Israel if they obeyed him as King of Israel: "Jehovah will also make you overflow indeed with prosperity in the fruit of your womb and the fruit of your domestic animals and the fruitage of your ground, on the ground that Jehovah swore to your forefathers to give you. Jehovah will open up to you his good storehouse, the heavens, to give you the rain on your land in its season and to bless every deed of your hand." (Deuteronomy 28:11, 12) As including a global paradise, Jehovah's will is certain to be done on earth.

²² Long ago down in Egypt faithful Jacob and his family, seventy souls, took up residence to stay there for a while. In the course of 215 years down there and in spite of the tyranny of later Pharaohs, the children of Israel came to number millions, with "six hundred thousand able-bodied men on foot, besides little ones." (Genesis 46:26, 27; Exodus 1:1-5, 12; 12:37) After Armageddon there will be, not seventy, but likely hundreds of thousands of surviving "other sheep" on hand with which to begin filling the earth with righteous offspring. With no devilish Pharaonic tyranny to defy, but under the blessing of God's kingdom, these far more than seventy "other sheep" survivors should reproduce and become millions in no great length of time. No obedient ones will be dying.

²³ At the proper time the glorified Son of man, the "last Adam," will cause childbearing to cease. He will not let those survivors of Armageddon overpopulate the earth, or even fully populate it. Why not? Because he will fulfill what he said:

---

22. In the light of what experience of the Israelites down in Egypt for 215 years, why may the "other sheep" surviving Armageddon expect to increase to millions in no great length of time?
23. (a) How and why will the "last Adam" not let the surviving "other sheep" then overpopulate or fully populate the earth? (b) When may the past doers of good come forth, and to what will the unrighteous come forth?

"The dead will hear the voice of the Son of God and those who have given heed will live. . . . the hour is coming in which all those in the memorial tombs will hear his voice and come out, those who did good things to a resurrection of life, those who practiced vile things to a resurrection of judgment." (John 5:25, 28, 29) Past doers of good things, like Daniel, Abraham, Isaac and Jacob, and Moses and King David, and sheeplike ones dying now before Armageddon, will come out of the memorial tombs, doubtless early during the thousand-year reign of Jesus Christ with his 144,000 joint heirs. (Luke 20:35-38; Hebrews 11: 2, 39, 40) In agreement with this, the apostle Paul said: "There is going to be a resurrection of both the righteous and the unrighteous." (Acts 24:15) The unrighteous, the former practicers of vile things, who come forth to a resurrection with judgment in view, will come forth to opportunities for everlasting life on earth under the kingdom. Providently enough room must be allowed on earth for these to dwell, bringing the earth to a full-ness of population, to a comfortable density and spread of population.

[24] The thousand-year reign of Christ is a judg-ment day. (2 Peter 3:7, 8; Acts 17:30, 31) Never-theless, Psalms 96:12, 13 and 98:8, 9 call upon the earth to exult and cry out joyfully because Jehovah comes to judge the peoples with right-eousness and faithfulness. In ancient times when Jehovah was King over Israel he raised up judges according to the need. Those judges were used to deliver the Israelites from their enemies and to restore them from false worship to the true worship of their God and King. (Judges 2:18) So Jesus Christ the King he makes the Judge, to deliver all earth's inhabitants from their inherited weaknesses and imperfections. He will apply to

24. What kind of day is the thousand-year reign of Christ, and yet why do Psalms 96 and 98 tell us to rejoice because it will be such a day?

the obedient believers the benefits of his perfect human sacrifice toward perfecting them physically, mentally and spiritually. He will not let the billions of resurrected practicers of vile things form a "sea" for the development of wicked organizations on earth. He will judge toward their improvement even to human perfection, that they may show themselves worthy to dwell in complete happiness in the earthly Paradise forever.—Isaiah 11:1-9.

[25] During the thousand-year "day of judgment" any unrighteous ones that resist the uplifting judgments and stubbornly refuse to reform and do God's will, the Judge Jesus Christ will execute as deserving no further opportunity. They will not be permitted to defile the holy Paradise, the Edenic sanctuary, as opposers and stumbling blocks to the righteously disposed "other sheep." They will be punished with the "second death" of complete, everlasting destruction. Thus by the end of the thousand years all who then live in the earth-wide Paradise will be humans as perfect as Adam and Eve were when created and put in the garden of Eden. By then the prophecy of Revelation 21:3, 4 will have been realized: "God himself will be with them. And he will wipe out every tear from their eyes, and death will be no more, neither will mourning nor outcry nor pain be any more. The former things have passed away."

[26] That is the time when Christ's millennial reign ends and "he hands over the kingdom to his God and Father, . . . For he must rule as king until God has put all enemies under his feet. As the last enemy, death is to be destroyed." This handing over of the kingdom to God will be that "God may be all things to everyone." (1 Corin-

---

25. What will be done to those resisting the uplifting judgments, and so by the end of the thousand years what will be the condition of all those living on earth?
26. At that time, what will be done with the kingdom, and at the same time who appear on the scene?

thians 15:24-28) However, at this time of human perfection and Paradise perfection Satan the Devil and his demons appear on the scene. It is God's will that "he must be let loose for a little while" at the end of the thousand years spent in the abyss. (Revelation 20:1-3, 7) So release of these wicked spirit forces must come to pass at that time. Why? it may be asked in surprise.

²⁷ At man's beginning Adam and Eve were permitted to be put to a test by that original Serpent, Satan the Devil. Not otherwise, all perfected humankind in the future earthly Paradise sanctuary must be put to a final decisive test. To make sure that all who are favored with the gift of everlasting life in Paradise will forever do God's will on earth as it is done by loyal angels in heaven above, the King of eternity must put these perfected humans to the determining test. They are now directly in his hand.

²⁸ That is why "Satan will be let loose out of his prison, and he will go out to mislead those nations in the four quarters of the earth." He will war against the kingdom of Jehovah God over the earth. The question that he puts in dispute will be Jehovah's universal sovereignty, as to whether it takes in the Paradise earth. How he and his demons will proceed to try to mislead perfected humanity is not revealed. However he tries it, each person will have to decide for himself whether he will be for all time fully committed to Jehovah's universal sovereignty. Will he be true to his dedication to God through Christ for time without end?

²⁹ The number of those who selfishly let themselves be misled is left as indefinite as the sand

27. At man's beginning in Eden, what was permitted, and now what must be determined respecting perfected mankind in Paradise restored?
28. What question will Satan then put in dispute, and what decision will each one have to make for himself?
29. How many will let themselves be misled, and what will happen to them and also Satan and his demons?

particles of the seashore. All such will be destroyed so completely that it will be as if they were plunged into a lake of fire and sulphur, as if fire came down from heaven as it once did upon Sodom and Gomorrah and destroyed them irrecoverably. They will suffer the "second death," a death that Jesus Christ will not destroy. (Revelation 20:7-9, 14, 15) Then, too, Satan the Devil and his demons, having served the purpose of their being let loose for only a "little while," will themselves be forever consumed in that same lake of fire and sulphur, "the everlasting fire prepared for the Devil and his angels." (Revelation 20:10; Matthew 25:41) Hallelujah! The Serpent and his seed visible and invisible are thus at last bruised in the head to their eternal destruction. Heaven and earth are free of them forever!

³⁰ Those who keep their hearts perfect will pass this soul-searching test. Fully assured now of the incorruptible loyalty and exclusive devotion of these, the Supreme Judge Jehovah will express his joyful approval of these ever-faithful ones. He will justify them or pronounce them perfectly righteous. They have followed the example, not of the "first man Adam," but of the "last Adam," their beloved Father for eternity, Jesus Christ. Together with the judicial declaration of their being righteous, Jehovah God will confer upon them the gift of eternal life, with the right to it. Forever they will enjoy their Paradise in Jehovah's new world, doing his will on earth as it is done up in heaven.—Romans 8:33; 6:23.

³¹ According to Jehovah's unchangeable purpose from the beginning, his holy, perfect and loving will will thus have "come to pass, as in heaven, also upon earth." The prayer that his dear Son taught us to pray will have been fully answered.

---

30. Who will pass this final test, and how will the Supreme Judge express his approval, with what result to the approved?
31. What prayer taught by God's Son will thus be fully answered?

CHAPTER 15

Whose Will Do You Favor?

EVERY practical-minded, right-hearted person wants to put himself on the side of the will that is bound to win out. Today political rulers and parties are bitterly fighting to dictate their will to the people or to make their will the one supreme on earth. Which will or purpose will at last win? Which will should a person choose? In the matter of choice, man seems to be caught between the jaws of a pincer movement, the communistic North and the democratic South closing in upon him. As each side fights to make its will prevail, uninformed people wonder which side will somehow win. Bible lovers, informed on Jehovah God's prophecies, know that neither side will win. Communism will not bury western democracy. Western democracy will not root out communism. Both sides will fail. Why, then, favor either one of them?

[2] To favor either one of them is to favor their unseen ruler, the god of this world of which they are a part. The Bible is plain-spoken regarding this ruler. It says that Satan the Devil is the 'god of this present system of things.' (2 Corinthians 4:4) It is his will that is being imposed upon the minds of all who conform to this world, this system of things, Satan's system. Whether of the Eastern bloc or of the Western bloc or of the neutral bloc, all nations are being gathered together by Satan's demons to the "war of the great day of God the Almighty." (Revelation 16:14, 16) All are being gathered onto one general side, for a universal war. By the political ideologies of all conflicting sides the "original serpent, the one called Devil and Satan, . . . is misleading the entire inhabited earth." (Revelation 12:9) It is plainer than ever that "the whole world is lying in the power of the wicked one." (1 John 5:19) God's Word cannot be denied in these observations.

[3] We cannot hide ourselves from the fact. We cannot dodge the fact. The decision we all have to make is not between the conflicting wills of men, as all men are subject to the one superhuman will of the opposer of Jehovah God. The final, all-important decision is between the will of Satan

---

1. In the choice between wills that the East and the West are trying to force upon all men, why are informed Bible lovers in no uncertainty as to whether to choose between the two?
2. To favor either will means to favor whom, and by means of what is this favored one misleading the entire inhabited earth?
3, 4. (a) Between whose wills is the final, all-important decision, and what will working together with the Devil mean to one? (b) What will conforming ourselves to this world mean, and what does Romans 12:2 advise us to do?

the Devil and the will of Jehovah God. We are pinned down to favoring either Satan's will or God's. We should ask ourselves: Do we want to be working together with Satan the god of this world? We can be workers together with Jehovah the God of the righteous new world, as the apostle Paul was, who said: "Working together with him, we also entreat you not to accept the undeserved kindness of God and miss its purpose." (2 Corinthians 6:1) One's working together with Satan the Devil means one's being destroyed with him when Jehovah's will triumphs.

⁴ Satan's world is nearing the close of its "time of the end." It is moving out. This is true according to the overwhelming evidence at hand. Why foolishly conform ourselves to this world or to any part of it and be disappointed with it and have to move out with it permanently? Advice from the Word of the winning God says: "Quit being fashioned after this system of things, but be transformed by making your mind over, that you may prove to yourselves the good and acceptable and complete will of God."—Romans 12:2.

⁵ Do we take the Lord's Prayer upon our lips and say: "Our Father in the heavens, let your name be sanctified. Let your kingdom come. Let your will come to pass, as in heaven, also upon earth"? If we do repeat this prayer, then we are praying for God's kingdom to destroy all the kingdoms and rulerships of this world. In this regard, is His will our own will? If it is not, then we should quit praying the Lord's Prayer. But if it is, then we should honestly make God's will the will of our lives. We should will to dedicate ourselves completely to him to do his will, to live in harmony with his will. It is not too soon to make this

5. When we repeat the Lord's model prayer for God's kingdom to come, for what are we praying, and if this is our own will, then what action toward God should we take?

dedication to Him through the Teacher of the
Lord's Prayer. The hour is late.

⁶ All earth is in a trouble the like of which has
never been known since the Flood. With good
reason this is so. Destruction of the seventh world
power, the Anglo-American dual world power, is
at hand. Think of it! As on the very night that
Daniel interpreted the handwriting on the wall
of King Belshazzar's dining room, a world power,
the mightiest in human history, is about to fall!
The end will not be as easy and peaceful as when
the House of Lords passed the Statute of West-
minster in 1931, creating the British Commonwealth of Nations, at which the London *Spectator*
said: "The old British Empire passed away with
the war, and its place has been taken by the
British Commonwealth." (November 26, 1931)
Additionally, the end of the Anglo-American pet,
the eighth world power, the United Nations, is at
hand. In times past the fall of world powers,
Egypt, Assyria, Babylon, Medo-Persia, Greece,
Rome and the League of Nations, was attended by
great trouble. Now the final world powers of all
history are about to fall, yes, communism also!
According to the pattern of history, trouble could
not be otherwise than expected. The trouble is
already upon us. But worse is yet to come. For
a destruction comes, not by the hands of men
raised in suicidal nuclear war, but by the hand
of Almighty God, by his kingdom with Christ
in power. A whole world will end!

⁷ If we want to repeat the Lord's Prayer without hypocrisy, it is needful for us to dedicate ourselves wholeheartedly to the heavenly Father, for
whose will to be done we pray. We should not
draw near to him with just our lips but having

---

6. What world powers are about to fall, and, according to the
pattern of history, why could nothing less than trouble be
expected, and by whom will the destruction come?
7. If we want to repeat the Lord's Prayer without hypocrisy,
what is it needful for us to do, and what will the doing of
this put into our lives?

our hearts far removed from him and his will. Dedicating ourselves to him puts an inspiring purpose into our lives, a living for God and his heavenly kingdom of the blessed new world, a purpose for eternity!

[8] This does not mean joining a so-called church or sectarian religious denomination of Christendom or of Jewry. It means following Jehovah's Right Shepherd, Jesus Christ himself. He was once a man, and as a man he set the perfect model for men to copy. When the kingdom of God was being proclaimed by John the Baptist, just as it is being preached everywhere today by Jehovah's witnesses, Jesus offered himself to do Jehovah's will in connection with that kingdom. He acted according to the prophetic scripture: "Then I said, 'Look! I am come (in the roll of the book it is written about me) to do your will, O God.'" (Hebrews 10:5-7; Psalm 40:7, 8) Then before God and his holy angels Jesus had himself baptized in public symbol of his dedication to God. The faithful fulfillment of this dedication led to his becoming Jehovah's now reigning King in that heavenly kingdom. His dedication to do God's will was in full accord with the prayer he taught: "Let your kingdom come. Let your will come to pass." So, too, let us honestly harmonize our lives with our prayer. God's kingdom is reigning!

[9] God's will for us is written down in the Holy Bible. Besides that, Jesus illustrated for us the doing of God's will. To find out what God's will is we cannot avoid studying God's Word itself. Religious books that turn us away from God's own written Word will not give us the truth about God's will. We must do as the believers in the Macedonian city of Beroea did when the apostle

---

8. Dedicating ourselves thus means following whom, and what model did he leave for us to copy now when God's kingdom reigns and is being preached everywhere?
9. To find out what God's will is, what cannot we avoid studying, and by this to whom will we be drawn that we may dedicate ourselves?

Paul was driven out of Bible-rejecting Thessa-
lonica and came and spoke to them: "Now the
latter were more noble-minded than those in Thes-
salonica, for they received the word with the
greatest readiness of mind, carefully examining
the Scriptures daily as to whether these things
were so. Therefore many of them became believers." (Acts 17:11, 12) Each one seeking to
know God's will for the purpose of doing it should
have his own copy of the Holy Scriptures, if possible. Said Jesus to possessors of God's written
Word: "You are searching the Scriptures, because
you think that by means of them you will have
everlasting life; and these are the very ones that
bear witness about me." Thus it is by the written
Word that Jehovah teaches us and draws us to
his Son Jesus Christ our Leader. (John 5:39;
6:45) Then it is that through Jesus we may come
in faith and dedicate ourselves to Jehovah God.
We now become Jesus' followers.

[10] In order to understand God's Word and discern his will we need help. In addition to prayer
we need his holy spirit. We also need the help
of his dedicated, organized people. The Ethiopian
Bible reader acknowledged that fact. When the
evangelist Philip asked him: "Do you really know
what you are reading aloud?" he replied: "Really
how could I ever do so, unless someone guided
me?" He invited Philip to guide him in study.
Thus helped, he discerned God's will, dedicated
himself without delay and had Philip baptize him
in water in symbol of his dedication through
Christ. (Acts 8:28-39) The apostle Paul helped
the Bereans in their Bible study, so that many
became believers. Now, in this "appointed time
of the end" since 1914, Jehovah has made manifest the "people that do know their God," his

---

10. To understand God's Word, what help do we need, and in
whom does God provide this needed help in this "appointed
time of the end"?

sanctuary class. With them many "other sheep" have associated themselves in dedication to the God whom they know, Jehovah. These too have become Jehovah's witnesses. In fulfillment of Daniel 11:32, 33; 12:3 these "intelligent" ones among the people "impart understanding to many." Yes, they "shine brilliantly like the brilliance of the expanse of the sky" and "bring many to righteousness." (*Le*) These witnesses of Jehovah are commissioned by him to help any reader of this book who desires and welcomes help.

[11] Jesus Christ has commanded them: "Go therefore and make disciples of people of all the nations, baptizing them in the name of the Father and of the Son and of the holy spirit, teaching them to observe all the things I have commanded you. And, look! I am with you all the days until the consummation of the system of things"— where we are now. (Matthew 28:19, 20) All who become Jesus' disciples by dedicating themselves to Jehovah God as he did must obey the command to be baptized in water. They must also accept teaching that God provides through his visible organization on earth.

[12] Even after dedicating oneself one has to continue studying the Bible to grow in the knowledge of God's will, in order that one may become fruitful by teaching still others. Paul prayed for Christian holy ones or saints. Why? "That you may be filled with the accurate knowledge of his will in all wisdom and spiritual discernment, in order to walk worthily of Jehovah to the end of fully pleasing him as you go on bearing fruit in every good work and increasing in the accurate knowledge of God." (Colossians 1:9, 10) With this aim a dedicated Christian must seek the company of

---

11. All who become Jesus' disciples by dedicating themselves must obey what command in harmony with Matthew 28:19, 20?
12. Even after dedication, why must one continue studying the Bible, and in harmony with this what is one under command to attend?

Jehovah's dedicated people and attend all their meetings, if possible, obeying the command: "Let us hold fast the public declaration of our hope without wavering, for he is faithful that promised. And let us consider one another to incite to love and right works, not forsaking the gathering of ourselves together, as some have the custom, but encouraging one another, and all the more so as you behold the day drawing near." (Hebrews 10:23-25) In this safe manner one will be able to worship Jehovah God at his sanctuary.—Psalm 150:1.

¹³ We do not want to be "workers of lawlessness" and be rejected for salvation. To be saved, it is God's will that we must do. Said Jesus: "Not everyone saying to me, 'Master, Master,' will enter into the kingdom of the heavens, but the one doing the will of my Father who is in the heavens will." —Matthew 7:21-23.

¹⁴ What, chiefly, is Jehovah's will for us in this "time of the end"? Jesus foretold it in these words: "This good news of the kingdom will be preached in all the inhabited earth for the purpose of a witness to all the nations, and then the accomplished end will come." (Matthew 24:14) We must give this final witness. We must be Jehovah's witnesses by preaching this good news, down to the end.

¹⁵ Eternally rewarding to us is the doing of Jehovah's will now on earth. It means life forever in his favor. "The world is passing away and so is its desire, but he that does the will of God remains forever." (1 John 2:17) With loving loyal obedience to our Father in the heavens may we continually live up to our prayer: "Your will be done on earth as well as in heaven"—forever!

---

13. To avoid being rejected and to be saved, what is it that we must do?
14. What, chiefly, is Jehovah's will for us, now?
15. How rewarding to us is our doing Jehovah's will now on earth, and to what prayer may we obediently live up?

CHRONOLOGICAL CHART OF WORLD POWERS (THIRD TO SEVENTH) — 607 B.C. to A.D. 1926

MIDDLE EAST	THE WEST	EGYPT	JUDEA
BABYLONIAN EMPIRE (607-539 B.C.) Nebuchadnezzar Evil-merodach, 582 B.C. Nerilissar Nabonidus Belshazzar, died 539 B.C.			Jerusalem and temple destroyed, 607 B.C.
MEDO-PERSIAN EMPIRE (539-331 B.C.) Darius the Mede Cyrus the Great (Persian)			Jerusalem's temple altar rebuilt by restored Jewish remnant, 537 B.C.
Cambyses [Usurper Magian Gaumata, pretending to be Smerdis, 522/1 B.C.] Darius I (Persian) (Hystaspes), 521-485 B.C.		Pharaoh Psammetichus III Darius I redigs the Suez Canal	Jerusalem's temple rebuilt, 520-516 B.C.
Xerxes I (Ahasuerus) Artaxerxes I (Longimanus)	Roman Republic is set up with praetors, 509 B.C.		Jerusalem's temple visited by priest Ezra, 468 B.C. Jerusalem's walls rebuilt by Governor Nehemiah, 455 B.C. Seventy weeks of years begin counting
Xerxes II Darius II (Ochus; Nothus)			
Artaxerxes II (Mnemon) Artaxerxes III (Ochus) Arses	Philip II, king of Macedonia, 359-336 B.C.		
Darius III (336-331 B.C.) (Codomannus)	Alexander III, the Great, King of Macedonia, 336 B.C.		

MIDDLE EAST	EGYPT	THE WEST MACEDONIAN (ALEXANDER'S) EMPIRE (336-323 B.C.)	JUDEA
	Conquered by Alexander the Great, 332 B.C.		Conquered by Alexander the Great, 332 B.C.
	PTOLEMAIC KINGDOM	Alexander the Great dies at Babylon, 323 B.C. Philip Aridaeus (323-317 B.C.)	Comes under control of Ptolemaic Kingdom of Egypt, 323 B.C.
	Ptolemy I, son of Lagus the father of the Lagidae (323-285 B.C.)	Alexander Allou (317-311 B.C.)	
SELEUCID KINGDOM Over Syria and Mesopotamia Seleucus I Nicator (312-280 B.C.)		Heracles (Hercules) (311-309 B.C.) Cassander, king of Macedonia	
	Ptolemy II (285-246 B.C.) (Philadelphus)	Antigonus Gonatas, king of Macedonia, 277-239 B.C.	
Antiochus I (280-261 B.C.) Antiochus II ("Theos") (261-246 B.C.) husband of Laodice Seleucus II Callinicus (246-226 B.C.) Seleucus III Ceraunus (226-223 B.C.) Antiochus III the Great (223-187 B.C.)	Ptolemy III Evergetes (246-221 B.C.)		
	Ptolemy IV Philopator (221-203 B.C.) Ptolemy V Epiphanes (203-181 B.C.)	Philip V, king of Macedonia, 220-179 B.C. Roman General L. Scipio Asiaticus defeats Antiochus III at Magnesia, 190 B.C.	Taken under control by Syrian King Antiochus III the Great, 198 B.C.
Seleucus IV Philopator (187-175 B.C.) Antiochus IV Epiphanes ("God Manifest") (175-163, B.C.)	Ptolemy VI Philometor (181-146 B.C.)		Seleucus IV Philopator sends Heliodorus to Jerusalem to pillage the temple treasure, c. 175 B.C.

Syria (Seleucids)	Rome / Greece	Egypt (Ptolemies)	Palestine (Maccabean)
			MACCABEAN REVOLT (167 B.C.) Temple rededicated by Judas Maccabeus, 165 B.C. Feast of dedication instituted
Antiochus V Eupator (163-162 B.C.) Demetrius I Soter (162-150 B.C.)	Macedonia becomes dependent upon Rome, 168 B.C.; is made a Roman province, 146 B.C.		Judas Maccabeus negotiates a treaty with Rome, 161 B.C. Jonathan, youngest brother of Judas
Alexander Balas (150-145 B.C.) Antiochus VI Dionysus (145-141 B.C.) Demetrius II Nicator (145-139/8 B.C.) Antiochus VII Sidetes (139/8-129 B.C.) Seleucus V Antiochus VIII Grypus	Greece made a Roman province, 147/146 B.C.	Ptolemy Eupator (146 B.C.) Ptolemy VII, surnamed Evergetes II (Physkon) (146-117 B.C.)	Simon, of original Maccabean family (143/142-134 B.C.)
	Attalus III, king of Pergamum, wills his kingdom to Rome, 133 B.C.		John Hyrcanus (134-104 B.C.)
Antiochus IX Cyzicenus Antiochus X Eusebes Antiochus XI Epiphanes Philip II Antiochus XII Dionysus Tigranes, king of Armenia, acquires Syria, 83 B.C. (83-69 B.C.)		Ptolemy VIII, surnamed Soter II (Lathyrus), and Cleopatra his mother, 117-81 B.C. Ptolemy IX (or, Alexander I) (107-89 B.C.)	Aristobulus I assumes title of "king," 104 B.C. Alexander Jannaeus (103-76 B.C.)
		Ptolemy X (or, Alexander II) (81-80 B.C.) Ptolemy XI Auletes (80-51 B.C.)	Alexandra (76-67 B.C.) Aristobulus II (66-63 B.C.)
Antiochus XIII Asiaticus (69-65 B.C.) Dethroned by Roman General Pompey. Syria made a Roman province, with capital at Antioch, 64 B.C.	Roman General Pompey defeats Mithridates and Tigranes, 64 B.C. Romans occupy Egypt, 55-51 B.C., after restoring Ptolemy XI to throne Julius Caesar defeats Ptolemy XII, who drowns	Ptolemy XII and his sister Cleopatra (51-48/7 B.C.) Ptolemy XIII and Cleopatra (47-43 B.C.)	Jerusalem captured by Roman General Pompey, 63 B.C. Roman control established over Palestine

MIDDLE EAST	EGYPT	THE WEST	JUDEA
	Cleopatra, with her son Caesarion nominally coregent under the name of Ptolemy XIV (43-30 B.C.) Egypt becomes a Roman province, 30 B.C.	Battle of Actium, 31 B.C., in which Octavius defeats Mark Antony	Herod the Great (son of Antipater) takes Jerusalem by storm, 37 B.C., to become king
		ROMAN EMPIRE as Sixth World Power (30 B.C.-A.D. 800) Octavius, as sole ruler of Rome, is styled Augustus by the Roman Senate, 27 B.C.	
P. Sulpicius Quirinius, governor of Syria, 2 B.C.			Birth of Jesus at Bethlehem-Judah, 2 B.C.
			Archelaus, son of Herod the Great, ethnarch of Judea
P. Sulpicius Quirinius (A.D. 6)			ROMAN PROCURATORS:
Q. Caecilius Metellus			Coponius, A.D. 6-9
Creticus Silanus			Ambibulus, A.D. 9-12
M. Calpurnius Piso			Annius Rufinus, A.D. 12-15
C. Sentius Saturninus		Tiberius Caesar, emperor of Rome, A.D. 14-37	Valerius Gratus, A.D. 15-26
L. Pomponius Flaccus			Pontius Pilate, A.D. 26-36
L. Vitellius, Roman proconsul of Syria (A.D. 35-39)			Marcellus, A.D. 36-37
		Gaius Caligula, emperor A.D. 37-41	Marullus, A.D. 37-41
			[Herod Agrippa I, king of Judea, A.D. 41-44]
		Claudius, A.D. 41-54	Cuspius Fadus, A.D. 44-46
			Tiberius Alexander, A.D. 46-48
			Ventidius Cumanus, A.D. 48-52
			M. Antonius Felix, A.D. 52-58 (?)
		Nero, A.D. 54-68	Porcius Festus, A.D. 58-62 (?)
			Albinus, A.D. 62-64
C. Cestius Gallus (A.D. 65-67)		Galba, A.D. 68-69	Gessius Florus, A.D. 64-66
P. Licinius Mucianus (A.D. 67-69)		Otho, A.D. 69	Jewish war with Rome, A.D. 66-73
		Vitellius, A.D. 69	

	Vespasian, A.D. 69-79		Jerusalem and temple destroyed, A.D. 70
			Jewish fortress of Masada falls, A.D. 73
	Titus, A.D. 79-81		
	Domitian, A.D. 81-96		[John the apostle, on isle of Patmos, writes The Revelation and three letters and Gospel, A.D. 96-98]
	Nerva, A.D. 96-98		
	Trajan, A.D. 98-117		
Emperor Trajan adds Armenia, Mesopotamia and Assyria to Rome	Septimius Severus, A.D. 193-211 Builds a Roman wall in Britain		
Septimia Zenobia (Bath Zabbai), queen of Palmyra, A.D. 266/7-272	Aurelian, A.D. 270-275	Queen Zenobia's army occupies Egypt, A.D. 270	
Queen Zenobia and son captured by Emperor Aurelian, A.D. 272			
CONSTANTINOPOLITAN RULE Emperor Constantine founds New Rome or Constantinople, and makes it the capital, A.D. 330	Constantine the Great, A.D. 324-337		
Theodosius, A.D. 379-395 Arcadius, A.D. 395-408 Theodosius II, A.D. 408-450	Honorius, A.D. 395-423 Valentinian III, A.D. 423-455 Romans quit Britain, A.D. 436	Egypt comes under the control of the eastern division of the Roman Empire, A.D. 395	
Zeno, A.D. 474-491 Becomes ruler of the whole Roman Empire, A.D. 476	Odoacer, of Imperial bodyguard, takes Rome and becomes king of Italy, A.D. 476		
Heraclius, A.D. 610-641		Alexandria falls to Mohammedan Saracens; Egypt becomes province of Mohammedan caliphs, A.D. 641	Jerusalem captured by Moslems under the caliph Omar, A.D. 637 Dome of the Rock built by amir Abdalmalik, A.D. 688, in Jerusalem
Constantine V, and his mother Irene, A.D. 780 Constantine VI, A.D. 792 Empress Irene alone, A.D. 797-802	Charlemagne, the Frank, crowned Emperor of the West, by Pope Leo III, at Rome, A.D. 800		
EASTERN ROMAN EMPIRE Nicephorus I, A.D. 802-811	**WESTERN ROMAN EMPIRE** Emperor Charlemagne, A.D. 800-814 Lewis I, A.D. 814-840		

MIDDLE EAST	EGYPT	THE WEST	JUDEA
Romanus II, A.D. 959-963		**HOLY ROMAN EMPIRE OF THE GERMAN NATION** Otho I crowned by Pope John XII as emperor of the Holy Roman Empire, A.D. 962	Jerusalem captured from Crusaders by Saladin, sultan of Egypt and Syria, October 2, 1187
Nicephorus II, A.D. 963-969		Frederick III, as head of the House of Hapsburg, is elected emperor of the Holy Roman Empire, A.D. 1440. Reigns till A.D. 1493	
Constantine Palaeologus XII, A.D. 1448-1453 Constantinople is captured by Mahomet (Mohammed) II, May 29, A.D. 1453. It becomes capital of Ottoman Empire, and the Byzantine Empire ends	Selim I, emperor of the Turks, conquers Egypt, A.D. 1567	British Queen Elizabeth I charters East India Company A.D. 1600 Virginia begins to be settled, A.D. 1607, as Great Britain's first American colony Seventh **World Power** emerges in Great Britain, A.D. 1763 Francis II succeeds his father as Holy Roman Emperor, A.D. 1792	Jerusalem taken by Turks under Selim I in 1516
	Great part of Egypt is conquered by French under Napoleon Bonaparte, A.D. 1798-1799	**HOLY ROMAN EMPIRE** ends, as Francis II renounces title, and takes title of Francis I, Emperor of Austria, A.D. 1806	
Syria is restored to Turkey, A.D. 1840	British troops dispossess French, and Turkish government is restored, A.D. 1801	**GERMAN EMPIRE** re-established under William I of Prussia, A.D. 1871; signs treaty of alliance with Austria and Italy, March 13, 1887	
	Suez Canal opened, A.D. 1869 Egypt, under a native "Khedive," is virtually a British dependency from 1882 onward	Frederick III, German emperor, A.D. 1888 William II, German emperor, A.D. 1888-1918	

	Austria declares war on Serbia, July 28, 1914	
	Germany declares war on Russia, August 1, 1914	
	Great Britain declares war on Germany, August 4, 1914	
	America declares war on Germany, April 6, 1917	Jerusalem captured by British, December 9, 1917
Egypt declared a British Protectorate, December, 1914	World War I ends on November 11, 1918	
	Paris Peace Conference opens January 18, 1919	
	France ratifies Peace Treaty, with League of Nations Charter, October 13, 1919, to make it effective	In peace settlement Turkey, ally of Germany, renounces her sovereignty over Palestine
Syria ceases to be a Turkish province, is created as an independent state and is mandated to France by Supreme Council of League of Nations, A.D. 1920	League of Nations begins functioning at Geneva, Switzerland, January 10, 1920. Eighth World Power becomes alive	Palestine is mandated to Great Britain by League of Nations in 1920
	Germany is admitted to League of Nations, September 8, 1926	

PROPHETIC "TIMES" AND "DAYS":

"SEVEN TIMES," or "the appointed times of the nations" (Daniel 4:16, 23, 25, RS; Luke 21:24):
    Began in 7th lunar month (Ethanim—September–October), 607 B.C.
    Ended in 7th lunar month (September–October), A.D. 1914

"TIMES, TWO TIMES, AND HALF A TIME" (Daniel 7:25; 12:7, RS):
    Began in first half of November, 1914
    Ended May 7, 1918, at arrest of Watch Tower Society's officers and companions
    (Compare the 42 months of Revelation 11:2.)

"A THOUSAND TWO HUNDRED AND NINETY DAYS" (Daniel 12:11, Le):
    Began the end of January, 1919
    Ended the first half of September, 1922, at the second Cedar Point (Ohio) convention

"THE THOUSAND THREE HUNDRED AND THIRTY-FIVE DAYS" (Daniel 12:12, AT):
    Began the first half of September, 1922, at the second Cedar Point (Ohio) convention
    Ended in the month of May, 1926, at the London (England) International Convention

"TWO THOUSAND AND THREE HUNDRED EVENINGS AND MORNINGS" (Daniel 8:14, RS):
    Began in the month of May, 1926, at the London (England) International Convention (May 25-31)
    Ended on October 15, 1932, with the official publication of notice in The Watchtower

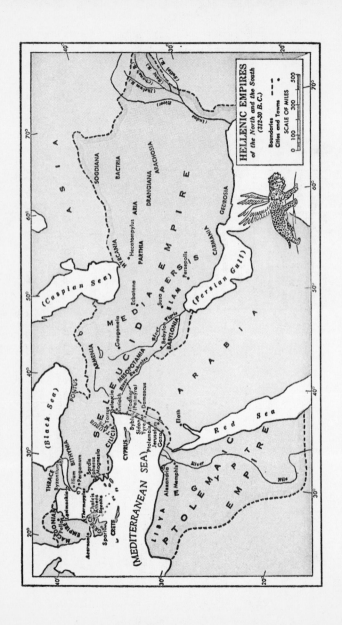

HELLENIC EMPIRES
of the North and the South
(312-30 B.C.)

Boundaries · · · · · ·
Cities and Towns •
SCALE OF MILES
0   100   300   500

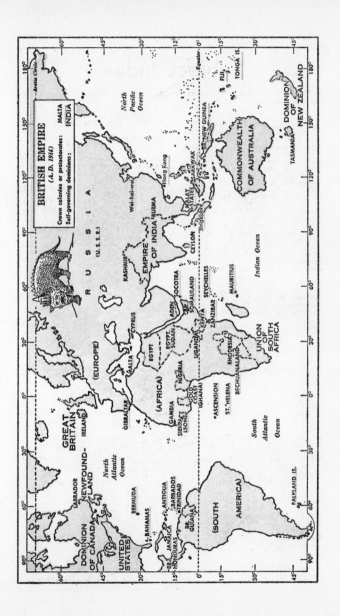

BRITISH EMPIRE
(A.D. 1914)

Crown colonies or protectorates: MALTA
Self-governing dominions: INDIA

Subject Index

Index to Scriptures Cited

379

WATCHTOWER BIBLE EDITIONS

God's Word, the Bible, is a special gift to all who desire to do His will. For this reason the publishers of the book you hold have made available the most popular Bible versions in fine yet inexpensive editions. All are printed on thin Bible paper with hard-bound gold-embossed covers.

Particularly valuable is the *New World Translation*. It is accurate and literal, yet reads with grace and ease in modern English. Printed in large clear type, it has copious cross references, helpful footnotes, maps and drawings. Bound in green leatherette, the size is 7 5/16" x 4 7/8". A truly handsome edition for only $1 each volume.

Now available are the following Bible books:

Christian Greek Scriptures. From Matthew to Revelation.

Hebrew Scriptures, Volume I. From Genesis to Ruth.
Volume II. From 1 Samuel to Esther.
Volume III. From Job to The Song of Solomon.
Volume IV. From Isaiah to Lamentations.

Other top-ranking versions are also available:

American Standard Version. A familiar translation of the entire Bible, this edition has a 95-page concordance of 3,000 listings; also maps and footnotes. In light-brown leatherette, it measures 7 3/8" x 5 1/8" x 1 3/8". $1.

SPECIAL POCKET EDITION. *American Standard Version* as listed above but measuring only 6 5/16" x 4 3/16" x 1". In blue leatherette with red-edged pages. $1.50.

Authorized (King James) Version. A complete Bible version, this edition excels in helpful marginal references, concordance and index of proper names and expressions with their meanings. In maroon leatherette, it is 7 5/16" x 4 7/8" x 1 1/8". $1.

The Emphatic Diaglott. Greek text of the Christian Scriptures with English interlinear, also a new English translation, footnotes, cross references, alphabetic appendix. Size: 7 5/16" x 4 7/8" x 7/8". Blue leatherette binding. $2.

For ordering the above see addresses on the last page.

HARD-BOUND BOOKS — 50 Cents Each

Reading the Bible with understanding calls for help such as you have received in this book *"Your Will Be Done on Earth"*. You can share your pleasure in this book. Obtain another copy for 50c and send it to a friend or relative with encouragement to read it.

Other helpful books are also available for 50c a copy. Each contains vital information clarifying God's will. All are hard bound with gold-embossed cover.

You May Survive Armageddon into God's New World. You will be gripped with overwhelming proof that the greatest catastrophe of all times impends, yet the way of escape is at hand. 384 pages.

"New Heavens and a New Earth". Learn why a completely new world is necessary, when and how its foundation was laid and why it is truly reliable. Learn how to share in its blessings. 384 pages.

What Has Religion Done for Mankind? When and how false worship began, how to recognize its influence and avoid its snare, how the prospects and hopes of clean worship can affect your future—this is indeed a revealing study. 352 pages.

"Let God Be True". This basic study of Bible doctrine removes the shroud of mystery many persons believe surrounds the Scriptures. Now in its 16 million edition. 320 pages.

"Equipped for Every Good Work". Do you know how the Bible came into being? how it has been preserved through centuries to our day? Do you know the main contents of each Bible book? Read this 384-page book.

Qualified to Be Ministers. Now you can receive simple and practical training in speaking clearly and forcefully in behalf of the faith, in arranging private and group study and bringing others on to Christian maturity. 384 pages.

From Paradise Lost to Paradise Regained
Here is a truly delightful book from its artistic cover to the simple and direct message it carries. An ideal book for young and old, it will thrill you from beginning to end. 256 pages; 7 x 9¼ inches in size; 75c.

For ordering the above see addresses on the last page.

CHIEF OFFICE AND OFFICIAL ADDRESS OF
Watch Tower Bible & Tract Society of Pennsylvania
Watchtower Bible and Tract Society of New York, Inc.
International Bible Students Association
124 Columbia Heights, Brooklyn 1, New York, U.S.A.

ADDRESSES OF BRANCH OFFICES:

ARGENTINA: Calle Honduras 5646-48, Buenos Aires 14. AUSTRALIA: 11 Beresford Road, Strathfield, N.S.W. AUSTRIA: Gallgasse 44, Vienna XIII. BAHAMAS: Box 1247, Nassau, N.P. BELGIUM: 28 Ave. Gen. Eisenhower, Schaerbeek-Brussels. BERLIN, WESTERN GERMANY: 49-50 Bayernallee, Charlottenburg 9. BOLIVIA: Casilla No. 1440, La Paz. BRAZIL: Rua Licínio Cardoso 330, Rio de Janeiro. BRITISH GUIANA: 50 Brickdam, Georgetown. BRITISH HONDURAS: Box 257, Belize. BURMA: P.O. Box 62, Rangoon. CANADA: 150 Bridgeland Ave., Toronto 19, Ontario. CEYLON: 35 Beach Rd., Mount Lavinia. CHILE: Moneda 1702, Santiago. COLOMBIA: Apartado Nacional 147, Barranquilla. COSTA RICA: Apartado 2043, San José. CUBA: Avenida 15 Núm. 4608, Almendares, Marianao, Havana. CYPRUS: Box 196, Famagusta. DENMARK: Kongevejen 207, Virum Copenhagen. ECUADOR: Casilla 4512, Guayaquil. EGYPT: Post Box 387, Cairo. EIRE: 86 Lindsay Rd., Glasnevin, Dublin. EL SALVADOR: Apartado 401, San Salvador. ENGLAND: 34 Craven Terrace, London W. 2. FIJI: Box 23, Suva. FINLAND: Vainamoisenkatu 27, Helsinki. FRANCE: 3 Villa Guibert, Paris 16e. GERMANY (WESTERN): Am Kohlheck, (16) Wiesbaden-Dotzheim. GHANA, WEST AFRICA: Box 760, Accra. GREECE: No. 6 Kartali St., Athens 6. GUADELOUPE: B.P. 239, Pointe-à-Pitre. GUATEMALA: 11 Avenida 5-67, Guatemala 1. HAITI: Post Box 185, Port-au-Prince. HAWAII: 1228 Pensacola St., Honolulu 14. HONDURAS: Apartado 147, Tegucigalpa. HONG KONG: 312 Prince Edward Rd., Second Floor, Kowloon. ICELAND: P.O. Box 251, Reykjavik. INDIA: 167 Love Lane, Bombay 27. INDONESIA: Postbox 2105, Djakarta. ISRAEL: 31 Uno Ave., Haifa. ITALY: Via Monte Maloia 32, Rome 742. JAMAICA, W.I.: 41 Trafalgar Rd., Kingston 10. JAPAN: 1 Toyooka-Cho, Shiba-Mita, Minato-Ku, Tokyo. KOREA: P.O. Box 7, Sodaemun-ku P.O., Seoul. LEBANON: P.O. Box 1122, Beirut. LEEWARD ISLANDS, T.W.I.: Box 119, St. Johns, Antigua. LIBERIA: P.O. Box 171, Monrovia. LUXEMBOURG: rue Antoine Meyer 14, G.D. Luxembourg. MAURITIUS: 2 Arnaud St., Beau Bassin. MEXICO: Calzada Melchor Ocampo 71, México 4, D.F. MOROCCO: Alvaro Berecochea, B.P. 1028 Principal, Tangier. NETHERLANDS: Koningslaan 1, Amsterdam-Z. NETHERLANDS ANTILLES: Breedestraat 12, Otrabanda, Curaçao. NEWFOUNDLAND, CANADA: 239 Pennywell Rd., St. John's. NEW ZEALAND: 621 New North Rd., Auckland, S.W.I. NICARAGUA: Apartado 183, Managua, D.N. NIGERIA, WEST AFRICA: P.O. Box 194, Yaba, Lagos. NORTHERN RHODESIA: 84 King George Ave., Luanshya. NORWAY: Inkognitogaten 28 B., Oslo. NYASALAND: Box 83, Blantyre. PAKISTAN: 8-E Habibullah Rd., Lahore. PANAMA: Apartado 1386, Panama. PARAGUAY: Ayolas 394, Asunción. PERU: Pasaje Velarde 165, Lima. PHILIPPINE REPUBLIC: 186 Roosevelt Ave., San Francisco del Monte, Quezon City. PUERTO RICO: 704 Calle Lafayette, Pda. 21, Urb. Hip., Santurce 34. SIERRA LEONE: Box 136, Freetown. SINGAPORE 15: 33 Poole Road. SOUTH AFRICA: Private Bag, P.O. Elandsfontein, Transvaal. SOUTHERN RHODESIA: P.O. Box 1462, Salisbury. SURINAM: Box 49, Weidestraat 82 B, Paramaribo. SWEDEN: Jakobsberg. SWITZERLAND: Allmendstrasse 39, Berne 22. TAIWAN (CHINA): No. 5, Lane 99, Yung-Ho St., Taipei. THAILAND: Box 67, Bangkok. TRINIDAD, T.W.I.: 21 Taylor St., Woodbrook, Port of Spain. UNITED STATES OF AMERICA: 117 Adams St., Brooklyn 1, N.Y. URUGUAY: Casilla de Correo 1375, Montevideo. VENEZUELA: Avda. Honduras, Quinta Luz, Urb. Las Acacias, Caracas, D.F.

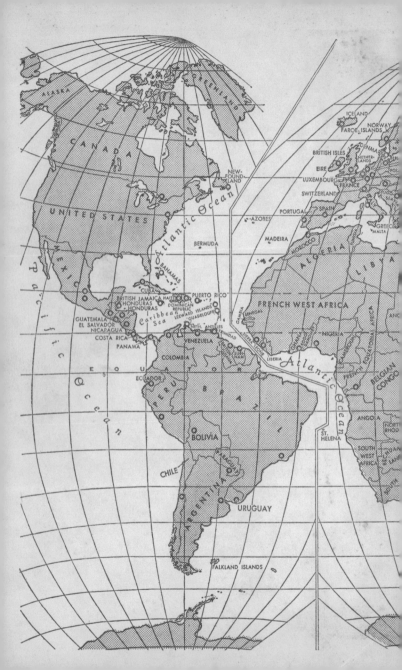